The Highly Sensitive Person in Love

Also by Elaine N. Aron, Ph.D.

The Highly Sensitive Person
The Highly Sensitive Person's Workbook

*How Your Relationships
Can Thrive When the World
Overwhelms You*

The Highly Sensitive Person in Love

Elaine N. Aron, Ph.D.

Broadway Books
New York

BROADWAY

Visit our website at www.broadwaybooks.com

Library of Congress Cataloging-in-Publication Data
Aron, Elaine.
  The highly sensitive person in love: how your relationships can thrive when the world overwhelms you / by Elaine N. Aron.
    p.   cm.
  Includes index.
  1. Man-woman relationships. 2. Love. 3. Sensitivity (Personality trait)
  HQ801 .A747 2000
  306.7—dc21   99-054965

FIRST EDITION

Designed by Susan Hood

ISBN 0-7679-0335-8

00 01 02 03 04 10 9 8 7 6 5 4 3 2 1

To my husband, Art
To my son, Elijah
To similar loving persons in the lives of my readers

Acknowledgments

I am so fortunate to have had Tracy Behar as my editor and Betsy Amster as my agent—both have been kindly and intelligently exacting during the long process of coaxing me to put down and clarify everything that my buzzing HSP brain had worked out in such depth about love and temperament. Editor Sarah Whitmire also gave the manuscript a good going over, as did my husband, Art. I also appreciate the work on the text done by my son, Elijah.

Great thanks also go to the HSPs who were willing to be grilled by me for hours about their relationships and to the many more who answered my surveys. I am also grateful to those who have come to me for psychotherapy. When I needed to tell a part of their stories in these pages, I jumbled the facts wildly while preserving the insights. These stories were the only way to add the depth this book required. I feel highly privileged to have been present while they unfolded.

Contents

Introduction

The effect of the inherited personality trait of high sensitivity on love is not a purely scientific interest of mine. I have lived it, and it has taught me, whether I wanted to learn or not. So while my own case illustrates only one way in which sensitivity affects a relationship, it does bring to life the deep reach of this neglected influence on love.

SCHOOLED BY DIFFERENCE

My husband, Art, a social psychologist, is a restless sort. If he goes out for a walk alone, he wears a Walkman. But he'd rather walk with me.

I am rather fond of walking alone. And I can drive five hours by myself and never turn on the radio. I'm just thinking.

Art is great when under pressure. There's no one I'd rather have in a crisis; he walks in and handles it all. But he can also enter the same room a hundred times and not notice that turning off the fluorescent lights and straightening the rug would make it nicer. Sensing the subtle ways to improve a situation comes naturally to me.

When we go to a conference, he's out there socializing from breakfast until two in the morning, going from group to group. I go to the sessions, maybe join him at dinner or for a party, but mostly I am in my room, outdoors walking, or having a long conversation with some other loner.

To Art, every action is spiritual. Everyday life is sacred. I am always wanting to withdraw, feeling torn between outer demands and the rich, spiritually tantalizing world I only find when I turn within.

I tease him about the time he asked me where I got that beautiful "new" print in the kitchen—the one that had been hanging there for a year and a half. But he doesn't tease me about much of anything—I would take it too hard.

We both can work sixteen hours straight if we have to. I hate it; he's okay with it. When I go to rest, I'm wide awake, too overstimulated to sleep. He gets into bed beside me and in half a minute he's slumbering like a grizzly in winter.

Art does not dream as often as I do. His dreams are happy, or they are about organizing things. My dreams are powerful, sometimes disturbing.

So for years we both thought of me as strangely intense, him as "not very in touch." But of course I thought about all *that* more intensely too. I vacillated between seeing myself as sick and him a miracle of mental health, and me as a genius cramped by a husband who was frustratingly shallow and unconscious. Of the two viewpoints, I actually preferred seeing myself as the problem. I so much wanted to love my husband. But sometimes I longed for a deeper partner, one who could lead me to God perhaps. Meanwhile, Art might have enjoyed a more spontaneous, outgoing mate—one who would talk more, take more pleasure in life. But he was not really bothered by our differences. I was.

I was unhappy with myself too. I truly thought there was something wrong with me, although to Art's credit, he never did. He liked my intensity, creativity, intuition, preference for deep thinking and conversation, awareness of subtleties, the intense emotions. I saw these as acceptable surface manifestations of a terrible, hidden flaw I had been aware of all my life. From my perspective, by some miracle he loved me in spite of it.

In other ways we are hardly total opposites, of course. Nor is this book only about love between a highly sensitive person (HSP) and a non-HSP. Much of it is about HSPs loving themselves and one another. Further, Art is not highly *non*sensitive. He dislikes crowds, hates violent movies, loves the arts. He's very conscientious and consistently seeks to be attuned to others and to his inner life. On the HSP Self-Test on page 11, he scores around a nine—a middle score (middle scores are actually not the most common—mostly people are HSPs or not). And he loves love, intimacy, closeness. In fact, our main area of research has been and still is love and close relationships.

Yet until a few years ago, privately I wasn't always sure I wanted to be close or could be close to anyone. Mostly I reined in my negativity, another part of the seeming flaw, until a midlife crisis spewed it all over. This period was very hard on Art, as I became pretty blunt about my dissatisfactions. But it also broke open the way toward a resolution of our difficulties, and to this book.

ENTER THE HIGHLY SENSITIVE PERSON

The breakthrough came when the psychotherapist I turned to at this time casually mentioned to me that I was "highly sensitive." The lights went on. Could this be my apparent flaw? And not a flaw after all? And so began my study of highly sensitive persons.

For those of you new to the concept, HSPs are that 15 to 20 percent of the human population born with a nervous system genetically designed to be more sensitive to subtleties, more prone to deep reflection on inner experience, and therefore inevitably more easily overwhelmed by outer events. We'll get to the details of the trait in chapter 1. By the way, this is not just my idea but one well established through research by others too. The main point to understand in this introduction is that I am not talking about a little quirk here, but a major, normal, *inherited* difference in how the entire nervous system functions, affecting every aspect of life. It is present in about a fifth of the population, and to some degree in a much larger percentage; thus if people were matched randomly, the chance of a relationship being affected by the trait is at least 36 percent.

What matters to you right now, of course, is whether you and/or your partner is an HSP. Take the HSP self- and partner-tests on pages 11–14, along with the second pair of tests on pages 17–19, which involve another inherited trait—sensation seeking—also discussed in chapter 1. By the way, just as many men as women are born highly sensitive, even though women are stereotyped as being sensitive to subtleties and men as being tough and not noticing much. Stereotypes about men, women, and sensitivity are addressed in chapter 2.

As I have interviewed, conducted surveys, consulted with, and gathered questionnaires from thousands of people, I have found that both my own life and my marriage make infinitely more sense to me now. More and more, I can love and respect both myself and my husband, different as we are. Indeed, I can see now that facing our deep-rooted temperament differences has schooled us, developed our characters, and added passion and pleasure to our lives in a way that nothing else could have.

This book speaks from my strong personal experience that we HSPs and our partners, HSPs or non-HSPs, need help thinking through the meaning of our intensity and our differences. Without this help, love and close relationships can bring HSPs bitter disappointment, and in the process we can unwittingly inflict suffering on others. But with help, we HSPs are ideally designed to make an unusually bountiful contribution of love to our families and the world.

SO THIS BOOK SAYS IT'S ALL IN THE GENES?

I would never argue that being an HSP, or not being one, decides one's happiness or success in relationships. Certainly Art and I had many other issues to deal with besides our difference in sensitivity. But I can say confidently that one's degree of sensitivity, and inherited temperament in general, is the most neglected factor in understanding the success of relationships.

This neglect is going to end soon, however. For example, although little was made of it, in 1992, psychologists Matt McGue and David Lykken at the University of Minnesota found that about 50 percent of the risk of divorce is genetically determined! Although in a moment I will dispute the meaning we should give to that figure, that's an astounding amount of genetic influence. The issue is bound to receive more attention soon, given our culture's increasing interest in genetics.

Do genes really decide whether your love relationships work out? Obviously not, you say. People learn attitudes and values as they grow up, and they can change them too—for example, by following the guidance of a self-help book like this one. But the genetics-of-divorce study is part of a general trend asserting that most of your current psychological situation—such as how happy you are with your job and home life—is the result of genes, not your experiences or upbringing.

I think we are right to be skeptical about emphasizing genes so much. First, marriage and divorce are obviously social in nature. (Surely genes are not the reason for more people divorcing in California than Minnesota.) Second, this trend of thinking that behavior is controlled by genes can lead to a subtler but more insidious idea: Let's forget about trying to help people change their lives or holding them accountable for their behaviors because, poor things, they were "born that way." Then come the labels for "that way"—neurotic, fearful, pessimistic, low in intelligence, violent, having an attention deficit disorder, and so forth. Yes, there are studies showing that genes are a factor in each. But how are they a factor, and what should we learn from this? And why does one member of a pair of identical twins, both with identical genes, often lack the other's "inherited" problems?

Well, while I may be hunting mushrooms in the same woods as the temperament researchers who see most of our psychology decided by genes, I am certainly coming home with a different harvest. First, I think relationship problems are still social, not genetic. The heritability of divorce only means that *something* about people's genetics is influencing divorce—I believe it's not our inherited temperaments that are causing trouble, but that we deal with some temperaments poorly. Second, the more I learn about temperament, the more I think *learning* about it is the key to changing people—to making them less stressed and more tolerant of themselves and others. Temperament is not a reason for leaving people unchanged and viewing them as unchangeable.

Nevertheless, 50 percent of your risk of divorcing has something to do with your genes. This makes inherited temperament a very important and neglected factor in relationship harmony.

HOW TO USE THIS BOOK

Remember, People Are Complicated

Like anyone writing about human psychology, I have to make generalizations. HSPs are especially suspicious of generalizations, labels, and stereotypes because we are always reflecting on their implications and the other possibilities. Maybe you are already saying to yourself, "I thought I was an HSP, but I'm really more like Art—I sleep great, I'm extroverted, restless, optimistic."

The fact is, there are HSPs with all of those qualities. For example, 30 percent of HSPs are socially extroverted. We are all unique individuals, thanks to our different experiences, genetic complexities, and perhaps a dash of personal destiny as well. Every relationship is also unique. So please read this book with many grains of salt, taking only what is useful.

You also may be thinking, "Just what the world needs—another basis for prejudice." Good for you. That's the "shadow," the inevitable downside of generalities—they become stereotypes and then prejudices. We start thinking HSPs are this way, the good way, and non-HSPs are that way, the bad way.

We HSPs know about prejudice—when we haven't been simply ignored, we have been pitied or denigrated as shy, timid, or neurotic (traits I believe no one is born with). Of course we need a compensating infusion of pride, a sense we have some superior aspects to ourselves. But in this book especially, where we are trying to learn to honor difference, you and I must be very careful to value ourselves without devaluing the non-HSP. So use this book thoughtfully, as I trust you will—keep brief the times (we all slip) when you reduce yourself or others to a single score on a single trait or feel superior or inferior because of it.

Use This Book for Love and Friendships Both

Although this book mainly addresses romantic relationships, we obviously love friends and relatives as well. Much of what is here applies equally to those relationships—meeting friends, staying close to relatives, deepening collegial connections, communicating well with HSPs and non-HSPs you are fond of. I believe romantic relationships cannot survive the long haul without these other kinds of close relationships to augment them. No partner can be everything to the other or enjoy everything about the other. And HSPs can have particularly rich, complicated personalities and interests that they need to talk about and have appreciated. You will especially need some HSP friends if your partner is a non-HSP, and your partner will need some non-HSP friends. If you are both HSPs, both of you will enjoy having some separate non-HSP friends.

Adapt the Book According to Where You Are with Love

Love happens to be about as big a topic as I could have chosen. Your needs will vary widely, depending on whether you are falling in love, happily living with someone, having trouble with a long-term relationship, or not in a relationship at all and perhaps wanting to be or perhaps not. So for a moment I would like to address some of you separately.

If You Are Reading This Book with Your Partner (Another HSP or Not)

Good for both of you—this is the best plan. Maybe you can even read some or all of it out loud to each other. I think you will be surprised by how much thinking together about your temperaments can soften and smooth your relationship.

If You Have a Partner Who Probably Will Not Read This Book

This is fine too. You can share what you have learned, perhaps read the juicy-for-you parts out loud, but spare your partner the time involved in reading the entire book. If he or she is not even slightly interested, don't let it trouble you too much. Usually people resist an idea because it threatens them in some way, so you will have to think about what your partner fears about reading this book. Then perhaps you can gradually build his or her trust enough for you to be confided in. If you are angry and hurt, you will not receive that trust.

To be so understanding is a tall order, of course, and not always a wise one. If you are deeply upset by your partner's lack of interest, you probably cannot and should not hide your feelings. But remember, interest comes and goes, as do fears. People open to new ideas when they are relaxed and secure that they are appreciated. Keep the big picture—the things you love about your partner—and let's see how it goes.

If You Are Not in Love Right Now

Please know that you were often on my mind as I wrote, because I meet so many HSPs who are not in close relationships—by choice or not. But whatever the state of our current relationships, we HSPs tend to be more sculpted by our loves than others are. We tend to fall in love harder than others. So we can always benefit from reflecting on our past loves. Goethe is supposedly the source of a sentiment I like: I love you, and it has nothing to do with you. I called this a book about love, not relationships, for just this reason—love seems a far richer, more personal and subjective "HSP topic" than relationships. I don't think books on relationships are often written by inward-oriented, solitude-requiring lovers such as myself or many of you, who can do much of their loving in private. I thought a book for us was needed, and that you as a group would particularly appreciate it.

Also remember that we all need close friends, and love is a force in human psychology that never disappears. All day long we think of people, even if we are alone. Those we can think of, we can love. People certainly need to be loved, yourself included. I hope this book will help release in you more of the self-love and other-love that is there.

If You Are Not an HSP

How good of you to want to learn more about your HSP partner and friends. I apologize for addressing this book to HSPs—I do not mean to exclude you non-HSPs—but I think you will understand.

THIS BOOK IS BASED ON RESEARCH—AND MORE

HSPs will want to know that much of this book is based on solid research—both my own and that of the leading researchers in the fields of adult temperament and close relationships. These fields have grown enormously in the last decade. But much of this research fails to reach the general public, which instead receives a steady stream of non-research-based opinions on personality, gender, and "what makes love last." This book will inform you about many of the facts being gathered in research settings as I connect those facts to HSPs in relationships.

Data from All Over

I began my own research for this book by interviewing HSPs in depth about their relationships. Then I devised research studies and questionnaires to explore specific questions. One questionnaire was completed by one thousand people, HSPs and not. Another sent out to all the subscribers of the HSP newsletter *Comfort Zone* requested not only information from them but also from a non-HSP acquaintance, to provide a comparison group. I also had the opportunity to include measures of sensitivity in long-term studies of couples done by other researchers, and to analyze those results.

My goal has been to provide some authentic answers, not just my opinion, to questions such as: Are HSPs likely to pair up with other HSPs? And if they do, are they happier? What are the typical problems of two HSPs versus an HSP and a non-HSP? What are HSPs' strengths and weaknesses in relationships? How does being highly sensitive affect one's sexual life or one's likelihood of ending a relationship?

Yet love does not like to yield its secrets to a pure number cruncher. That is why this book is also grounded in my very personal experience, as I revealed at the beginning of this introduction, and in my experience as a psychotherapist. Finally, it is also informed by depth psychology.

Data from Below as Well

Depth psychology is that part of psychology dedicated to the study of aspects of life that have been overlooked, repressed, or even despised. Like sailors keeping an eye on the surface weather of the sea, research psychologists use methods that tend to keep them looking for the general principles of conscious thinking and behavior. Depth psychologists are the scuba divers and Jacques Cousteaus, trying to get below the surface, to the unconscious "rest of the story." Both approaches are valuable, but to know only the surface gives a very one-sided view of the ocean, even if at first glance or for some purposes it seems to suffice.

I happen to be one of those rare psychologists who uses both research and depth approaches. The study of sensitivity needs this because sensitive people are unusually attuned to and sometimes overwhelmed by the unconscious. Their more vivid dreams are just one example.

Depth psychology is also needed for plumbing the seabed of love, those dark places that are home to what is scary, strange, forbidden, forgotten, sometimes violently repressed. Indeed, to depth psychologists, sudden deep love is almost always an eruption from these depths. We will return to this in chapter 4.

This book, then, looks at love and sensitivity from the surface, through numbers and data, and also from the depths, from the unconscious and the seldom spoken of. This is the approach best suited to HSPs, I believe. We are not ones to accept easy answers, especially about love. The longer we reflect, the more rich, subtle, and complex our topic becomes.

For example, HSPs know well that love, even romantic love, is not mainly about sex, whatever some biologists say. This is evident from the fact that falling in love is no more or less likely at any age, from kindergarten to senior citizenship.

Further, reflecting deeply, as we do, most HSPs would not agree with the easy answer that love is or should be all about lasting relationships or marriage, since many profound loves remain secret, are never reciprocated, or flash briefly and die.

We can agree with those who say that love transforms people, but we know it doesn't always. And *if* love transforms, we would be glad to agree that the change is for the better—except we know that's not always true, as when the chosen lover betrays or abuses.

We'd like to agree with those optimists who say that if we stay in a love relationship long enough, we will learn important things about ourselves. But that's the saddest joke of all—there are many who stay in relationships and seem to get blinder and blinder to their own role in any problems they are having, their partner just providing them with someone to blame.

After much reflection, this HSP has decided that all we can say for sure about love is that it is always an *opportunity* to step inside and grow in our integrity and insight. We may fail to use the opportunity, but it is being given, every time. Even if the relationship is long over, the opportunity remains, if you wish to reflect with me. So let's begin.

Are You Highly Sensitive?

A SELF-TEST*

Answer each question according to the way you feel. Answer true if it is at least moderately true for you. Answer false if it is not very true or not at all true for you.

T F   I seem to be aware of subtleties in my environment.

T F   Other people's moods affect me.

T F   I tend to be very sensitive to pain.

T F   I find myself needing to withdraw during busy days, into bed or into a darkened room or any place where I can have some privacy and relief from stimulation.

T F   I am particularly sensitive to the effects of caffeine.

T F   I am easily overwhelmed by things like bright lights, strong smells, coarse fabrics, or sirens close by.

T F   I have a rich, complex inner life.

T F   I am made uncomfortable by loud noises.

T F   I am deeply moved by the arts or music.

T F   I am conscientious.

T F   I startle easily.

T F   I get rattled when I have a lot to do in a short amount of time.

T F   When people are uncomfortable in a physical environment, I tend to know what needs to be done to make it more comfortable (like changing the lighting or the seating).

T F   I am annoyed when people try to get me to do too many things at once.

T F   I try hard to avoid making mistakes or forgetting things.

T F   I make it a point to avoid violent movies and TV shows.

T F   I become unpleasantly aroused when a lot is going on around me.

T F   Changes in my life shake me up.

T F   I notice and enjoy delicate or fine scents, tastes, sounds, and works of art.

T F   I make it a high priority to arrange my life to avoid upsetting or overwhelming situations.

T F   When I must compete or be observed while performing a task, I become so nervous or shaky that I do much worse than I would otherwise.

T F   When I was a child, my parents or teachers seemed to see me as sensitive or shy.

....

To score, see the box after the Partner Test.

....

Is Your Partner Highly Sensitive?

THE SAME SELF-TEST, TO BE COMPLETED BY *YOUR PARTNER*

(If you are not in a relationship or your partner does not want to take this test, you can fill it out yourself, answering the questions as you would imagine your partner would, or as someone would whom you have been close to in the past and want to think about as you read this book.)

Answer each question according to the way you feel. Answer true if it is at least moderately true for you. Answer false if it is not very true or not at all true for you.

T   F   I seem to be aware of subtleties in my environment.

T   F   Other people's moods affect me.

T   F   I tend to be very sensitive to pain.

T   F   I find myself needing to withdraw during busy days, into bed or into a darkened room or any place where I can have some privacy and relief from stimulation.

T   F   I am particularly sensitive to the effects of caffeine.

T   F   I am easily overwhelmed by things like bright lights, strong smells, coarse fabrics, or sirens close by.

T   F   I have a rich, complex inner life.

T   F   I am made uncomfortable by loud noises.

T   F   I am deeply moved by the arts or music.

T   F   I am conscientious.

T   F   I startle easily.

T   F   I get rattled when I have a lot to do in a short amount of time.

T   F   When people are uncomfortable in a physical environment, I tend to know what needs to be done to make it more comfortable (like changing the lighting or the seating).

T   F   I am annoyed when people try to get me to do too many things at once.

T   F   I try hard to avoid making mistakes or forgetting things.

T   F   I make it a point to avoid violent movies and TV shows.

T   F   I become unpleasantly aroused when a lot is going on around me.

T F   Changes in my life shake me up.

T F   I notice and enjoy delicate or fine scents, tastes, sounds, and works of art.

T F   I make it a high priority to arrange my life to avoid upsetting or overwhelming situations.

T F   When I must compete or be observed while performing a task, I become so nervous or shaky that I do much worse than I would otherwise.

T F   When I was a child, my parents or teachers seemed to see me as sensitive or shy.

....

SCORING

If you answered true to twelve or more of the questions, you are probably highly sensitive. But no psychological test is so accurate that you should base your life on it. If only one or two questions are true of you, but they are extremely true, you might also be justified in calling yourself highly sensitive.

....

1

Are You an HSP? Temperament, Love, and Sensitivity

"I fall in love so damn hard."

"I feel like an alien sometimes. Everyone else seems to be in a relationship. But what they call love just doesn't appeal to me."

"Investments, cars, sports, getting ahead at work—I don't say it, but I've zero interest in those things compared to my love for my wife."

When highly sensitive people (HSPs) confide about love, there is notable depth and intensity. They fall in love hard and they work hard on their close relationships. Yes, sometimes non-HSPs sound similarly enthralled and confused by love, but on the average, HSPs have a more soul-shaking underlying experience.

None of this is too surprising. As I said in the introduction, HSPs are that 15 to 20 percent of the population born with nervous systems that pick up on subtleties, reflect deeply, and therefore are easily overwhelmed. So of course an HSP in love notices every nuance of another, reflects deeply on the other's charms, and is overwhelmed by the whole experience.

Even if it's not surprising that HSPs have these reactions, how little has been said about it. People are reading about psychology more than ever—I think we are awakening to the fact that our happiness and the world's survival depend on a deeper knowledge of the psyche and of love in particular. And this very basic trait of sensitivity, along with the entire neglected topic of inherited temperament, are absolutely essential for that deeper knowledge. Yet the topic is largely ignored, as if it is undemocratic to say we are born different.

In this chapter we will thoroughly explore sensitivity as well as another inherited temperament trait, sensation seeking. At the end we will return to you as an HSP and what you need for yourself before we take up the concern of the rest of the book, your relationships with others.

WHAT TEMPERAMENT ARE YOU?
TIME TO FIND OUT

If you haven't already, take the HSP Self-Test on page 11 and score it. Then take the Sensation Seeker Self-Test here and score that as well—I will explain more about what it measures later in the chapter. (Taking these tests before you read further means your answers will be less influenced.) By the way, HSPs *can* score high on both tests.

If you are in a relationship and your partner is willing to take the same tests, now would be a good time for your partner to take the second copy of each test, which I've provided for that purpose.

If your partner is not going to take the tests for some reason, you can fill them out, answering the questions as you think your partner would.

If you do not have a partner, you can fill them out as you imagine a past partner would have—someone you were once close to and want to think about as you read this book.

Are You a Sensation Seeker?

A SELF-TEST

Answer each question according to the way you feel. Answer true if it is at least somewhat true for you. Answer false if it is not very true or not at all true for you.

T F   If it were safe, I would like to take a drug that would cause me to have strange new experiences.

T F   I can become almost painfully bored in some conversations.

T F   I would rather go to a new place I may not like than go back again to a place I know I like.

T F   I would like to try a sport that creates a physical thrill, like skiing, rock climbing, or surfing.

T F   I get restless if I stay home for long.

T F   I don't like waiting with nothing to do.

T F   I rarely watch a movie more than once.

T F   I enjoy the unfamiliar.

T F   If I see something unusual, I will go out of my way to check it out.

T F   I get bored spending time with the same people everyday.

T F   My friends say it is hard to predict what I will want to do.

T F   I like to explore a new area.

T F   I avoid having a daily routine.

T F   I am drawn to art that gives me an intense experience.

T F   I like substances that make me feel "high."

T F   I prefer friends who are unpredictable.

T F   I look forward to being in a place that is new and strange to me.

T F   To me, if I am spending the money to travel, the more foreign the country the better.

T F   I would like to be an explorer.

T F   I enjoy it when someone makes an unexpected sexual joke or comment that starts everyone laughing a little nervously.

. . . .

To score, see the box after the Partner Test.

. . . .

Is Your Partner a Sensation Seeker?

A SELF-TEST TO BE COMPLETED BY *YOUR PARTNER*

> *(If you are not in a relationship or your partner does not want to take this test, you can fill it out yourself, answering the questions as you would imagine your partner would, or as someone would whom you have been close to in the past and want to think about as you read this book.)*

Answer each question according to the way you feel. Answer true if it is at least somewhat true for you. Answer false if it is not very true or not at all true for you.

T F   If it were safe, I would like to take a drug that would cause me to have strange new experiences.

T F   I can become almost painfully bored in some conversations.

T F   I would rather go to a new place I may not like than go back again to a place I know I like.

T F   I would like to try a sport that creates a physical thrill, like skiing, rock climbing, or surfing.

T F   I get restless if I stay home for long.

T F   I don't like waiting with nothing to do.

T F   I rarely watch a movie more than once.

T F   I enjoy the unfamiliar.

T F   If I see something unusual, I will go out of my way to check it out.

T F   I get bored spending time with the same people everyday.

T F   My friends say it is hard to predict what I will want to do.

T F   I like to explore a new area.

T F   I avoid having a daily routine.

T F   I am drawn to art that gives me an intense experience.

T F   I like substances that make me feel "high."

T F   I prefer friends who are unpredictable.

T F   I look forward to being in a place that is new and strange to me.

T F   To me, if I am spending the money to travel, the more foreign the country the better.

T F   I would like to be an explorer.

T F   I enjoy it when someone makes an unexpected sexual joke or comment that starts everyone laughing a little nervously.

....

SCORING

For women, if you answered true to 11 or more of the questions, you're probably a sensation seeker. If you answered true to 7 or fewer, you are probably *not* a sensation seeker. If you answered true to 8, 9, or 10 of the questions, you are probably somewhere in between on sensation seeking.

For men, if you answered true to 13 or more of the questions, you're probably a sensation seeker. If you answered true to 9 or fewer, you are probably *not* a sensation seeker. If you answered true to 10, 11, or 12 of the questions, you are probably somewhere in between on sensation seeking.

Yes, you *can* be an HSP and score high on sensation seeking too.

....

HELP! "MY PARTNER AND I ARE TOTAL OPPOSITES." OR, "WE'RE LIKE TWINS"

What if you and your partner scored as near opposites on these traits?

Relax. There is no reason to think you can't have a wonderful relationship. Indeed, your differences may make your relationship stronger and happier than most. This book is not about the importance of having compatible temperaments.

What if you are highly similar? That's fine too, although it may come as a surprise and require adjusting some long-standing views of each other.

Okay, I will be honest here: The research shows that there is a slight tendency for people to choose others with similar personalities—by personality I mean that which results from inherited temperament plus all your life experiences. And there's a slight tendency for those with similar personalities to be happier together. By a slight tendency, however, I mean there's considerable overlap, as when we say men tend to be taller than women but realize that many women are taller than many men. That's why we all know so many spectacular violations of this tendency—so many couples unlike each other in basic temperament but very happy. What fun to be the exceptions to somebody's rule. In particular, personality dissimilarity is a very poor predictor of a relationship's demise.

What does strongly determine the success of a relationship—the length of it or the happiness it brings—is the personality of each person, whether matched or not. Specifically, even if one person in a couple is kind, reasonable, hopeful, and so forth (traits not measured by the self-tests), you have a good chance of working well with your differences. And most important, you need to understand how your temperaments work together—the topics of chapters 5 and 6.

Most of you were only moderately different—perhaps different on one trait but not both. Your situation could be the best of all.

Again, the point of this book is not that some people ought to be together and others ought to avoid each other, but that many of the problems couples have, whether well matched or not, are due to ignorance of how to live with each other's temperaments. Let's see some examples of such problems and their solutions.

DEENA, DANIEL, BLAKE, AND THE OTHERS

Deena wants with all her heart to love Daniel. This husband of hers is funny, kind, successful, responsible, and great with the kids. And boring. And so clueless. To her, he interrupts her at the wrong times and says the wrong things. If she discusses these "flaws" with him, he is understandably hurt and surprised. Further, when she has carefully inquired, she finds that her friends don't find him either boring or clueless. But she is often disappointed by them too, so she thinks it must be her problem. Maybe she just can't love anyone. But it isn't really about not loving Daniel. She loves him, she thinks. But she doesn't respect him. She finds his interests shallow, too practical. This makes her feel ashamed, because she knows she benefits from his practicality and that he both loves and respects her.

To truly complicate matters, Deena recently met "the man I should have married" at a yoga retreat—a quiet, deeply spiritual person who said little, and all of it profound. She knows she would never leave Daniel, but she feels cursed to live out her life with the wrong man, unable to discuss this with either of them, or with anyone.

Then there's Blake, a single parent who is not in a relationship right now and does not expect to be soon, if ever. Blake feels ill at ease in the whole dating scene. Even meeting by computer feels wrong for him—putting one's private self out into the marketplace and waiting for someone to take an interest or shopping among descriptions that seem vapid. The problem is, Blake does want a companion. He knows he was scared off by his last relationship, knows he has to put himself out there, yet he can't. So naturally he feels there's something wrong with him—who would want him anyway? Blake's dreams are full of dates and weddings that go awry, or else nightmares about tidal waves, floods, or muggers.

What about Terry and Jess? They should be happy as clams. They were delighted to find each other. Both like quiet evenings at home; both find the world stressful, even a little alarming. Both like to ponder things like death and the meaning of life. But as the years have passed, Terry has tried to get the two of them out into the world just a little more, to bring some excitement into their lives. Instead, it is usually Terry who goes out, alone, with Jess's blessings, because Jess is too tired. In the process, Terry has met someone quite fascinating—outgoing, adventurous, upbeat. Suddenly Terry realizes how much she has felt like a perennial spectator to life. She is now thinking of leaving Jess, but she fears Jess might not survive the breakup.

We can also get to know David. He loves Jill almost too much, he thinks. She's so deep, so interesting. The trouble is, he never feels her equal. Jill has this uncanny way of knowing what's going on—whether its the weather, the meaning of a film, or what their friends are going through. Worse, she knows what's going on with him before he does. He feels insensitive, stupid. Lately he fears that she feels the same way about him, and her occasional criticisms are always right on target. He wonders if his self-esteem will survive this relationship, wonderful as it is.

Finally, Jordan and Chris. Jordan has had three jobs in different states in six years. Chris has moved with him every time, but with great reluctance. Moving is traumatic for Chris, who has begun thinking that Jordan has trouble committing, putting down roots, being satisfied. Chris even wonders if Jordan has Attention Deficit Disorder, given this impulsiveness around work and where he lives. This week Jordan has been talking about a transfer to the London office of his current employer. Chris is threatening not to move to London with him and thinks they need to see a couple's therapist—hopefully someone who will diagnose Jordan's underlying dysfunction.

What a painful inventory of cases. And they can be multiplied by millions.

THE MYSTERY OF UNRESOLVABLE CONFLICTS

Here's a mystery: Research psychologist John Gottman finds that 69 percent of the conflicts couples have turn out to be perpetual and unresolvable, and happy and unhappy couples have the same percentage of these unresolvable conflicts. So much for the theory that happy couples have fewer long-standing troubles because they are more skilled at solving their problems—they have just as many and are just as stuck by them.

The mystery is only partially solved by the data gathered so far: Couples in the better relationships understand the perpetual problems differently; they dialogue *about* them rather than fighting *over* them. But what kinds of conflicts could be so perpetual and unresolvable, even for happy couples? A likely answer would be those arising from innate differences in temperament, such as one liking an active social life, or city living, and one liking "just us two," or country life. Perhaps the happier couples have found ways to talk about and accept their permanent temperament-related conflicts.

Deena, Daniel, Terry, Jess, and the others you just met have not yet figured out the cause of their unresolvable conflicts. They are still intent on blaming each other for not changing, or they are silently losing respect for each other or themselves. According to any measure of unhappy relationships, they are in deep trouble. But their problems are not around communication or their own neuroses. I know their backgrounds enough to say that none had a truly traumatic childhood or problematic adulthood, in the sense of being unable to work, make friends, or think well of themselves outside of their relationships.

What's happening to them? They are experiencing temperament-related conflicts. They are wanting themselves or the other to be different, to change. But the changes they are asking for are like asking for a change of blue eyes to brown or left-handedness to right-handedness. If they understood this, they and any marital counselor they might consult could approach their situations very differently. But innate temperament is one of the most neglected topics in psychology. Temperament is finally being appreciated among those working with children, but rarely by those helping adults, and never until now by those dealing with relationship problems.

As a result of this ignorance, Deena and the others could easily end up in individual or couple therapy focused on the wrong issues entirely.

What should they focus on? Temperament. High sensitivity in particular.

DIAGNOSING DEENA AND COMPANY

Deena, the woman torn between her love for her "boring" husband, Daniel, and her attraction to a quiet man she met at a yoga course, is an HSP with a normal reaction to a perfectly normal, charming non-HSP husband. She loves Daniel for what are, for an HSP, the many assets of a non-HSP. But she dislikes him for the aspects of a non-HSP that can be unpleasant for an HSP like herself. She mulls the whole situation over, in typical HSP fashion, knowing better than to leave, especially knowing better than to betray him, but finding it so difficult to truly respect this difference in Daniel. We will carefully consider situations like Deena's in chapter 5.

A word about boredom: I see signs from research and my practice that boredom with the other person or the relationship, or what feels like boredom, is one of the most frequent problems couples encounter, and it is usually related to temperament issues. Couples come for help after boredom has led to fighting, lack of respect, or an affair, and so it is never directly confronted. In this book we will confront it.

Turning to Blake, the HSP without a partner: He is expecting himself to behave like a non-HSP, as have his past partners, no doubt. He needs to value himself more, something very difficult for sensitive men especially; chapter 2 will help with that. Blake's valuing of himself needs something else as well—work on his relationship with his own psyche. This relationship must be right for the outer ones to work and must continue to sustain an HSP no matter how alone he or she is or how well the outer relationship is going. Chapter 9 gives most attention to this relationship.

Terry and Jess, so happy until Terry became restless, are two HSPs who have made the classic error of letting their relationship become too much of a safe haven, without enough excitement to balance it—the problem of boredom again. In addition, an unwritten rule has been that neither distresses the other, so Terry cannot even talk about it. Only a full exploration of their resentments, so dreaded by them both, will save this pair. The fear that Jess will "not survive" is a failure to respect the trait both of them possess. Chapter 6 is for such couples.

David, the husband in awe of his wife, is a non-HSP struggling to live with an HSP. He is too impressed by Jill's specialties, forgetting his own. Thinking in depth-psychology terms, we can say that David is projecting his own inner lover, the soul part of himself, onto Jill. This is a double mistake. Because of this projection onto her, he overvalues, almost worships Jill's mysterious abilities—her intuition, emotional and artistic expressiveness, rapport with children and animals, and ability to take time to just be. And he rues their absence in his own life when they are already there, in their own potential seed form, in himself. Indeed, given our culture, a man may be much more comfortable forever admiring them from afar than risking developing them in himself.

Finally, Chris, who thinks Jordan is sick because he wants to relocate yet again, is another HSP who is misunderstanding a non-HSP partner, pathologizing what is different, probably out of true fear of what is so painful for Chris, so easy for Jordan—moving. We will revisit them when we discuss sensation seeking later in this chapter.

THE CASE BEFORE US—HIGH SENSITIVITY

High sensitivity is an inherited tendency to process what comes to HSPs through our senses in a very deep, subtle manner. It's not that our eyes and ears are better, but that we sort what comes in more carefully. We like to inspect, reflect, ponder. This processing is not necessarily conscious. We may be aware of reflecting (or "ruminating" or "worrying," depending on the mood we are in and the issue we are processing), but more often, this goes on without awareness. Hence we are very intuitive, meaning that we tend to know how things came to be the way they are and how they will turn out, but without knowing how we know all that.

We are also good at using subtle cues to figure out what's going on with those who can't communicate with words—animals, plants, infants, unconscious parts of people, those who are ill (bodies don't use words), foreigners trying to communicate with us, historical persons long dead (from our reading their biographies).

HSPs also have a close connection with our own unconscious, evidenced by our vivid dreams. With attention to our dreams and bodily states, HSPs can develop not only respect for the unconscious but a wise humility about motivations, knowing how much of what people do is caused by unconscious impulses.

Our tendency to reflect also makes us more conscientious—prone to think about "what if I don't get this done?" or "what if everybody did that?" Compared to less sensitive people, my research finds that we are more concerned about social justice and threats to the environment (although probably less prone to be comfortable on the political front lines, demanding changes). We also get greater pleasure from the arts and from our own inner life. And we tend to think of ourselves as spiritual, so that, for example, we are on the average more willing than non-HSPs to sit at the bedside of a dying stranger and give comfort (an actual question on one of my surveys).

The bad news is that if we are going to pick up on all the subtleties around us, we are also going to be easily overwhelmed by high levels of persistent, complex stimulation. It's a package deal. We are easily stressed in today's world.

We are also more sensitive to criticism; we process all input deeply, including information about our shortcomings. We are more easily made depressed or anxious due to traumas, processing those more deeply too. As a consequence, we may feel less hope and greater insecurity than those who do not reflect on experiences as thoroughly.

Finally, our sensitivity goes somewhat beyond a deeper processing of information in the brain, in that we tend to be more sensitive, for example, to alcohol, caffeine, heat, cold, itchy fabrics or other irritants, changes in the amount of daylight, medications, and allergens affecting the skin and sinuses.

THE IMPORTANCE OF AN OPTIMAL LEVEL OF AROUSAL

Nobody works well or feels good when over- or underaroused (I mean here arousal in general, not sexual arousal). This is true of all animals, from birth. Infants cry when overstimulated by pain, hunger, noise, or just a long day. And they cry when they are bored and understimulated. Adults do not like being overstimulated either—by noise, chaos, pain, deadlines, social pressure, fear, anger, grief, or even too much pleasure, as when people on a vacation can't stand to see one more view, shop, or museum. Besides being physically and psychologically uncomfortable, overarousal can make people feel like they will mess up—fail a test, make an error, have an accident. Everyone dreads overarousal. We all dread underarousal too—being bored, restless, having to wait with nothing to do.

All organisms like an optimal level of arousal, and all day we humans make adjustments to stay there—we put on the radio to increase arousal, take a nap to decrease it, call a friend to increase it, turn off the TV to decrease it, and so forth. We do this over longer intervals too—change jobs to increase it, avoid divorce to decrease it, travel overseas to increase it, move to the country to decrease it.

The only difference for HSPs is that we get overaroused a little sooner than others. This means that a situation that is optimally arousing for someone else is too much for us. And what's optimal for us may be boring for them. We want the radio off when our non-HSP partner wants it on. We want to stay in our hotel room after a big day of touring when our non-HSP friend wants to check out the nightlife. You can see the potential for conflict.

IS SENSITIVITY THE SAME AS INTROVERSION? YES AND NO

The psychiatrist Carl Jung defined introversion as the tendency to turn inward, away from things in the world, and to prefer the subjective realms, to reflect deeply. To Jung, an introvert finds the inner world as real or more real than the outer one. This is one of the fundamental aspects of what I mean by sensitivity—this preference for reflecting deeply on an experience, so that this reflection, yielding so much rich meaning, is almost more valued than the original object of experience.

But when most people speak of introversion, they mean social introversion—not liking to meet strangers or socialize in large groups. Even tests of Jungian typology tend to make this shift. Using this definition (*social* introversion), and the tests of it, 30 percent of HSPs are not introverts. They are actually extroverts. So I will stick by the idea that the fundamental trait, as most people define it, is not introversion but sensitivity. That way the many socially extroverted HSPs are not turned away by a confusion in terms.

Why does social introversion *almost* but not quite define sensitivity? I think 70 percent of HSPs are socially introverted because it is a good strategy for reducing our stimulation and spending our time doing what we do best—processing things deeply alone or with a close friend, which is something you usually can't do with strangers or in large groups. However, if HSPs grow up in an environment where groups and strangers are common, these become familiar and even calming, and these HSPs are extroverts. Similarly, if an HSP grew up being punished for being introverted or highly praised for being extroverted, extroversion would be the preferred, familiar, least-anxiety-provoking style. So again, many HSPs are extroverts. Social introversion and extroversion themselves are not inherited.

IS SENSITIVITY THE SAME AS SHYNESS? NO

There is no evidence I know of that anyone, human or animal, is born shy—that is, afraid of being socially judged and rejected. Like introversion, shyness develops as one possible adaptation to some of life's situations and does not define the inherited trait itself. Yes, HSPs become shy and fearful more easily than non-HSPs, but only under certain circumstances. The basic trait is sensitivity. Sensitivity only causes HSPs to pause and carefully check out new situations, noticing all the subtleties and considering all their implications. Others mistake this pause as fear, or the pause may turn into fear if the situation seems to warrant it.

It is really quite easy to see the difference between an animal or child that was born sensitive and one that has become timid, shy, or frightened through bad experiences. The sensitive one just wants to watch carefully and reflect on a new situation before advancing into it. If you are a stranger, the child or animal will watch you, all senses tuned to you. Then, if you are "okay" and do not resemble anyone who has caused it trouble in the past, it will come forward, knowing all about you. You are friends for life.

The chronically fearful animal or child will be quite overwhelmed by your presence, not alertly curious but restlessly, anxiously on guard, not really sensing very many details about you. If it ever comes forward, it must repeat the whole process next time. Almost no one is a friend for life.

A sensitive individual who is also fearful due to past experiences is very shy, of course. In particular, my research has repeatedly found that having had troubled relationships with one's parents in childhood leads to more shyness in HSPs than it does in non-HSPs. But again, shyness is a result of experience and not a basic, inherited trait. In fact, in some of my studies, HSPs with good childhoods have turned out to be *less* shy than non-HSPs.

WHY SENSITIVITY IS SO IMPORTANT

The focus of this book is temperament, but through an HSP lens. This lens of sensitivity is for three reasons: Sensitivity is perhaps the most basic inherited trait, its presence particularly affects relationships, and appreciating this trait is crucial for human survival. We'll look at these three bold claims one at a time.

Sensitivity Is Most Basic

High sensitivity is a new name for the most widely researched inherited personality difference (known in the past as introversion-extroversion, shyness-boldness, etc.), both in humans and in all higher animals. The topic has a long research history because it highlights differences in the basic wiring of the nervous system. Even the new name for the trait is not that new. Psychiatrist Carl Jung talked about sensitivity in an early phase of his work. Psychologist Albert Mehrabian came up with an idea like sensitivity in the 1970s, which he called "low screening." In 1988 psychiatrist Burton Appleford published *Sensitivity—Agony or Ecstasy?* (But don't look for it—his publisher folded and the book was never distributed.) Appleford fully appreciated the advantages of the trait, seeing it as just as important and as variable as I.Q. Sensitivity in children was described by child psychiatrists Alexander Thomas and Stella Chess in the 1950s as one of nine fundamental traits, and a book on *The Sensitive Child* by Janet Poland appeared in the same month of 1996 as the first printing of *The Highly Sensitive Person.*

Sensitivity is far more widely recognized than by these few writers, however. It has just been traveling under the wrong names, as shyness, fearfulness, inhibitedness, or introversion (as in "that's a shy puppy" or "he was born timid"). Whatever the term for it, after gender and age it is the most common distinction made among individuals, human or animal, in all cultures.

HSPs Are Important to Relationships

The second reason to focus on high sensitivity is that when a relationship includes an HSP, I believe it has the potential to be exceptionally successful or quite unsuccessful. And although we represent about 20 percent of the population, the chance of a relationship including an HSP (if we assumed people were matched randomly) is around 36 percent. If we include moderately sensitive people, the percentage is higher. If we include friendships as well as romantic relationships, probably every non-HSP is trying to love some HSP, and certainly every HSP is trying to love at least one non-HSP. You could also say that knowledge about differences in sensitivity is relevant to every pair, in that one of them will always be more sensitive than the other.

The reasons HSPs are valuable in relationships are fairly obvious—for example, we are conscientious, intuitive, aware of others' moods, and eager to think deeply about what is going on.

HSPs also can be dismal partners for many reasons, none of them incurable. But all of them are topics for this book. For example, since HSPs hit overload sooner than other people, we can either try to ignore it, which is deadly for us and sure to build our resentment, or we must thwart some of our partner's desires, building their resentment. Further, for reasons I will explore in chapter 3, HSPs can be unusually afraid of both intimacy and conflict. And in several carefully designed research studies, I have found that HSPs growing up in stressful, unhappy families are more likely than non-HSPs to have the characteristics that other research has found to be most dangerous for relationships: pessimism, low self-esteem, depression, anxiety, and an insecure attachment style. HSPs without these stressors are not more likely than others to have these characteristics. By separating out the effects of personal history from temperament, we can attend to both issues better, making each less overwhelming.

Sensitivity Is Crucial to Human Survival

The Need for Two Breeds

Biologists once assumed that evolution meant that each species evolved toward a single ideal form, perfectly adapted to its environment. If the environment changed, the ideal changed or the species became extinct. But theory notwithstanding, it turns out that most species have found a better survival plan: two (or more) ideal forms, two ways of surviving. If one "breed" of the species can't handle things, the other might do fine.

The two temperaments I am calling sensitivity and nonsensitivity are thought to serve exactly this clever plan for surviving. Sensitive individuals process more information before acting, checking things out carefully and taking fewer impulsive risks. Those without the trait take more risks. The HSP lives by the adages "look before you leap" and "a stitch in time saves nine." The non-HSP is guided by "he who hesitates is lost" and "opportunity only knocks once." Both approaches to life work, although one will be an advantage in some situations, the other in others.

This difference in strategies has been found in many species—primates, dogs, goats, rats, and elk, to name a few. It is probably in all higher species. As one example, some pumpkinseed sunfish will enter traps set in ponds and others will not. The two types of sunfish differ not only in this behavior but also in mating, foraging, and predator-avoidance behaviors. They even have different parasites. I was told that when California Fish and Game experts do a census of deer by setting out cameras with trip wires that the deer cross in the dark, about 20 percent (the sensitive ones, I presume) will avoid these trip wires, and so that number of deer have to be automatically added to the census.

Every Culture Favors One Breed Over the Other
It makes sense for social animals such as humans to have a certain percentage of careful, alert-to-the-subtle individuals in a given group. They are the ones who first sense that there are lions in the bushes. Then it's the nonsensitive individuals who eagerly rush in to drive off the lions. But most cultures tend to favor one over the other. Immigrant cultures or those choosing or needing an aggressive approach to survival tend to favor the risk takers. Cultures living close to the earth value most their sensitive herbalists, trackers, and shamans, and many old, highly civilized, stable cultures value most their sensitive judges, priests, historians, healers, visionaries, artists, scientists, scholars, and counselors.

In an aggressive culture, non-HSPs are favored, and that fact will be obvious everywhere. Even in the study of pumpkinseed sunfish described above, the U.S. biologists writing the article described the sunfish that went into the traps as the "bold" fish, who behaved "normally." The others were "shy." But were the untrapped fish really feeling shy? Why not smug? After all, one could as easily describe them as the smart sunfish, the others as the stupid ones. No one knows what the sunfish felt, but the biologists were certain because their culture had taught them to be. Those who hesitate are afraid; those who do not are normal. (Science is always filtered through culture—the true image is not lost but sure can be tinted.)

Here's a good study to remember: Research comparing elementary school children in Shanghai to those in Canada found that sensitive, quiet children in China were among the most respected by their peers, and in Canada they were among the least respected. HSPs growing up in cultures in which they are not respected *have* to be affected by this lack of respect.

Our Importance Is Even Greater in Aggressive Cultures

While cultures naturally favor one trait a bit more than the other, it is dangerous when this goes too far, as is the case with much of Western culture, which keeps paying dearly for its overvaluing of impulsive aggression. One important historical reason for this overvaluing is that all Western (and some Eastern) cultures are derived from a small group of tough, nomadic people who originated on the steppes between Europe and Asia. They lived by conquest, taking other people's herds, and eventually most of the world, forming the foundation of the Greeks, Romans, Gauls, Germanic tribes, and the upper castes of India, among others—hence they are called the Indo-Europeans.

Anthropologists have observed that Indo-European culture and every culture to come out of the steppes after that, and most aggressive cultures in general (such as the Aztecs), have two ruling classes: the warrior kings and the priestly advisors. Warrior kings are the impulsive leaders of raids and builders of empire. The equivalent today are our high-powered business, political, and military leaders. The priestly advisors—usually HSPs, I believe—are, again, the teachers, healers, judges, historians, artists, and so forth. They counsel the warrior kings. An HSP can even be a nation's president—consider Lincoln, an HSP who perfectly balanced his warrior-king Civil War generals.

The priestly advisor's function is to see that the warrior kings reflect a bit on the consequences of their actions—for example, starting a war they can't win or that will do more harm than good. When the power between these two groups is balanced (as in the executive versus the judicial branch of government), all goes well. For this balance to exist, however, the priestly advisors, usually we HSPs, have to assert ourselves. To do this, we must value ourselves and our *type* of power and influence.

Getting Back to Balance, and How Relationships Can Help

Instead of asserting ourselves, however, in the last fifty years we HSPs have been losing influence. This is not due to some conspiracy but is simply because our traditional fields *seem* to have changed, to demand the sort of people who can thrive under high levels of stimulation and stress. In fact, these fields need HSPs in them more than ever. Anyone can see the negative consequences of there being fewer sensitive doctors, nurses, lawyers, teachers, and artists.

In business and government, too, everyone suffers when leaders with nervous systems *not* inclined to reflect are making impulsive, aggressive decisions for the rest of us. Here especially, some of these decisions may affect our very survival. For example, I am confident that HSPs are far more concerned about global warming than are non-HSPs. A species that does not take advantage of both of its "breeds" or types puts itself at a grave disadvantage.

As you proceed through this book, reflecting on your loving relationships, you are not simply helping yourself and those close to you. Your relationships also help you fulfill your critical role in the world. First, you have a direct influence on those you love, and they in turn repeat your views to others. But even more important, they can give you the confidence, support, and practice you need to be an influence among a broader circle of people. Finally, while this may not apply to you personally, the more HSPs in close relationships, the more HSPs there will be who have children or raise or influence the children of others.

SENSATION SEEKING

If the priestly advisors are usually highly sensitive, it makes sense that the warrior kings are low in sensitivity, and perhaps also high in a different trait. (And those high on both are perhaps the best mediators between the two groups.) Look back now at the Sensation Seeker Tests (pages 17–19) to see if you or your partner scored high on these, because these are the measures of the trait we are about to discuss.

Remember Chris, so upset with Jordan for wanting to change jobs yet again? It might have been as Chris saw it—a fear of commitment, or even Attention Deficit Disorder—but knowing Jordan well, I would say it is mostly the result of a normal variation in temperament. Jordan was born with a nervous system that makes him easily bored, and so he is willing to take more risks than Chris in order to get ahead or have a new experience.

HSSs Want Change

Marvin Zuckerman, who has most researched this other trait, calls it high sensation seeking. According to Zuckerman, high-sensation seekers (HSSs) seek "varied, novel, complex, and *intense* sensations and experiences" and are willing "to take physical, social, *legal,* and *financial* risks for the sake of such experience." Genetic studies have found that this trait is as much determined by genes as is a person's height, so that's a lot. And these physical differences are seen in the first days of life, as high levels of activity in babies who will become HSSs. Is it more common in boys and men? Maybe, but it is very difficult to write a test of sensation seeking that does not contain some gender bias, so men as a group score higher because they tend to answer the way "real men" are supposed to feel.

Being an HSS, easily bored and therefore eager to take risks in order to try new things, would seem to be just the opposite of a highly sensitive person. But it is not at all. These two traits are completely independent of each other. You can be high on one, high on the other, high on both, or low on both. And some people have moderate levels of one or the other, although moderation seems to be more the case with sensation seeking than sensitivity. However, the most surprising result, again, is that someone can be an HSP *and* an HSS.

For those of you who are both, we will discuss the implications in a moment. But first, let's understand sensation seeking better.

Two Systems in the Brain

While no one knows for certain what in the brain makes an HSP or an HSS, the best guess is that there are two independent brain systems, each varying independently in their strength or efficiency. The system that decides the degree of sensitivity is what some researchers call the Behavioral Inhibition System, but it would be better to call it the Pause-to-Check System. This system helps you take in the current situation and see if it is anything like past situations before deciding what to do. Having a strong Pause-to-Check System, as HSPs are said to have, requires making very fine discriminations among situations, resulting from long and deep processing, all of which HSPs seem to do.

The other system, the Behavioral Activation System, makes us curious, eager to explore, and excited about rewards. The parts of the brain and the main neurotransmitter (dopamine) involved in this system are quite separate from the pause-to-check parts of the brain and its main neurotransmitter (serotonin). When this system is highly efficient, you are an HSS.

While risk taking is associated by Zuckerman with being an HSS, I think it is actually associated with *not* being an HSP—being low in pause-to-check. Being an HSS is about liking new experiences. HSSs may seem more willing to take risks than HSPs because if you really want something—a novel experience in the case of an HSS—you'll take more risks to get it. You take more risks even if you are also an HSP, although mostly an HSP/HSS will choose to enjoy novelty in safe ways. If you were an HSS but not an HSP, you'd take many more risks because you would be less likely to pause to check.

Sensation Seeking and Love

Zuckerman has found that the love relationships of HSSs tend to be "casual and hedonistic with a lack of strong commitment and a history of many relationships." However, Zuckerman was surprised to find that sensation seekers do marry (usually other HSSs), which seems to contradict their casualness. But this may be explained by the fact that HSSs can also be HSPs. Maybe the married HSSs reflected and came up with a compromise—plenty of casual romantic adventures for the HSS part before settling down to the long-lasting relationship that the HSP part senses will lead to the deepest love. Throughout this book we will return to HSSs as another way to use an appreciation of temperament to improve relationships.

NOW WE HAVE FOUR TYPES

We now have four types of people:

1. *HSPs/non-HSSs*. They are usually reflective and tend to be happy with a quiet life; not impulsive, not seeing much reason to take risks.
2. *HSSs/non-HSPs*. They are usually curious, eager, impulsive, quick to take risks, and easily bored; not very aware of subtleties in a situation or even interested in them.
3. *Non-HSPs/non-HSSs*. They are low in curiosity, low in the tendency to reflect deeply, just living their lives in a simple, natural way.
4. *HSPs/HSSs*. They certainly have versatility, a combination of the HSP's vision and the HSS's drive, but their optimal level of arousal is very narrow because they are easily overwhelmed *and* easily bored; they are often conflicted, in that they want new experiences but do not want to be overaroused or take big risks. As one HSP/HSS said, "It feels like I always have one foot on the gas, one on the brakes."

Four types of people make sixteen possible combinations in a relationship: a pair of HSP/non-HSSs, of HSPs/HSSs, an HSP/non-HSS with a non-HSP/HSS, and so forth. If we added a few more important traits, like intelligence level or analytic versus artistic thinking styles, an exploration of all the possible relationships would make this book rival the *Encyclopaedia Britannica* in length.

Still, you can see that an appreciation of this particular trait of sensation seeking is important for working with the trait of sensitivity. Obviously an HSP/non-HSS paired with a non-HSP/HSS will have many more differences to work out than an HSP/HSS with a non-HSP/HSS. Another important reason for introducing sensation seeking is that those who are both HSPs and HSSs need some extra attention, individually and in their relationships (which I will begin to give them in the final section of this chapter, on taking care of yourself).

For example, Terry and Jess are clearly both HSPs, but Terry is more of an HSS as well. It is easy for HSP/HSSs with HSP/non-HSS partners to let their partners carry their own HSP part. It lessens the HSP/HSS's inner conflict. So it is Jess, the "pure" HSP, who comes to represent the "brakes" in the relationship. Now Terry can blame and resist Jess rather than feel an inner conflict, even though if Jess were not there, Terry might stay home almost as much. If Terry could see this, she would blame Jess less for their quiet life.

MAKING SENSE OF ALL THESE TERMS

It may be time to show you a blueprint. This book uses a host of general concepts, like temperament, personality, and gender, plus specific traits like sensitivity, sensation seeking, introversion, extroversion, and shyness, and soon to come, fear of intimacy, attachment style, depression, anxiety, and preferences in sexual behavior, just to name a few. How do they fit together?

I like to think of our personalities as having three levels. On the ground floor, we find what I call inherited temperament, the basic wiring. Sensitivity and sensation seeking are the big examples, along with energy level, general intelligence, and some specific talents, perhaps. These bottom-floor temperament traits permeate the nervous system, influencing everything from how easily you startle to how much you are disturbed by social injustices.

On the second-floor we find personality traits. Personality is the enduring part of you, coloring or flavoring most of your behaviors. Personality arises from the interaction of the first-floor temperament with social influences and personal history—it is how your inherited temperament has played out for you, uniquely, through your social and personal experiences. Personality traits include introversion, extroversion, optimism, pessimism, attachment style, desire or fear of intimacy, shyness, and so forth. As we saw, HSPs tend to be introverts because they have found from personal experience that it protects them from overstimulation. HSPs become shy if they have had distressing social experiences. Cultures contribute to personality by making it a little more comfortable and ideal to have certain traits rather than others. For example, extroversion is favored in the United States, Australia, and Israel but is not so important in Japan, Sweden, or Tibet. Creativity is highly valued in the United States but is not so critical in India.

Finally, the third floor has the visible behaviors, habits, and preferences that persist for at least a while but not as long as personality traits. Examples are exercising regularly, going to parties every weekend, procrastinating, having many sexual partners, drinking coffee every morning, or being generous in donations to charities. These behaviors change more easily and often, but not always, as each is a product of the floors beneath them too.

The first-floor basic inherited traits are both more and less influential than those on the second and third floors—more because they are the basic wiring, less influential because they are only the backdrop for social and personal experience. We all tend to underestimate social and in particular cultural experience because everyone in a particular culture experiences these somewhat the same; like the air we breathe, we do not notice our own society unless we happen to get to know well a Zulu or an Inuit.

I hope the blueprint helps.

WHAT HSPS NEED

Now you understand your trait of sensitivity and another trait you or your partner may have, sensation seeking. Let's take a moment to think only about you, an HSP. What do you need? Although this is the central topic of *The Highly Sensitive Person* and *The Highly Sensitive Person's Workbook,* a reminder is still in order. Happy HSPs make happy partners.

1. *You need information about your trait*—a constant stream of it. It should be neutral to positive information, to offset negative views from those who do not understand it. Otherwise, since it is not the cultural ideal, you will soon go back to trying to behave like others and criticizing yourself when you can't. Your difference is real—others have it, most species have it, and it is scientifically validated.

2. *You need to reframe your past in light of your sensitivity,* especially those events that have reduced your self-confidence. This means you need to recall these events and actively consider whether what happened may have been due to your sensitivity. For example, perhaps you were in a state of overarousal or trying to avoid one—which was no fault of yours, but just part of the package deal.

3. *You need to heal the effects of a difficult childhood or dysfunctional family* (and also of traumas experienced at a later age). Not only were we as children more vulnerable to negative events, but if our families were under stress, they could not manage the delicate task of helping a sensitive child feel secure in the world. And however fine our families were, we still must heal the effects of subtle prejudice, of not being seen as the ideal. This healing takes time, but there is plenty of excellent help available. And if you are being made anxious or depressed by all of this, you should seek treatment for those symptoms too, in the same way a non-HSP would, through reading well-researched books and getting some brief psychotherapy, long-term psychotherapy, medications, or other complementary physical treatments. Or you may benefit from a combination of these. But do not accept treatment for the trait of sensitivity itself. It is not a problem.

4. *You need help learning to handle overarousal.* This means learning how to avoid it when possible, survive it when it is happening, and recover from it when it is over. Overarousal is the greatest problem for HSPs, and while there's plenty written on stress management, little of it is specialized for us. We need more than a few new techniques. We need an entire lifestyle that suits our trait and a strong sense of being justified about doing what we need to do.

5. *You need help being out in the world,* while still maintaining your optimal level of arousal. HSPs should be out there, involved, and successful, and we can be; but it must be in a balanced way—neither too protective of nor too brutal with ourselves. Our vocations must meet our requirements for calm and downtime, bring the respect we deserve, and make best use of our trait. HSPs typically have to try a number of jobs or even whole careers before finding the right niche, often opting for self-

employment or going back to school. All of these topics need to be seen as temperament-related issues.

6. *You need ample permission to turn off some of your sensitivity to the needs of others.* This is not selfish—for example, it could make your partner a far happier person. When you try to behave like a non-HSP and help everyone whom you sense needs it, you are bound to succumb to overarousal. This leads to insomnia and anxiety due to high levels of the stress hormone cortisol, which leads to low levels of the neurotransmitter serotonin, and bingo, you are a mess—anxious, depressed, irritable, and no help to anyone. There goes your loving kindness anyway. So choose who you will give it to and save it for them. If you can't, start exploring why.

7. *HSPs who are also HSSs need special help finding their optimal level of arousal.* You are easily bored *and* easily overwhelmed. You are often in conflict about going out or staying home, doing more or doing less, and it isn't just about wanting to be like the non-HSPs around you. It's a "hardwired" inner conflict, and it can be intense. For example, you have a business scheme you love and know will work but also know how much stress is involved in starting any new enterprise, and you are already overloaded. What to do?

ESPECIALLY FOR HSP/HSSs

First stop blaming yourself for your "neurotic" or "self-destructive" tendencies when you start off in multiple directions even when knowing it will be too overstimulating. Yes, you *could* be behaving self-destructively, but when you honestly cannot see reasons in your past for self-destructiveness, thinking in terms of an HSP/HSS temperament instead can lead to a whole new realm of solutions. You can satisfy the HSS part with travel, not new work projects. You can hire an assistant for the HSP part to cut down on overstimulating hassles, and let the HSS go ahead and take on more projects. Above all, learn to forge major deals, not do-it-halfway compromises, between your two traits—don't start the business, but ask over the charming next-door neighbor whom the HSS in you has wanted to meet, while the HSP part has been deliberating and dithering.

A LAST THOUGHT

You've come to know your sensitivity better. But it takes time to work that knowledge down deep into your psyche. For example, even after writing *The Highly Sensitive Person,* I still have had to work on my own dislike of myself for my sensitivity. Then, as that has improved, I have had to face not always liking my partner for being a non-HSP! Changing these attitudes requires time to reflect, alone, and then time to discuss your new viewpoint with those you love, and even to argue the ideas with them. But be patient too. Stay with the process.

Changing your temperament prejudices (temperamentism? sensophobia?) also requires time to become alert to outside forces that undermine your respect for yourself and others. For example, those traits that are less than ideal in an aggressive culture are easily pathologized. We hear he has a social phobia, she's obsessive-compulsive, he's codependent, she's a depressive personality. It's a matter of degree, isn't it? Actually, less valued differences do often become problems just because those with them will indeed experience more social rejection. But from a temperament perspective, these supposed pathologies may be only the result of normal variation that causes some of us to withdraw to reduce stimulation, be neat, consider consequences, be sensitive to others' needs, or feel the tragedies of the human condition.

When we don't understand normal variations in temperament, and therefore do not respect them, we expect ourselves or our partners to shape up and change, become more "normal" (really, more like the culture's ideal). "Normal" (ideal) people in our culture are cheerful, outgoing, relaxed, success-oriented, and independent. We think it is our right to be like that, or to have a friend or partner like that. In fact, variations from the ideal are more common than the ideal and are very nice in their own way.

Then there are the differences that are not considered ideal for a particular gender, the topic of the next chapter. Men are supposed to be decisive, stoic, logical, and not really sensitive. Women are supposed to be gregarious, good with kids, skilled at expressing feelings, and deeply sensitive. It is implied that if you don't have a "real man" or "feminine woman" for a partner, you have been shortchanged. It's time to work on this—sensitivity has been confused with gender for too long.

2

Gender-Shyness and Sensitivity: Finding Your Self, Forgetting the Stereotypes

This chapter aims to rescue and protect your love—the person you love, your feelings of love generally—from the effects of the damage that can be done by gender stereotypes. Rigid gender stereotypes and prejudices cause trouble for everyone, but more trouble for HSPs. We fit the stereotypes less and suffer from all the effects of the prejudices more. As a result, we can have special difficulties with the other gender—mistrust, fear of rejection, misunderstandings. These have to be faced before going any farther in this book.

For obvious reasons, this chapter has to focus mainly on close relationships between men and women. This is where gender difficulties rear their subtlest, ugliest heads for most people. However, same-sex relationships of all kinds, which for some of you are your closest relationships, are just as embedded in a world where gender is the "great divide." Thus everything said here can be useful for same-sex relationships too, with a little adjustment.

WHY HSPS FEEL ESPECIALLY UNEASY AROUND THE OTHER GENDER

The animal world is divided into male and female, and humans are divided into men and women, and what a tangle of trouble this has created. What delight too. Each desires the other, dreams of the other—both for biological reasons and for the pleasure, safety, and excitement of a long-term relationship. However, often standing in the way of that relationship is sexism.

Cultural Reasons

To review this annoying problem, in our culture a woman feels pressured to be physically attractive to men. Of course she is also told to respect herself and achieve her own goals. But attracting a man remains a subtle priority. When all goes well, a woman succeeds in that, and the two enjoy her attractiveness, her other accomplishments as well, and accept the changes in her appearance as she ages. But often a young woman's beauty seems insufficient to her, brings the wrong kind of attention, becomes her only currency in the world, or "fades." Meanwhile, men seem valued mainly for their accomplishments and are able to find women all their lives. So women feel treated unfairly, or refuse to be victims—with great stridency—or become indifferent, or "masculine." Through all of this, women develop a conscious or unconscious distrust of men.

Meanwhile a boy grows up trying to act in charge, to become a "real man." At the same time he waits sensitively and patiently to understand what seem to be the hopelessly subtle, indirect, incomprehensible expressions by women of their needs. What a contradiction in what is expected of him. He feels unjustly blamed for the effects of a patriarchy he did not create and for the blatant sexism and violence of a few men. Each gender's difficulties are intensified for HSPs, partly because we are so much more aware of the subtleties behind these stories.

Biological "Strangeness"

According to Jungian analyst Polly Young-Eisendrath, the roots of each gender's distrust of the other go back to our basic differences—men can never be women, women can never be men. Each is always a stranger, a "strange gender," to the other. In childhood we learn that the two sexes are exclusive clubs, and rumors start in our own club about what goes on in the other—rumors augmented of course by our culture's sexism. As we mature, we have our own particular images of the Others we have come to both fear and desire. In Young-Eisendrath's words,

They may be angels or demons, seductive or celibate, but they have enormous power because of their imagined difference. As adults, we . . . project one or several [of these images] onto people of the opposite sex for a variety of reasons—to defend ourselves, to fall in love, to blame another. . . . These [images] prowl through our nights and catch us unawares during the day. They are evoked by others of the opposite sex around us, but they carry no real knowledge about those others.

The point is that the differences are not nearly as great as each sex imagines, but let's face it: the "strangeness" will be more intense for HSPs, with our tendency to process everything deeply, imagine vividly, and sense others' feelings—in this case including the anger and suffering of the other gender. With all these reasons for tension, distrust, and arousal, we can be quite uneasy about what's going to happen when we are alone with the other gender.

Not Feeling Like the "Ideal" of Manhood or Womanhood

Our tension around the other gender can also be profoundly affected by not feeling like the "ideal" man or woman. Never mind the fact that as many boys as girls are born HSPs—if you are a man, you are not supposed to be sensitive. Yes, there's a new interest in the "sensitive man," but mostly as a source of jokes.

If you are a woman, you can be sensitive, especially to the needs and desires of others. In fact, you are supposed to have been born sensitive in this way, mostly interested in being with people and perfecting your attractiveness, even if in fact you are deeply introverted or love your work more than socializing or nurturing. Further, you should not be so sensitive that you need any downtime. "I am *woman; I am strong.*" In short, in this culture, desirable women are outgoing, flexible, and strong in a non-HSP way. So actually, as with men, sensitivity is at odds with our culture's ideal of women.

This sense that we are not the ideal of manhood or womanhood begins in childhood. Research has found that mothers often describe a daughter who is shy—usually a misnomer for highly sensitive—as their favorite child. But there is a price for such favoritism: these girls are often overprotected and come to feel different from other girls and less competent. Meanwhile, mothers often describe a "shy" son as their least favorite, literally loving these boys less. Ouch. These mothers don't mean to be prejudiced against their own children, but their culture subtly shapes them to see a sensitive boy as not the ideal.

When mothers overprotect sensitive girls, these girls grow up feeling they will always need this kind of overprotection—later a man's protection—and gladly give up their authority for it. Sensitive sons, loved less by their mothers, grow up expecting to be loved less by everyone unless they can somehow hide their sensitivity. In short, HSPs of both genders can grow up lacking confidence and doubting themselves as men and women, all of which undermines their ability to be authentic with the other sex.

A Final Point—How Different Are We?

After analyzing results from several different surveys I have conducted, I have found no consistent differences between highly sensitive women (HSWs) and non-HSWs or between highly sensitive men (HSMs) and non-HSMs in their relationship success or satisfaction. The potential specific problems I will discuss are not meant to imply that we have any more problems overall than non-HSPs of our gender. But the problems we have are, I think, quite different.

Fortunately, one of the few advantages for HSPs living in our high-pressure culture is that it increasingly encourages men and women to do whatever they do best—what matters is who gets the job done, not that traditional gender roles be maintained. This ought to give HSPs greater freedom to express our unique personalities. Still, since humans love to make generalizations—such as men are better at this, women are better at that—I sometimes suggest the half-facetious solution of having four genders: HSWs, HSMs, non-HSWs, and non-HSMs. (Add HSS into the mix and you get eight.) That arrangement makes us completely different! Four genders give us twice as many socially constrained ways to be, twice as much freedom and flexibility.

More seriously, I will begin by considering the struggles of HSWs and HSMs separately, but I strongly suggest that you read about each other. HSWs and HSMs are marvelously similar. And before this chapter ends, we will discuss how to heal the effects of gender prejudice on both HSMs and HSWs.

HOW GENDER PREJUDICES DAMAGE RELATIONSHIPS FOR HIGHLY SENSITIVE WOMEN

DIANE'S FLIGHT INTO MARRIAGE

When I interviewed Diane as part of my research, she was forty-six and deeply aware of how her sensitivity had determined her choices, especially given her upbringing. Diane's childhood was painful—her mother was depressed and not fond of children, and her naval-officer father was often away at sea. When he was at home, he sided with Diane's mother on every issue without exploring what might actually be going on. So it is not surprising that at school Diane was always looking for a solid place for herself, always in love with someone, but always from afar. She did not date in high school, partly because she felt she could not bring anyone home—her depressed mother would refuse to let anyone in—but also because Diane just could not let anyone near her. She sold candy bars at the school dances and went home alone.

Diane met Ron the first week of college. She would talk to other men in her classes, but the existence of Ron spared her having to date. From the start, she doubted he was the right one for her, but they were married when they graduated. "I had nowhere else to go. I couldn't go home."

After the wedding, they moved to Ron's hometown. "After one week, it felt like we had been married twenty-five years," she told me. "He worked fourteen hours a day and spent his weekends with his high-school buddies. We were never close. In fact, I guess you could say he was verbally abusive. I guess he hated me. And I would just try to placate him."

Given her sensitivity, however, to her any alternative seemed even more out of reach, especially after the birth of her two children. "I knew it would be impossible for me to make it as a single mother." Diane also admitted that "I stayed married because it gave me my freedom—I could keep my own schedule."

But she was never happy, and she finally left Ron after twenty-four years of marriage. She did not date for four or five years; then she met her current boyfriend, Stan, an HSM, at a personal-growth workshop. A year later they met again at a meditation course. Since then they have been seeing each other regularly but living apart.

Sexism's Damage to Women Damages Love

Diane's story demonstrates the common plight of the HSW who has no example from her mother and no coaching from her father about how to be in the world. So she accepted her culture's traditional solution for women—marry, unhappily if necessary, so that a man will protect and support you. It was a sellout that for twenty-four years brought her little joy and no doubt hurt Ron as well.

Sensitive or not, women have a more difficult time in life—research indicates that they are more affected by troubled childhoods, have lower self-esteem, have trouble speaking up in class and exerting their influence, underestimate their abilities, are paid less for the same work, are far more likely to live in poverty in their old age, and so on. The reasons are obvious. Yes, change comes and the scars heal slowly, generation by generation. But Diane's mother was undoubtedly damaged in part by sexism and, in her case, could not prevent damaging Diane too.

A feminist subculture strives to correct all of this and to encourage women not to do as Diane did. A less sensitive woman with some feminist insight might have just gone out on her own after college, or after a few years of this sort of marriage, and learned how to manage by trial and error. But for an HSW, sudden, unsupported independence can seem overwhelming. Further, all the independence, activism, anger, and group activities urged by feminism can seem personally risky, and as an HSP you tend to pause to reflect on the dangers before taking risks, especially if you lack the support of your family.

Sexism has probably also affected you more because as an HSW you are bound to pick up on and process more deeply all the negative messages that still reach you about women—whether in sexist language, in the use of women's bodies to sell products, in differential treatment in school or on the job, or in learning to be cautious so you aren't raped or appear to be asking to be raped. If you also learned to feel bad about yourself for your other difference, your sensitivity, you carry two reasons to feel less than okay, and to love, or hate, the first unsuspecting man who approaches you. To state the obvious, sexism damages one's ability to love.

Where's Daddy?—Absent or Dismissive Fathers

We HSPs, both women and men, are especially affected by how involved our fathers were in our growing up. This makes sense since, right or wrong, traditionally fathers have been associated with going out into the world and making it. Therefore fathers are the ones to teach those making-it skills. And three cheers for the ones who did.

However, fathers tend to teach these skills less to daughters. Diane's absent and dismissive father was a particularly clear example. Not only did her father not teach her how to be in the world, but his harshness caused her to orient her life to pleasing and placating—something HSPs can do all too readily anyway. Meanwhile her mother role-modeled that women have no choice but to depend on domineering men like her father and Ron.

Even the best-intentioned fathers, however, often err on the side of letting their sensitive daughters avoid challenges. Perhaps they hold the conventional (patriarchal) view that girls should be sheltered; mainly bear and raise children; be more delicate, sensitive, and dependent on others; and be discouraged from going out into the world and possibly being "taken advantage of" sexually. So a sensitive daughter may seem to her father to be especially suited (or doomed) to depend on men her whole life. When I was a child, my father often told me I'd be better off not taking the math classes my brother took—I'd be so smart no man would want me. He did not say this as much to my less sensitive sister. As an HSP, I processed deeply both the advice and the underlying message about sensitive women.

Besides your attitude toward being in the world on your own, your feelings about men in general and how you think they will feel about you was largely determined by your father. If your father was absent, dismissive, or not interested in teaching you skills, you may unconsciously assume you were unattractive or boring to him. Again, if you already felt flawed for being sensitive, you were even more affected. So, you came to expect to be uninteresting and unappealing to all men. Expecting rejection, you may feel awkward and overaroused in men's presence. Even in a relationship, you may continue to doubt your attractiveness, or else your partner's worth (since he is attracted to you, and you do not value yourself).

Another problem that can arise with fathers is that too much of the wrong kind of sexual attention can convince any woman, especially an HSW, that the only thing she has to offer the world is her sexuality, and that she may have no choice about giving it over.

Sexual Victimization

Rape, incest, sexual harassment—we have all read so much about it that we are weary of it, but this does not take away its effects on your psyche or on how you feel about men. Again, HSWs are naturally more cautious about potential dangers (even more so once we have experienced a danger firsthand) and may feel generally less confident out in the world. Thus our lives can be strongly ruled by the shadow of the violent male intruder and the potentially violent male within every man we meet—the part of a man that heard, even if he doubted it, that he is entitled to a woman's body or that women "really want it, and when they say no, they mean yes." Add the effects of any actual sexual abuse, which are nothing less than soul-destroying, and an HSW can find trusting, joyful sexual relationships with men all but impossible without much healing work.

Back and Forth with Men

As an HSW, you grew up knowing that men internalized all of this sexism too and surely were benefiting from the superior role they were allotted. One solution was to win men over, to coax them to share their power or their wealth, to let you be their servants or their sidekicks. On the other hand, as you became aware of having sold yourself for a small portion of the power that should have been shared with you all along, you probably also rebelled. You didn't want to trust any man. You may even have talked about women's superiority. But you still have sympathy for men as fellow human beings; none of this is really their fault. Back and forth—how to feel about them? Whatever you decide seems wrong, and some other women are doing the opposite, which can make you dislike women as much as men.

Not feeling sure of how to behave, or even of how you *will* behave in the moment, much less how he will behave, you are more aroused (in the nonsexual sense) around men, less clearheaded. Being an HSP, all this tension and arousal can make you want to avoid men altogether. But avoiding them makes them even more the "strange gender" and seemingly dangerous to your well-being, and you more awkward and overaroused in their vicinity. Meanwhile, across the gender abyss . . .

HOW GENDER PREJUDICES DAMAGE RELATIONSHIPS FOR HIGHLY SENSITIVE MEN

HSMs are trickier to study than HSWs. There are as many men as women born highly sensitive, but adult women score higher on the HSP Self-Test, no matter how I work to avoid sex-biased items. Given our culture, I am sure there is no way to write a self-test of sensitivity that men could answer without the interference of a conscious or unconscious fear of being seen as unmanly. So I know now I am writing mainly to men unscarred enough to embrace their sensitivity without defensiveness, or so sensitive they can't ignore it. As a result, most of you do not think of yourselves as "typical males." This turns out to be potentially very good for your relationships. But it is a source of many of your troubles as well, with the other gender and your own.

Feeling Like a Failed Man

"He's a real man"—somehow you have to prove that's you, or you'll be in big trouble. That's the burden of men in this culture, and much of this fear and need to prove takes place in boyhood, when sexism most narrowly defines the ideal male's behavior. At that age a "real man" should be tough and cool—that is, have no deep thoughts that do not conform to the crowd. He should be spontaneous, even recklessly impulsive, rather than reflective. He should be fiercely and successfully competitive, especially in team sports. He should be outgoing without needing people or showing any vulnerability—that is, not truly intimate. He never cries and rarely shows any emotion, especially not fear, shame, or remorse. In short, he is not highly sensitive. And by that logic, a highly sensitive man is not a "real man."

William Pollack, Harvard psychologist and author of *Real Boys,* has spent twenty years studying boys in our culture. He points out that, at birth, male infants actually seem to be more emotionally expressive than females. But by elementary school, most of that is gone, thanks to a gender straitjacket enforced by what he calls the Boy Code. According to the code, boys and men must not, above all, express their feelings. This rule constrains not only boys, "but everyone else, reducing us all as human beings, and eventually making us strangers to ourselves and to one another."

Spencer Koffman, a San Francisco psychotherapist and HSM writing for the HSP newsletter, *Comfort Zone,* describes his own experience with the Boy Code:

> Boys are enlisted into "gender bootcamp" at a very early age, where they are taught to be good Warrior/Kings. One of my earliest memories of this indoctrination comes from first grade. I fell off the jungle-gym. I wasn't seriously hurt, but the shock of the fall caused me to cry. The uniform reaction from every boy and teacher was not to console me, but to point out that boys do *not* cry. That was the first and last time that I cried in school. I was in training to become "a little soldier."

I do not want to claim that only HSMs suffer from the Boy Code, but HSMs have a far harder time living up to it. You are especially affected in your relationships with women, who bring the culture's prejudices home in hurtful ways they seem unaware of, such as confiding in you as a friend but not seeing you as sexually interesting. As a result, you can be as shy of the other gender as they are of you, but your "love-shyness" has more serious consequences.

Love-Shyness

Love-shyness is a term coined by sociologist Brian Gilmartin, who has studied that small but troubled set of heterosexual men who have become too shy to initiate a romantic sexual relationship or marry, although they desperately want to. If you are love-shy, you simply expect to be rejected romantically, mainly because of your sensitivity. Although most HSMs are *not* love-shy by this definition, most very love-shy men are HSMs. And I think love-shyness paints an extreme picture of what most HSMs fear or experience to a lesser degree.

Of course, the term can apply to many HSWs too, who both want and fear men's attentions as desperately as love-shy men want women's love. For either gender, love-shyness is a direct result of sexism, working with special toxicity on HSPs, with our extra reasons to fear being judged as not a "real man" or "real woman." However, love-shyness is a more devastating problem for HSMs, because in matters of romance, men in this culture traditionally are supposed to make the first move. It is more acceptable now for women to show interest first, but it is still expected that, being a man, you will then respond decisively and take charge. A woman can stall and "play hard to get," but you are not given that leeway. So what happens to your strong innate preference as an HSM to pause and check before acting, to see if you will like the person you are approaching and if she will like you? Having to leap before you look in order to seem manly means you must override your own temperament. If you can't, you are likely to remain without a partner.

Gilmartin interviewed 300 love-shy men, ages 19 to 50, and also compared the younger men with those who were older—still virgins after age 35. He also interviewed 200 college men who were not shy with women. The love-shy men had much more unhappy childhoods than the non-love-shy, and the older cases more than the younger ones. But most love-shy men also reported the numerous physical sensitivities that would be normal for all HSPs—allergies, a rapid knee-jerk response, and being unusually bothered by wool, insect bites, extremely hot or cold weather, the shorter days of winter, bright sunlight, pain, and sudden or annoying sounds, like that of chalk grating on a blackboard. The combination of unhappy childhoods and sensitivity was creating their intense love-shyness.

Where's Daddy? Absent and Dismissive Fathers Revisited

Sensitive boys definitely suffer from the absence or indifference of their fathers far more than non-HSMs. Fathers not only teach boys how to be in the world, but in particular how to handle feelings successfully as men in this culture. A boy raised only by his mother can miss out on that help.

A great deal has been written about the negative effects on young men of the lack of involved fathers and the even greater lack of male mentors, who instead compete with young men and try to keep them down. Male elders are seen as betrayers who, for example, send young men off to wars they would not fight themselves and fail to see that these soldiers are honored and healed on their return. As an HSM, you may even believe you do not deserve better attention from older men, not having been able to adhere as well to the Boy Code. Maybe you believe you are not really a part of the exclusive male club everyone else admires.

The Complexities Created by a Sensitive Boy's Sympathy for His Mother

Seeing the harm done to women by men, possibly including harm done by your own father, you may have felt a deep division in your loyalties, and great compassion for your own mother in particular. This may have been generalized to all women, so that you saw them as being, like you, bullied by tough guys. But this sympathy can obviously alienate you from your own gender. You will feel, in a sense, a traitor in the gender wars—and in the end admired by neither side. This feeling can be augmented if you sensed subtle signs that your mother may have appreciated you as a confidant or companion, but again, not as a "real man"—remember the research on "shy" sons being their mothers' least favorite children.

Finally, if you had this kind of strong connection with your mother, in our culture you probably saw yourself as a "mama's boy," which means being feminine, which means in our culture being weak, inferior. It would be easy to come to hate, perhaps only unconsciously, both the "weak, second-rate" gender you have been relegated to and your own gender, for its aggressions against you and women. You are left in a literal no-man's-land. And whom do you trust, with whom do you confide your deepest feelings? Men? Women? Or neither?

More on the Fear of Being Weak or Feminine

As I sat down one day for lunch with an HSM, the waiter brought us our menus and said, "May I get anything to drink for you ladies?" I was flooded with embarrassment for my friend, who is slight of build but otherwise looks and acts, to me, like a totally typical male.

I was furious as well. Another HSM put the anger into words for me, in response to my telling him about the incident:

> See, the Boy Code becomes the Man Code—subtle, but always waiting to undercut you just when you let down your guard. Why was he seen as feminine? Because HSMs are being human beings—not iron-driven robots—and the real name for being human *in this culture* is "feminine." What's wrong with being feminine/human? Nothing. But the reality is, in our culture, being like a woman is seen as an insult. So any man, HSM or not, if he does not want to be marginalized, has to play the game and learn to be okay with this robot role (or to find corners of society where it is not so emphasized). But I hope we HSMs know inside that we are the leading edge of a new, nonpatriarchal world.

Besides happening to be slight of build like my friend (not even an HSP trait), I suppose an HSM might be perceived as feminine for seeming to show, as many women do, an understandable subtle alertness to the possibility of physical attack—a vigilance augmented by all HSPs' sensitivity to pain. As Gilmartin says, sensitivity to pain "can have an extremely negative affect upon a male's ability to get along successfully with his same-sex peer group. Such fears can render a male child highly vulnerable to persistent bullying," that is, it makes him as easy to bully as a girl, especially a sensitive girl.

Or maybe HSMs seem feminine because you do not control or subtly dominate others, or because you seem to be a person who shows your feelings—something not done by those who must always be in control. Or because you seem to be more sad or anxious than other men. As I already said, my research indicates that HSPs with troubled childhoods will evidence greater depression and anxiety. This result is mainly due to the fact that non-HSMs seem unusually unaffected by childhood problems. Women and HSMs with troubled childhoods feel the resulting feelings.

Maybe non-HSMs handle troubled childhoods better because life is just easier for them. But many do not truly handle the pain better—they simply stuff down their feelings. When an I'm-fine-I-don't-need-anyone attitude is used to cover up a deep sense of inadequacy, it is called a narcissistic defense, and it is employed far more by men than women, and far more by non-HSMs than HSMs. Again, HSMs and all women (HSPs or not) with troubled pasts on the average *react* to their troubles. They are disturbed. But this is interpreted as feminine.

The trouble with a narcissistic defense, in a man or woman, is that when feelings about fear or need are shut off, one must be sure those feelings stay forgotten by shutting off awareness of anyone else's fears or needs too. As a result, a narcissist can use people without seeming to see the effect on those he or she uses—hardly the sort of person one wants in a close relationship. It is almost as if men with troubled childhoods are given a strange choice of either rigid narcissism or not being seen as "real men." Personally, I like less narcissism, what most HSMs choose. I'd far rather live in a world where people do not deny their basic human feelings, even if these are fear or sadness.

ADDITIONAL DAMAGE, TO HSWS AND HSMS ALIKE

There are some additional ways in which gender issues create problems in HSWs and HSMs that are very similar, so I will discuss these for both genders together.

Foreclosed Options

All HSPs without parental support in childhood and self-confidence in adulthood tend to be overly cautious, turning down opportunities out of excessive fear. HSWs often seek shelter in the first career they happen to stumble into, or in a religious movement they are not ready for, or most often, in a hasty marriage, as Diane did. Once inside their safe ports, they stay put longer, even if the situation is not satisfying. HSWs tend to marry younger than other women, in spite of the fact that in high school or college they were unusually independent and creative. Meanwhile, HSMs marry and achieve their career goals later on the average than other men, in part reflecting their lack of tutoring in how to go forth into the world successfully as HSPs.

Low Self-Esteem

If Diane had more confidence in herself, she might not have needed to marry Ron, or if she had, she certainly would not have placated him. By standing up for herself and the needs of their marriage, she might have made him into a more attentive husband—research indicates that wives often have to teach their husbands relationship skills, and those husbands who accept this influence have happier marriages. But to have influence requires confidence in yourself and your gender's rights and strengths, which Diane lacked.

For HSMs, this same lack of confidence seems to emanate from failing to meet the Boy Code. Maybe you violated it by being too creative and "different," crying or blushing easily, or being bothered by things "tough guys" don't notice—heat, cold, water in your eyes, itchy clothing.

Further, both HSWs and HSMs can have trouble being "cool," that strange cultural ideal. We are easily overaroused by stimulation, so instead of looking cool, we often look nervous and perform poorly in competitive or high-pressure situations, including with a romantic partner we are just getting to know. As a result of all the pressure and low self-esteem, we may develop anxiety-related problems—a "nervous stomach," rashes, phobias, stuttering, shyness. These lower confidence and a sense of being attractive even more.

Poor Boundaries

All HSPs, men or women, are more aware of what other people are feeling, what they want and need. Thanks to your spontaneous deep processing, you also can sense what will happen if others don't receive what they need—they may suffer, fail at what they want to do, become angry with you, feel disappointed with you. And being more sensitive, when they feel bad, you will be bothered too—far more than others. So, you tend to try to give everyone what they want, for your own sake as well as theirs.

HSWs in particular are also taught by our culture to take care of others—as mothers, sisters, wives, friends. Except suddenly the rules have changed. Considerate women can be called "codependent." And so as an HSW you may be accepting yet another reason to be ashamed of your natural inclinations.

For HSMs, the issue is that "real men" are expected to have overly rigid boundaries—to pay little attention to others' needs, their emotional needs especially. At the same time, men *are* expected to meet the needs of women in particular—especially their need to be protected. It's that impossible contradiction again. No matter how overwhelmed a man is himself, he must perform. But in what way? So this is another case where, as an HSM just trying to be yourself, you may be accused not only of being codependent but of being feminine as well if you attend to the emotional needs of others. Or you may be accused of allowing yourself to be controlled by a woman, if it is a woman's emotional needs you are attending to. Or else you are seen as "not up to" *fully* meeting *all* of a woman's needs, always. And if, due to overarousal and conflict, you shut down completely, you are seen as not sensitive!

Being highly sensitive to others' emotional needs, including your partner's, is *not* codependency. Codependency arises when you make the wrong response to the other's needs. Especially in the word's original meaning, you would never be called "codependent" for recognizing that your friend is an alcoholic and needs help, but only for failing to confront him or her.

Still, for some of you, there's something in this label of being codependent that rings true, because being highly sensitive absolutely demands that you develop good boundaries—boundaries that let in what is useful and keep out what is not. What's not useful includes others' needs for you to respond in ways *they* want rather than in ways good for *both* of you.

Unless, however, you have been encouraged and taught to develop good boundaries, they are probably anything but. You are overworked. Your conscientiousness is taken advantage of. You are constantly saying yes and resenting it later. Or you go to the other extreme—now and then, or almost always—by putting up boundaries that shut out everyone and everything. Finally, you let others tell you that you are weak, nonassertive, and codependent—or else insensitive, rigid, and arrogant—rather than deciding for yourself what sort of person you are or what boundaries you want to have. In short, in attempting to be a "real" man or woman, many of you use your sensitivity to please others too much, or go to the other extreme and accept the idea that you are weak—unless you shut your sensitivity down.

The Highly Sensitive Superperson—At Risk

Over and over I have seen HSPs compensate for their not being the "ideal" man or woman by becoming Superman or Superwoman. The organizations they work for love it, of course.

Considering "super HSWs" first, we all know that these days the "ideal" woman shows real gumption. How handy for everyone else. Quite a few women now make themselves work long hours, probably travel for their businesses, relish competition, handle stress like warriors, and fit in family lives too. For nonsensitive, sensation-seeking women this can work out all right. It's high time they were free to express their temperaments. No more long skirts and knitting.

But many HSWs are also trying to meet these demands. You may have the good upbringing, confidence, education, and talent required for it. Maybe you are also high in sensation seeking—easily bored, full of ideas. And so, being an HSP too, you are often the bright visionary in your organization, on your way to the top. The star. You seem to have both the sensitivity and the toughness they want. But in trying to fit this new gender stereotype of Superwoman, you are violating who you are and risking your health.

HSMs may be even more at risk for trying to be "Super HSMs," because men in fast-track careers are even less respected than women if they express any need for personal downtime or uninterrupted periods with their partners and families. You are also even more likely to be driven to prove your manhood and overcome your "secret flaw" of sensitivity by showing you can work circles around others. And with your intuition and creativity, you can certainly think of new projects.

So, is this you? Then I probably know more about you, HSW or HSM, and about your relationships. You have no energy left for anything but work and often complain privately that life is hell, hardly worth living. It is pretty hellish for your partner too, if you have found time to have one. Or your partner is equally driven, in which case it is probably not much of a relationship. Yet you fear that admitting your exhaustion would be a display of vulnerability and low drive that would soon get around and probably cost you your job, and possibly the respect of your partner, family, or friends, as well, or so you think. It is my observation that it is usually your health that stops you, around forty. Adhering to rigid gender ideals can be deadly.

Good Parents Who Feel Like Bad Ones

When I was first searching the psychology literature for anything on "sensitive" or "sensitivity," I found only three references, and two of those held that sensitive was the only way to describe those who are best at taking care of infants. This ability has little to do with whether one is in fact a parent, but has everything to do with the ability to read an infant's subtle cues along with the appreciation of an infant's perspective and helplessness. Not surprisingly, once HSWs and HSMs recover from the birth of their children (I've seen both react strongly), they usually become highly responsive parents. Some may not notice their ability, but most, being subtly attuned to other parents as well, probably do.

At the same time, however, HSPs can have a strong sense that they are terrible at parenting. If you are a highly sensitive parent, you know what I mean. You are often irritable, depressed, lack energy, want to get away, want to express your other talents, or secretly think how much better life would be without children. Parenthood is a huge responsibility and source of stimulation. To be sensitive during pregnancy and childbirth is indescribably intense, for both parents, in the best and worst senses, especially the first time. Your body and inner life feel completely altered. All this multiplies after the birth, when you are constantly needed by your baby and sleeping so little. You wonder how you will ever survive. You may also wonder if you made the right decision even to have a child. You definitely doubt you are always or even often a Good Mother or Good Father.

Additionally, a sensitive father often feels left out of the first stages, and ashamed and bothered by that, yet profoundly moved by it too. And fatherhood carries an extra burden—not only will you strive to be a nurturer and a brilliant child psychologist, but you are likely to take with great seriousness the responsibility of protecting and providing financially for your children, no matter how much your partner helps. Meanwhile, what happens to your own need for time alone and time alone with the mother of your children?

Once again the traditional gender stereotypes, still alive in all of us, have undermined HSPs' relationships—this time as parents. This time the stereotypes are of the ideal mother or father—an ideal no one could meet, but especially no HSP. For non-HSPs, feelings of inadequacy may show up only in the dreams typical of new parents, but in HSPs the feelings tend to be closer to consciousness and more distressing. I hate to think of the generations of HSPs who have felt guilt-ridden with their secret awareness of the Good Parent and Terrible Parent lurking so closely together inside of them.

WHERE DOES SENSATION SEEKING FIT IN?

Before we turn to solutions to these difficulties, let's think a moment about the effects of gender prejudices on HSPs who are high in sensation seeking. Sensation seeking is obviously part of the ideal personality in this culture. If you are a high sensation seeker (HSS), being more like the ideal man or woman, you will have a bit more confidence. This is especially true for men, who are supposed to be eager for adventure. Being an HSS will also help an HSM in particular with love-shyness, pushing him to make the first move and have the varied sexual experience men are expected to have before they settle down.

The disadvantage, of course, is that the HSS/HSP is even more likely to try to be superman or superwoman, being driven both by outer forces and these conflicting inner temperament traits. The sensitive side receives little support, until the body votes with an illness. An important caution: as an HSS/HSP, you are no less likely to experience overarousal and exhaustion. Do not be seduced into trying to fill a gender stereotype that does not suit you, no matter how close you may come in a limited sense because you are an HSS.

WORKING ON GENDER TROUBLES

I have led you through some dark places. Now let's consider how to bring in more light. Just as many of the effects of sexism are remarkably the same for HSWs and HSMs, so are the ways to heal, in spite of the generalizations our culture still loves, such as "When women feel bad they want to talk about it, but when men feel bad they want to go into their caves and work on projects." Or, "When women have problems, they just want to be listened to, but men want to give and get solutions." The fact is, the last generation may have behaved this way, although even that is not clear, but on the average gender differences have declined with each generation.

We all need to express our feelings *and* find solutions to problems, including these gender-related problems. We still make the generalities, however, which give them a bit of a life of their own. It helps to know the facts, so you can correct the generalizations when you want to. For example, research shows with perfect consistency that people in relationships are happier when women *and* men behave in what in the past has been seen as a traditionally "feminine" way—that is, warm, nurturing, emotionally expressive, and eager to discuss the relationship. As my anonymous friend said, what's called "feminine" is simply "normal human." Fortunately, most men do behave that way too—contrary to stereotypes. Recent videotaped research of newlyweds found that at least these men and women did not differ at all on how much they sought or gave support to each other. Even the kind of support men and women gave—sympathy and encouragement versus suggestions—did not differ. So much for *that* stereotype.

HSPs, fitting these generalizations even less, are in a position to disregard them more easily, which then makes change easier for everyone still behaving in the old ways. We are the leaders, changing society in a way that is much needed. Research indicates that those who stick to traditional male-female roles on the average have the least happy marriages and are less responsive to marital therapy. A large part of this troublesome tradition is that the "man rules the roost." There is strong evidence that such marriages are less satisfying to both partners and are more likely to end in divorce.

Another part of "male supremacy" in a relationship is that the man ignores any requests from a woman partner that he change. How does this "demand/withdraw pattern" affect a relationship? Withdrawing occurs when one partner tries to speak honestly or intimately, including expressing a demand for change, and the other refuses to talk, turns away physically, or turns off emotionally. The fact is, although both genders do it, it is mainly when women demand and men withdraw that relationships are highly troubled, polarized, and likely to end.

To explore the demand/withdraw pattern, Christopher Heavey, Christopher Layne, and Andrew Christensen at UCLA videotaped married couples in two discussions—one about something the wife wanted the husband to do differently, and one about something the husband wanted the wife to do differently. Typical issues were "go out with me more" or "give me more time to myself." The researchers found that when the discussion was about a change the husband wanted in the wife, there was no demand/withdraw during the discussion. But men did withdraw in the discussions of what the wife wanted the husband to change—the men were refusing to change. (But I doubt that was true of many HSMs, right?)

The point of these two examples is that traditional male-dominant relationships are definitely not typical of successful relationships. So HSMs who do not feel comfortable ignoring others' feelings could not be more on the right track. In the long run, the only mold people should try to fit, whatever their sex, is the one that makes their relationships satisfying and intimate.

So, what can you do to heal the effects of sexism and gender stereotypes? Quite a bit. In one chapter I cannot go into solutions in detail, but I have provided some suggestions:

1. *Work on your low self-esteem*. Reframe that sense of being inferior because you are a woman plus an HSP, or because you are not a "real man" due to being an HSP. Chapter 1 discusses reframing briefly, and both *The Highly Sensitive Person* and *The Highly Sensitive Person's Workbook* work on self-esteem as well.

2. *Improve on your boundaries*. Good boundaries are flexible, neither allowing in every demand from the outside, nor shutting out everyone because you cannot trust them or it isn't cool to care. Discernment is the key here—each person who approaches you is unique, not merely a man or a woman or even an HSP or non-HSP, but an individual approaching you at a moment in time when you may or may not be able to respond.

3. *Replace stereotypes with knowledge of actual men and women*. The only way to reduce the strangeness of the other gender is to listen to members of that exclusive club and see what they are actually like. Hearing their difficulties, you'll be inclined to empathize changing your perspectives from mistrustful to understanding. You may even be able to help. For example, HSMs can go out of their way to give HSWs confidence that they can be in the world successfully, and HSWs can watch out for their own prejudices about "ideal men" and refuse to abide by any tradi-

tional views that, for example, a man who cries sometimes or makes slow, careful decisions is unattractive.

4. *Work on your love-shyness by, for example, vowing to meet some-one every week.* This is a relationship work, not inner work, you'll have to go out and *do* it. But be patient with yourself along the way. As we have seen, HSMs and HSWs both have reasons to expect rejection.

First, consider whether you have unconsciously protected yourself from rejection by looking or behaving in ways that put you totally out of the running, causing you to be completely overlooked as a possible date. "Nothing ventured, nothing lost." I have seen many HSPs who do this.

Second, it helps to prepare a little, planning what you'll say when you meet someone, and then what else you'll say if the other seems positive, negative, or hard-to-read. We HSPs can actually seem more spontaneous if we rehearse a little—it removes the squeaks in the voice, the shake in the hands. You'll have to prepare, too, for the inevitable rejections, and for the pain of having to exit relationships that turn out to have been mistakes.

5. *Confront your ideas about HSMs and homosexuality.* Being "feminine" and being gay are terribly confused in this culture. Five to 10 percent of men are homosexual, but while I have no data on it, I am fairly certain that there is no association with being an HSM. In a chapter in *Real Boys* on being "different," Pollack notes that many "tough" boys turn out to be homosexuals, and many sensitive boys who prefer quiet activities instead of rough-and-tumble play or contact sports turn out to be heterosexual. Gay men have made the same observation to me— the gay community is as full of macho men as it is of sensitive ones, and it is a definite mistake to expect an HSM to be gay. When people assume that, and imply something negative, combat it when you can. "Gay? I almost kind of wish I were—I do like men a lot." Or "That's an odd idea—I wonder why it was on your mind?"

6. *To avoid being a superman, superwoman, or superparent, identify what's causing you to try to be so perfect.* Are you compensating for your "flaw"? Trying to please everyone at once? Refusing to admit you have limits? Too excited about all the opportunities to give up any of them? Once you have acknowl-

edged the source of this striving, you will find it easier to reject a life that is too stressful for you. Your new attitude may require developing new vocations or new ways of leading, based on aiming for the highest quality of work or of parenting, not the quantity of time put in. Your new approach will definitely balance self-care with other-care to optimize both. (By role modeling, you may do more for society than you do through your actual work.)

An efficient way to achieve balance is meditation. I learned to meditate (in my case, Transcendental Meditation) when my son was about one. Just twenty minutes deep within myself, especially in the evening, made all the difference. Dinnertime was transformed from a nerve-shattering experience—with a sensitive mother and child outdoing each other in their overarousal— to a time of happy calm. Meditation helps immeasurably with work too. We all have seen how solutions often appear only after time away from the problem. You will be surprised how much more ready you will be to be productive or loving after some time being nothing.

7. *Find a sensitive mentor of your gender.* William Pollack and other educators have been emphasizing mentoring for boys. Boys can gain a great deal from being with men in addition to their fathers, men who share their specific interests, to teach them more about how to be in the world. Thus a sensitive boy who, for example, prefers reading to soccer could be mentored by a writer or English teacher who could introduce him to the joys of being a man of letters and who might share stories of his woes as a less than enthusiastic athlete. But mentoring can benefit anyone, especially HSPs. So find a sensitive man or woman in your profession or someone who has coped with your current situation, and ask if you can meet to share experiences and ask some questions. (For an HSP to agree, however, you will have to demonstrate that you will not be too demanding—request just one meeting to start with. If one potential mentor says no, try another.)

8. *Protect yourself from those who do not respect you.* I have come to think of the world as having certain areas of very dense, strong gender and temperament prejudice, such as I imagine might exist in some parts of the military. There are other areas

where it is so thin that it is hardly there at all, as with my own husband, who likes women and likes very much the type of woman I am, an HSW. I have made up my mind that it is absolutely essential to protect myself as much as possible from the dense spots.

Since it is not very acceptable these days to exhibit prejudice directly, it may be hard to detect. Become familiar with enough men and women to be able to sort them out, because many of them do make almost heroic efforts to avoid sexism, even if they sometimes make mistakes. If they want to overcome their prejudices, what more can you ask? They did not choose to be born into a sexist world any more than you did.

9. *Remember and then forget the four genders.* Earlier in this chapter I suggested that by having images of four genders, not two, there would be more room for HSWs and HSMs to be who we are. As I described in chapter 1, it seems that all species are meant to have two breeds—sensitive and not. Your breed should matter at least as much as your gender. Take a minute to think of your favorite examples of HSWs, HSMs, non-HSWs, and non-HSMs (admitting we can't know from afar, for sure, who are HSPs and who are not). For me, "real" HSMs might be the U.S. Presidents George Washington, Abraham Lincoln, and Jimmy Carter, plus candidate Robert F. Kennedy and director Ingmar Bergman, poets Rainer Maria Rilke, Robinson Jeffers, and Stephen Spender, and the psychologist Carl Jung, just for starters. Among HSWs, the mystic Teresa de Avila, U.S. First Lady Eleanor Roosevelt, poet Emily Dickinson, sculptress Camille Claudel, authors Jane Austen and the Brontë sisters, and archeologist Marija Gimbutas (who did the decisive scientific work on the goddess cultures).

We can all supply equally illustrious lists of "real" non-HSMs and HSWs. Your favorite entrepreneurs, athletes, explorers, or leaders of nations or of movements were probably non-HSMs, and all the hard-fighting suffragettes and feminists, plus many of the first women doctors, nurses, and scientists, were probably non-HSWs.

Then, when you are ready to graduate from gender stereotypes entirely, try this: A real man or woman is whatever any man or woman is at those times when he or she is living authentically, in accord with his or her true self and temperament. There is no truer definition of your gender than you.

10. *Use your dreams to heal gender hurts.* I always recommend that HSPs get to know their dreams—we dream vividly and are well suited to the deep personal reflection dreams can initiate. I offer lengthier advice about dream work in *The Highly Sensitive Person's Workbook,* but I suggest dream work here too. To heal gender hurts, here are three ways to use dreams:

First, pay attention to the sex of every dream figure. It always carries a message about your current relationship to that gender or to the qualities that gender represents for you. If you dream about someone of your own sex, generally that person's attributes are close to your own, easy to integrate or recognize. For example, when I dream of a certain woman friend of mine who is very extroverted, I know I am dreaming about my extroverted self, who is not very difficult for me to access. On the other hand, when you dream of the other gender, it generally represents attributes you may never have, or believe you can't. So when I dream of a certain male friend of mine who displays special assertiveness, endurance, and strength, I know I am dreaming of the sort of forcefulness I long to have or need right now in my life, but believe that I as a woman can never muster.

Second, use the gender of dream figures to help pinpoint how you are out of balance. For example, suppose you and a friend have tried to work through some issue, and that night you dream of a pale, thin woman drowning. Whether you are a man or a woman, you might want to think back over the evening's discussion to see whether some feminine part of you, in the traditional sense or as you personally define it, was overwhelmed, washed overboard, flooded, or sunk into the unconscious during the talking. By the way, better treatment of the gendered parts of yourself will translate to better treatment of persons of that gender.

Third, imagine new endings to your dreams that change your relationship with the other gender. This is called active imagination—discussed more in *The Highly Sensitive Person's Workbook* and also in Robert Johnson's *Inner Work.* With this technique you neither force a particular ending to a dream nor idly daydream, but return to a dream with an intention to *allow* more to happen in your imagination, which, after all, created the dream in the first place. Your further intention is to take some action too, in your imagination. This method can lead to valuable breakthroughs around gender.

In the case of the drowning woman, you might put yourself into the water with her and try to rescue her. If she can be revived, ask her how she came to be drowning. If you had anything to do with it, you may want to apologize and talk with her. If someone else caused her near drowning, you should begin by considering whether this person could represent a part of yourself. And if she wanted to kill herself, she needs serious attention from you—Why would she want to take her life? If she was swept away by natural forces, you might consider ways to protect her in the future, and what those forces might symbolize in your waking life.

In active imagination it is essential that you not force any issues or judge what comes to you. Like a dream, active imagination should be respected as a useful message from the psyche. No matter how distressing an image may seem at first, its intention is always that you should know more. Its intention is ultimately kind.

FINAL THOUGHTS

There seems to have never been a time in human history when more than a few odd men and women were equal partners. Men and women trying for equality now are pursuing something new, and they had better understand the daunting nature of their task. Recent research suggests that unconsciously our first reactions to a person are based on the prejudices we learned as children, no matter how unkind or unwanted those prejudices seem to us now. This is probably some very old human programing to help us protect our in-group by devaluing all the outgroups. But it certainly causes trouble now, in every corner of the world. This research also finds that the only real difference between racist, sexist people and those who are not is the *conscious* effort that the latter make to counteract their learned-in-childhood, unconscious prejudices.

A lack of prejudice does not mean sameness in all matters, however. Rather, it means that power is allocated equally, according to each person's interest and abilities. HSPs can lead in developing this kind of equality with the other gender because we are good at noticing our unconscious processes, including our prejudices, and can appreciate that gender, like temperament, requires everyone adopting a different-but-equal attitude. We are also excellent at realizing the consequences of all possible strategies, so that we can see that an inequality of power between the sexes will never lead to the trust and intimacy we are trying to develop in relationships.

In the next chapter I explore the HSP's natural tendency to be cautious about intimacy. We bring to that chapter from this one the appreciation that our hesitancies are often associated with a gender—"I'm deeply afraid of men" or "I will never trust a woman again." Our past, decisive intimate experiences always involved gendered others—not just parents or siblings, but mothers, fathers, sisters, brothers. As HSWs and HSMs, we responded to our intimates according to both our temperament and theirs, our gender and theirs, and how well we fit their idea of the perfect temperament and perfect man or woman. The question is, can the wounds due to these too-rigid ideals be acknowledged and healed?

For eons we humans have banished "the others" to the far side of a gulf of ignorance, then hurled/projected after them everything we disliked about ourselves, so that our side felt all good and theirs all bad. Men and women have been spectacular at it. Women say, "Men are aggressive, insensitive brutes," as if women are never like that. Men say, "Women are irrational, demanding, and only out to control men," as if men are never like that. We can fear, revile, and banish each other only so long. Now it is time to realize we actually fear, revile, and banish the other half of ourselves. And HSPs should be able to see this truth first.

3

HSPs and the Fear of Intimacy: The Reasons You Worry and the Ways to Security

As HSPs, you and I are by nature designed to take risk into account very carefully before we act. Intimacy with another person certainly involves risks—loss, betrayal, abandonment, or being used or controlled by the other person, just for starters. So while intimacy is highly praised these days and sounds wonderful in theory, in practice, all HSPs have their reasons to pause before plunging in—some reasons are conscious, some are less conscious.

Our goal in this chapter is to bring more of the unconscious reasons into consciousness where they can be examined. If "in the light of day" some fears seem exaggerated, you can face them more here and perhaps begin to adopt a strategy for reducing them.

First, however, take the Intimacy Self-Assessment about your reactions to opportunities to be intimate.

Intimacy Self-Assessment

Respond to these statements by thinking back about how you have tended to be in all of your close relationships, romantic or with friends.

T F   I feel uncomfortable discussing things from the past that I have felt ashamed of.

T F   There are things about me that, if the other person knew about them, would disgust him or her.

T F   I worry that something I reveal will make the other person angry.

T F   I would almost rather not love someone so that I do not have to worry about losing them.

T F   I tend to expect the other person to betray me in some way, in the end.

T F   I would be afraid to be spontaneous with the other person.

T F   Sometimes when I am close to another person, my feelings are so intense that even though they are positive, I want the feelings to stop.

T F   I am afraid that I might do something that hurts the other's feelings.

T F   I have avoided being close because I thought the other person was going to control me.

T F   A part of me would be afraid to make a long-term commitment to the relationship.

T F   I feel uneasy if another person starts depending on me for emotional support.

T F   I doubt I can be really close to anyone—little things always annoy me too much.

T F   It is difficult to tell this person that I care about him/her.

T F   I have avoided chances to become close to someone I wanted to be close to.

T F   I have held back my feelings in previous close relationships.

....

SCORING

Each true answer suggests a different reason that you fear intimacy— so the more trues, the more fear. Even one true is something to consider, and we will consider each in this chapter.

If you answered true to the first two questions, pay special attention to the first fear described in this chapter, the fear of exposure and rejection.

Question 3, pay attention to the second fear discussed, the fear of angry attacks.

Questions 4 and 5, the fear of abandonment.

Questions 6 and 7, the fear of losing control.

Question 8, the fear of your destructive impulses.

Question 9, the fear of engulfment.

Questions 10 and 11, the fear of commitment.

Question 12, the fear of being easily irritated.

Questions 13, 14, and 15—if you answered yes to any of these, give extra attention to the entire chapter.

....

How did you score? Notice I did not give you a number that means "above this you're fine, below this you're not," because saying yes to *any* of these questions points to some problem with intimacy. But none of them makes *you* a problem, or not fine. Each "true" simply highlights a topic for you. And if you said yes to more than three, you don't need me to tell you that you are very cautious about intimacy in general. You are not alone, however. Meet Max.

CLOSE-DISTANT MAX

Max has been seeing me weekly for psychotherapy for six years. He is an HSM in his mid-thirties who, as much as he can, directs films and plays. The rest of the time he designs web pages as an independent contractor. Many think he is an extraordinary director, but of course he "never compromises his vision," and we know what that can mean for an artist trying to make a living.

Max had a moderately happy childhood. He was the middle child of five and would have liked more of his busy mother's attention, but he was also the most sensitive of the five and her secret favorite (a nice exception to the pattern for mothers with "shy sons" described in chapter 2). So he caused her the least trouble and at the same time enjoyed an unspoken relationship with her that was very satisfying. He and his father also had a good rapport, but this sensitive man was often unavailable too. Being teased or lonely in school was more of a problem for Max, until he discovered the drama club in junior high. After that, his social problems were over. He developed several lasting close friendships in college, and more since. Romantically, he has been in two relationships, one for four years and one for three. He wanted both to last, but there were problems. There are problems with everyone he dates too.

Soon after he began psychotherapy with me, Max and I established a routine. He would bring in his amazing dreams, neatly typed, read them out loud to me for fifteen to thirty minutes, and we would discuss them in the time that was left. He found this so valuable that he was loathe to change any of it, but after five years of this (yes, it took a while), when his three-year relationship ended, we both began to look more at what was going on outside of this hour, in his "real life," and in the hour between us. A few incidents helped him see that some of the problems of those he dated could be better located within himself, as a fear of going beyond a certain level of intimacy. He especially feared being acutely attuned to another's needs and then feeling trapped into accommodating them, as he was by his parents' needs and as he believed himself to have been in his two relationships. Looking at our own relationship, we realized that the dreams were a way to share himself with me quite deeply, yet they had also become a way to avoid relating to me in a more spontaneous, direct way that might make him not "my favorite" (which he secretly imagined he was), or that through my spontaneous response might reveal some need of mine he would feel obliged to meet—the fears of his childhood. So we talked about these fears, as they arose with me and others. Some of what we discovered informs what follows.

HOW DO YOU FEEL ABOUT INTIMACY?

Maybe we need a definition. To me intimacy means being authentic, revealing to another your most private and true-at-this-moment self—thoughts, feelings, bodily self. In return, the other reveals his or her true self to you. This requires trusting each other. So intimacy equals authenticity, which is permitted by trust. Authenticity and trust are not easy matters.

Given this definition, does intimacy seem worth pursuing? Max began asking himself that, and I think that's a reasonable question seldom entertained by an extroverted, intimacy-obsessed culture. Researchers find that people in close, loving, intimate romantic partnerships are more likely to be happy and healthy, to find meaning in life, and to have high self-esteem and low anxiety, while people not in such relationships are unhappy, unhealthy, lonely, and so forth. So does that mean being in a close relationship *causes* all this good fortune and not being in one *causes* the bad stuff?

Not at all, although that is what most people assume. It can also be the other way around—being unhappy, unhealthy, and so forth causes a lack of close relationships, and being a happy person causes one to be able to have happy relationships. But being happy could also cause one to be able to have happy solitude. That is, maybe happiness can exist nicely without a lot of intimacy. I have met many HSPs, Max included, who claim to be happy having a few close friends but without a live-in, committed, or exclusive partner. Let's be open to this possibility, at least for HSPs, and not assume that romantic or live-in intimacy is the only way to be happy.

Still, most of us do want a relationship, live-in or not, in which each person sees the other as beloved and dear, a person who can be relied on through thick and thin and will love us no matter what dark feelings we share. (Note, I did not say, "no matter what we do," as some behaviors, as opposed to feelings, are going to be unacceptable in any adult-adult relationship.)

There's good reason for this desire for a beloved: We are born into another's arms and stay in that intimate, dependent relationship for years. Even as adults, we feel safer and more relaxed when there is at least one person who cares deeply about us—that is, unless closeness with another has been a source of great pain in the past. But even then, we probably all want intimacy at a deeper, instinctual level, even if that desire is overridden by fear at times.

Suppose you do believe you would be happier in a close relationship, and it makes sense to you that, like Max, your own issues are in the way? I would proceed with both assumptions behind the finding that happy people are more often in relationships—I'd trust that you'll be happier when you can be closer to someone, and you'll be more ready to be when you are happier. So you simultaneously do your outer work—trying to meet people, working on your social skills—and your inner work. By inner work I mean self-reflection using dreams, meditation, useful books, deep discussions with others, perhaps psychotherapy. This chapter should be a good start.

True, inner work is not always the formula given for becoming "happier," but I think it is usually the best one for HSPs. While the search for the right relationship will hopefully end with success, the inner work is your life's work, believe me. It will be just as necessary for beginning, maintaining, or revitalizing an intimate relationship—or for being content without one.

THE UNCONSCIOUS AND ITS FEARS

Inner work, as you may know, means exploring your unconscious, where many of your fears reside. Ironically, the more you respect the reality of the unconscious and grasp the enormous power of unconscious fears and assumptions, the easier it is to change or work around these. This is one reason I speak often of the unconscious throughout this book.

The unconscious holds, in part, the ideas and memories we have forgotten but could remember if we tried. Here resides also those experiences that we had so early we had no words for them, but that come back to us through symbols in dreams and bodily "memories" or reactions—the language of the unconscious. The unconscious also seems to serve to keep out of consciousness anything that seems too traumatic or shameful. And in the opinion of Jungians, the unconscious also contains all the archaic instinctual and symbolic "archetypal" knowledge that is often buried through our modern, outer-directed life, but comes with being human. Just as robins have instincts about nests and coyotes about howling, humans have instincts to help us respond to important age-old human experiences, like snakes, Mother, death, beauty, and Great Spirit. But modern, urban humans tend to lose contact with this part of the unconscious. When we are attuned to this knowledge, our life feels more satisfying and whole.

From childhood, HSPs seem to be, from my experience, more in touch with the unconscious, both our own and that of others. For us, the door into the unconscious world swings more easily. We are usually fascinated by this inner world and are aware that it has more influence over the conscious, rational mind than most people think. Naturally we have unusual respect for it, even awe and trepidation, as we also seek to explore it.

So let's tiptoe through your list of possible reasons for fearing intimacy, some of which may be quite unconscious until you think about them, and see which sleeping elephants wake up when you pass.

EIGHT REASONS AN HSP MIGHT FEAR INTIMACY

The first six fears discussed below were named by social psychologist Elaine Hatfield, famous for her pioneering research on love. Hatfield's six apply to everyone, but I have pointed out their special relevance to HSPs. Then, as an HSP aware of our particular issues, I have added two others, as well as thoughts on how to reduce each fear if it seems exaggerated.

One point holds true for all eight: The more you have experienced reasons for any of these fears in the past, the more likely you are, compared to a non-HSP, to feel them in the present. It's just part of the pause-to-check-and-reflect package deal.

First, Fear of Exposure and Rejection

Whenever you open up and are authentic, you risk exposing something that the other will find unappealing, silly, or even disgusting. Humans can rightly fear exposing many things—greed, envy, ignorance, moments of dishonesty, awkwardness, destructive impulses, anxiety so intense it leads to panic, forms of sexuality that at least somebody somewhere would disapprove of. And HSPs have something they may particularly fear exposing—their sensitivity, their core self. I have had prominent HSPs refuse to let me quote them as HSPs, fearing the public will see them as flawed, and a few subscribers to my newsletter have wanted it to come in a brown paper wrapper! Sometimes a sense of being deeply flawed becomes symbolized by a facial feature or bodily curve that we work on endlessly to hide or be rid of. Or we cannot let anyone study our face, look into our eyes, or see us less than fully dressed—important forms of intimacy. We can't expose ourselves.

It is difficult work to rid yourself of feeling so flawed that you can't expose your true self to anyone—the work is like digging out a tree stump with roots that have spread everywhere. As I mentioned in chapter 2 when discussing self-esteem, *The Highly Sensitive Person* and *The Highly Sensitive Person's Workbook* were especially designed to help with this, and this book will add what it can, through improving your relationships.

Relationships are critical to overcoming the fear of exposure because they can reduce your fear to a more realistic size. Even if you can't risk exposing your flaws yet, when you think about those you know well, you will probably have to agree that yours are not much more than theirs and are well within the range of normal if not always lovable human behavior. Since you tolerate flaws in others, you can imagine that those who love you will probably tolerate them in you if you take the risk of admitting your flaws. Maybe they will even be relieved and admit to more of their own "shadow" stuff. As you can imagine (if you try hard to override your assumption that you will be found to be a monster), that kind of self-disclosure increases intimacy rather than decreasing it. If your fear of exposure is very strong, however, consider group therapy or a process-oriented support group where you could test how people actually react to whatever you fear exposing, and hear how many skeletons others have stored away.

In long-term relationships, the stakes can be higher. What you expose may change your partner's trust of you or idea of who you are, and this can change a relationship forever or even end it. The only comfort is to ask yourself whether you want a relationship in which you cannot be authentic, in which your true self is not acceptable. Thinking this way, you may have little to lose. If you are fairly confident your partner will have a negative reaction to what you reveal, consider revealing it in the presence of a trusted third party, such as a marital therapist—preferably one you have seen before. It's good to have a skilled one handy, just like your family doctor. (For help in choosing one, see p. 196.)

Second, Fear of Angry Attacks

Anger is a highly stimulating emotion. HSPs are strongly affected by it, even when we just witness it. If we are expressing it or are the recipient of it, of course we will be aroused beyond our optimal level— our hearts pound, our minds become fuzzy. If the anger is toward us, we also may take what is said very seriously. We will process accusations deeply. The fear of angry attacks is greatly exacerbated for an HSP who grew up in a family where angry outbursts were common and led to nothing constructive. Family members can wound deeply with information gleaned from more intimate moments.

It helps to distinguish between "moral anger" and anger that is intended to attack, obtain victory, and annihilate the other person. This kind does not belong anywhere in an intimate relationship; it destroys trust, especially in an HSP. But what I've called moral anger is a more reflective kind that can be almost ethically required at times in close relationships. It involves one person letting the other know *clearly* that there are certain boundaries that cannot be crossed without violating something important to the one who is angry. For example, your partner, or you, may say "I *must* have a phone call if you are more than an hour late, because I love you and worry too much." And if next time that phone call still isn't made, some anger is justified and is needed to underscore the importance of the boundary.

I am not sure if moral anger can be entirely avoided in a close relationship, so if you fear anger so much that it keeps you from expressing your true feelings out of fear of the other's reaction, you need to explore that more. Maybe you can mostly avoid anger. Usually an HSP, yourself or an HSP partner, does not necessarily need to hear about another's boundary with an angry tone. A simple request ought to be enough. With non-HSPs it often is not, and it may be necessary with non-HSPs in particular for you to use a little anger—or strong words that to you sound like anger—for the purpose of making your boundaries clear. Since non-HSPs tend to deliver with the same emotional intensity they would need in order to receive a message of this sort, you will also have to make it clear that anger is not necessary with you or they will think they have to use some to get a message across to you. Perhaps if irritations were expressed before anger sets in, anger could be eliminated from a close relationship (if that's your desire, given your fear). It seems to be a question we'll all be exploring as we become more aware of our desire for less anger, kind of like asking whether a good restaurant exists that's not noisy, once you realize you'd like that.

My point here is that part of the assumption behind your fear of angry attacks is that you must give and receive anger (even moral anger), or give and receive it at higher levels than you would like—at the same levels that work for non-HSPs. But maybe you don't. Why not ask others to express their needs and complaints without anger? If they do turn up their emotional volume, why not tell them to turn it back down because "that doesn't work for me"? If they can't, why not say you need a time-out until they calm down? Why not a permanent time-out from a relationship that features excessive attacks meant to hurt, not help? Some people are habitually angry and almost can't seem to control it, or won't. When I find that an otherwise seemingly fine potential friend is going to insist on being very angry with me now and then, that's the end of the friendship for me. The threat of an angry attack hanging over a relationship just makes me too miserable.

But before you decide to exit, distinguish between anger meant to hurt—the kind you shouldn't tolerate—and anger that is moral, as well as anger that is defensive, or meant to keep you or the other from seeing something unbearable. In other words, another form of power in protecting yourself against anger is understanding and solving the problem it signals. Have you crossed a boundary you should not have? Have you stirred a sense of shame in your normally reasonable friend? What does he or she fear right now? See if you can use your sensitive intelligence to resolve the other's need to be angry.

Third, Fear of Abandonment

Of course we fear abandonment. If we don't fear abandonment—our partner leaving or dying—then we are in total denial. And HSPs don't tend to use denial as a defense. The idea of the death of your loved one is awesome—fear of this can be far more influential than we are ever conscious of. As for the breakup of a relationship, it is just that—the blending of two lives is sundered, and it feels terrible. HSPs often resist a breakup for just this reason. All sorts of endings hurt.

Then there's the insidious fear of betrayal, as when a partner you thought loved you has an affair with someone else. We all know people who have waited years or even a lifetime to trust anyone again after such an experience. And there are those shameful bouts of jealousy that can result and lurk for years afterward.

One form the fear of abandonment takes is the fear that we will become "too dependent" on someone. Of course we want to be able to live on our own if we have to, but other than that, I think the fear of dependency is a fear of what will happen if we lose the other person.

If we have experienced loss, abandonment, or betrayal early in childhood, before the self was strong enough to handle it, this deep-seated insecurity can pervade the entire personality; this is discussed later in the chapter. For HSPs, these fears are heightened and need to be faced head on. You can avoid intimacy in order to be safe from loss, but it is a far better strategy to risk intimacy, every day of your life, for you never know when your chance will be taken from you.

The assumption that someone may betray you is especially hard to shed if it has ever happened to you. As an HSP you will be superbly cautious, doubting both others and your own judgment of whom to trust. What I am about to say may sound impossible to accept, but I think it is the goal: You cannot predict or stop the sort of eruptions in a partner's unconscious that can cause even the seemingly nicest person to suddenly betray you, but to be fair, nor can you completely control your own. This is part of the unpredictability of life and of the human psyche.

The worst part of the fear of betrayal is the feeling that you deserved it, are worthless, unlovable, without power or resources. Low self-love is the fuel of these darkest thoughts. So for you to imagine that you can risk love because you know you would somehow survive even a betrayal, you need to return to thoughts of who you were before you were with your partner. If you were not worthless then, you will not be worthless in the future should your partner's life take one of these unexpected turns.

Fourth, Fear of Loss of Control

Were you ever tickled as a child? Or tossed into the air? Sometimes it was fun, but at some point it became overstimulating. This point comes sooner for the sensitive infant. The control of stimulation—not too little, not too much—is vital to every living being. But the loss of control in infancy is far more distressing because infants have no way to stop what's going on, and they also don't have a clear consciousness of themselves—a strong sense of "this is me, this is not me." Potentially this experience in infancy too often can leave a strong, primitive fear in adulthood—an unconscious dread of too much bodily stimulation in the presence of another, of physical intimacy leading to so much arousal that one loses all personal control.

As we get a little older, the sense of "this is me, this is not me" grows, becoming a boundary that goes with having ways to keep things out—by shutting our eyes, saying no, turning away. HSPs especially need such boundaries.

Falling in love, however, is about being tossed in the air by something bigger than us that has us in its grip; it is about breaching that boundary a little bit. Studies by my husband and myself found that people in close relationships literally get confused about which traits are theirs and which are their partner's. The me–not-me boundary has slipped. To have it go completely would mean a "psychotic break," a confusion about whether images are happening inside or outside, whether voices are our own thoughts or the words of another. But a true psychotic break is rare, just because we all carry some small, healthy terror of it that causes us to avoid a total loss of boundaries.

Still, humans do enjoy a Dionysian break from boundaries now and then, an overcoming of their separateness, such as through drugs, sexual passion, religious ecstasy, festivals in which social taboos are temporarily lifted, and creative "flow." One of the gentlest ways to break down the me-not-me barrier is by being intimate, being merged with another for a little while. HSPs can do it easily, if we don't fear it, because we are already used to a flexible boundary with the unconscious, and we need only include the conscious and unconscious of another. But we are often made anxious by the experience too—there's just so much of the other and of the unconscious getting in, so much not-me.

Being free to "soften" your boundaries when you would like to requires a well-developed relationship with your unconscious— which I discuss throughout this book—and with your partner. In both cases, the solution is having good "ego boundaries," as in the saying, "good fences make good neighbors." In particular, you need the kind of "ego strength" that lives in harmony with the unconscious, our powerful neighbor, rather than trying to defend the barricades against it. This in turn requires a strong "observing ego," the part that stands outside the fray and understands both sides, like a U.N. peacekeeper.

How about another metaphor? An HSP lives with the unconscious like a peasant on the bank of a great river. Or on the slopes of a volcano. Or on the shore of the sea. When rivers flood, volcanos erupt, or hurricanes pass over a coast, if you live nearby, you must be prepared to flee. But you expect it, and even know that later the mud or ash will make your fields far more productive—a blessing not enjoyed by those living in safer regions. And as for the sea, that great metaphor for the unconscious—those who fish the sea face many dangers, but famine is usually not one of them.

So try not to allow fear to keep you from living on your ancestral lands. Even after the worst flood or eruption or storm, the people return to start over. Even after being overwhelmed by the unconscious, that little conscious ego bobs back up to the surface soon enough.

As for a potential intimate causing you to lose control, the good news and the bad news is that no one is that powerful. As a child it seemed otherwise, which was good or bad depending on the intentions of those godlike adults, but you have gradually learned the truth: Extraterrestrials and other conspiracy theories notwithstanding, no one is in full control of the planet Earth or of you personally. In even the worst overarousing, loss-of-control situation, you retain some control. And moments of intimacy usually do not lead to such scenarios—although sometimes we HSPs behave as if they do.

Work with your partner on your need to feel more in control—for example, take time-outs, even from pleasant overarousal. Explain whatever intimacies are too much for you, right now or generally, like surprise hugs from behind, looking into each other's eyes or at each other's naked body, or long kisses, long lovemaking, or long intimate talks. Be gently honest and clear that this does not mean you love your partner less. Indeed, it may attest to your love's overwhelming intensity. And it is certainly true that all people have preferences; all people need to stay in an optimal level of arousal. Explore your partner's preferences and needs for the right level of arousal in the same spirit, and work out what's best for both of you.

Fifth, Fear of One's "Attack-and-Destroy" Impulses

Especially when we first fall in love, I think something in us hopes to become whole through our love. Love feels whole, energizing and integrating all parts of us. But wholeness would also mean integrating any repressed, split-off anger and destructiveness. So the first time we feel an aggressive, destructive, or sadistic impulse (a natural part of whole love) toward our loved one—in an argument, a passionate moment, or a fantasy—we may panic. Unconsciously we back off from the intimacy to be sure we do not hurt our loved one with the full energy of our repressed impulses. We may even have dreams of toxic waters, radioactive wastes, or atomic bombs, possibly symbolizing our rather inflated fear of what could erupt and contaminate everyone if we expressed these parts of ourselves.

In a long-term relationship the fear of these impulses may be a bit more justified. When you start expressing some issue needing discussion but sure to be hurtful to your partner, what if you notice some fleeting pleasure in the hurting? HSPs in particular may be aware of such deep, half-conscious instinctive desires—a desire to attack and hurt—and then squelch as evil the whole topic that brought up these feelings.

When you feel murderous due to pure frustration or irritation, remember that you can express anger before it seems overwhelming—or figure out why you can't. If your anger is defensive—due to feeling deeply attacked or shamed by the other person, so that you'd like to destroy this person before he or she can destroy your core you—then it could be that your core self is weak and needs strengthening through inner work and perhaps psychotherapy. Or else the other person is all too good at finding the part of you most easily wounded—in which case he or she is acting (not just feeling an impulse) to hurt you; this does not work and should not be tolerated in an intimate relationship.

If you fear that a destructive, aggressive instinct is built into you, its presence does not mean you must act on it in the first form it takes in imagination. Indeed, as an easily socialized HSP, you are the least likely to express it without reflection. Owning up to that side of yourself, however, can lead to its integration, making it even less likely to be acted out unconsciously and freeing you to use that instinct in useful ways. Owning up to it to your partner and accepting those instincts in each other may paradoxically lead to greater love, respect, energy, and intimacy because of the integrity such an integration brings.

To own up to these feelings often means becoming aware of your bottled-up rage from childhood, when your anger probably seemed all engulfing. Sensitive children in particular can really "lose it" when overaroused, having tantrums regularly until they learn how to protect and calm themselves. But if you sensed that those around you would not be able or willing to tolerate your anger, you bottled up these moments of total frustration, and the tiniest angry impulse may still seem truly dangerous, to you as well as others.

For those who are very good, as children or adults, however, spending intimate time with someone means being extra vigilant of the other's needs, always kind and thoughtful. How exhausting. As a compensation, you may have dreams full of bloodthirsty monsters and sadistic murderers. No one *we* know, of course—but for some reason they are out to get us and only us. While such dreams can have several purposes, in the case of the Always Good, such dreams may be saying that the repressed aggressive part of us wants to come into consciousness, which means the death of the helpless, innocent child we are when we hide all of our aggressiveness.

Now may be the time to reexamine your assumptions about what will happen when your aggressiveness shows. Your partner may not react as people did in your childhood—your partner may be more resilient, more understanding that such feelings are normal, more in love with you, even eager to see this dynamic, not-so-bland side of you. And you may be overestimating your true destructive power. After all, you have kept it split off from consciousness so long that all you really know about it is that it seems ready to explode. Once you explore it, you will find it is not infinite. Nor is it utterly lacking in purpose or value.

Sixth, Fear of Being Engulfed

We HSPs are so in tune with the needs of others and with their unconscious minds that, unless we have developed firm boundaries, it is easy for us to fear losing our entire identity, being absorbed by someone else's needs or pain, or having our compassion taken advantage of. Indeed, it may have happened to us in the past, particularly in childhood, if others sensed our eagerness to please and encouraged us to serve their needs totally.

Fortunately, your psyche will not tolerate the suppression of your individuality for long. Indeed, as with the fear of the loss of control, the fear of engulfment may be strongest if your individuality, security, and self-esteem are weak—you sense that you would readily sacrifice these under the pressure to please others and perhaps win a moment of love. But what you seek (and fear does not exist) is real love, the kind that would not wish for such sacrifices from you.

HSPs can also fear engulfment—or perceive it as that when someone else might just call it closeness—because we need more downtime than non-HSPs. A non-HSP partner can seem engulfing when he or she simply expresses a non-HSP's normal capacity to spend all day and half the night being intimate.

A milder form of the fear of engulfment is the fear of being overly influenced by the other. Consciously or unconsciously we HSPs sense that we are easily influenced, especially by people we love and who know us well. When they criticize us or argue with us out-right, we may feel we are completely losing our own perspective. But praise, too, influences us. Suppose your partner takes great pride in your professional accomplishments, but you would like to be able to take more time off. You may find it harder to slow your career just because of your partner's words of praise.

It is easy to say that we should not let others influence us, but social influence is subtle, strong, and is often not consciously processed so that we can spot it. Most people underestimate its in-fluence. HSPs do not. We know love means entering another's force field. We know it will transform us. So of course we hesitate before stepping within it.

Every therapist, researcher, or scholar writing about love will give you the same solution: You must be separate in order to be intimate. If you have no separate self, there's no one inside even to be au-thentic. Yet how can we claim to be intimate and love someone if we keep ourselves totally separate—if we don't share the other's de-sires and want to lessen his or her pain? This is the big question.

Suppose you were going to merge your aquarium with someone else's. It seems like a great idea because the two tanks together will be much larger and have more fish. But suppose your partner's tank has dozens of different spectacular fish and yours only has a few grey guppies. Merged, your fish will soon be overlooked, or eaten.

The fear of being engulfed assumes that you have a small aquar-ium, and if you allow anyone to take down the wall between the two of you, you will be gone. So, you need more fish—we will turn to this topic later, although you may already have your own ideas about what more fish would mean for you. In the meantime, check the actual number and size of your partner's fish. Have you "pro-jected" your own denied or undeveloped fish into the other tank, when they actually belong to you?

Another assumption to question is how much your partner actu-ally wants to engulf and devour your little fish. Look carefully at your childhood for those powerful caretakers who demanded that of you and ask yourself if you are projecting that onto your partner. No one who actually loves you would demand that of you. But does your partner, really? Or does your partner only want to be close, to see your fish swimming together?

If it is a matter of your partner wanting more time with you than you want with your partner (or anyone), this can be negotiated. Once you realize you can express your needs and your partner can accept them, you may find that your fear of being engulfed has vanished.

As for being overly influenced, use it to your advantage: Ask your partner to reinforce what *you* want reinforced. But do not entirely eliminate the influence of your partner—who can better see where you might need to change?

Seventh, Fear of Commitment

We hear about this fear all the time, forgetting it has many sources. Those who have been hurt in the past may fear commitment, as will those who had engulfing parents. Narcissists fear commitment because it means admitting they need someone. HSSs fear commitment because it curtails their freedom; they fear boredom. HSPs might have all these reasons not to commit, but in addition, we tend to fear making the wrong choice.

What a sensible fear. You know you will become deeply involved with someone you love, opening yourself to intense pleasure and pain. You want to be faithful to this person, perhaps for life. And HSPs have a genetically programed strategy, adopted by a minority within almost every species, which is to reflect before acting. You are going to reflect a long time before committing to one other person.

HSPs also fear commitment because we fear being responsible for others. Will we fail our partners? Hurt or betray them? What if they become too dependent? If we can't handle these responsibilities, will we be seen as failures? Feel like failures?

The only way I know to solve this fear is to accept that you cannot possibly be sure of your decision. With any important decision, at some point you must go ahead, because not to act also has consequences. And keep in mind where the exit is—what you would do if you found you had made a terrible mistake. While it would be very undesirable and painful to break this commitment, you could if you absolutely had to.

As for your justifiable fear of being responsible for another, the issue of boundaries applies once again. Aim for a balance of separateness and oneness, a healthy dependence, an interdependence.

Enjoy each other's strengths but don't assume those resources are the other's to command. Help each other if you can, but not because you must. With emotions, if you can make each other feel better, what a joy. But it is not one person's duty or the other's right to have good feelings quickly restored in every situation. The question is this: If you do not feel able or willing to help, can you stay separate enough to endure letting the other person work it through without your intervening? You may be surprised to find that not only is it okay with your partner that you do not respond instantly, but it is a relief not to have you hovering, helping when you didn't really want to, or helping only because you must reduce your own discomfort.

Eighth, Fear of Disliking the Other for Subtle Annoyances

HSPs can be bothered by all sorts of subtle things that are irritants only to us, and somewhere inside we know it and fear its effects on the other and on our own love. If we don't love, or only love from afar, we never have to deal with certain smells emanating from our beloved's body, little habits like a nervous cough or fidgeting with keys, some extra weight around the middle, or being interrupted at the wrong time with the wrong comment. One HSP confessed she couldn't stand to listen to the sounds her family made while eating. Another HSP related that he'd be telling his partner his dream and she'd start combing her hair or making coffee, spoiling the sacredness of the telling; and at the same time he felt ashamed for taking his dreams so seriously.

Often we HSPs mistake our "trivial" reactions for a true inability to "really love" and give up on ourselves as lovers, because being close really puts us in a quandary. If we don't mention these irritations, we are distracted from being fully present and feel dishonest. But if we do mention them, we suspect, often rightly, that we will be met with anything ranging from incredulity that we could be so fussy to anger that we could be so critical or harbor such feelings without mentioning them earlier. Further, we may feel terrible about being so petty and unaccepting, especially when the non-HSPs who love us are so generously oblivious to our own smells, nervous habits, interruptions, and so forth. So we may choose to be lovingly tolerant—and turned off. But that's not a close relationship, and so we decide there's something wrong with us. We may just not be able to love anyone.

What to do? Accept that you have the right excuse for being annoyed by small things—you are highly sensitive. My husband—who has been hassled by me for fidgeting while we meditate, talking too loud, asking too many questions, and a dozen other things—has pointed out that he is actually glad to comply if the request is in a spirit of love. How important it is for an HSP to hear this. Once a partner understands and appreciates your sensitivity, you really will be able to love someone and express your being bothered by these "little things" that seem so big.

A word of warning, however. There are times when it seems to my husband that no matter how much he changes, I will not be happy. We have learned that these are the times when I am disliking myself, and therefore him, who is so much a part of myself. When I can accept my temperament, I can accept his too. So check to be sure your annoyance is not part of an underlying self-loathing in which both you and the other, who is a part of you, are not worthy of love. That self-loathing, so hard to root out, is poison to both of you.

Again, it is part of the package deal that you will notice your partner's subtle needs and know how to meet them, and also have to ask your partner not to jingle the car keys. You may have to negotiate, remind, and smooth ruffled feathers. But there's nothing to fear here. It's just a normal desire to live without things that would annoy any HSP.

A WORD ABOUT SENSATION SEEKING AND THE FEAR OF INTIMACY

HSSs are, on the average, less likely to marry or commit to a long-term relationship—presumably because they want a variety of partners. But what about the HSP/HSS? You probably blend the desire for many partners with the desire, upon HSP-reflection, for deeper experiences. So you may have many partners during one period of your life and one partner for another. With the one, you may actually find it easier to be intimate and to commit, because as an HSS you tend to go after what you want with great energy, overriding some of your HSP cautions.

On the other hand, as we will see in chapter 8, as an HSP/HSS you may find it difficult to find a partner who can meet your fluctuating needs for both excitement and solitude.

DIGGING DOWN TO THE ROOTS OF THE DEEPEST FEARS OF INTIMACY

Now we shift gears, because for some of you my suggestions for reducing your fears of intimacy seemed pie-in-the-sky. Your fears remain, along with deep pain and inexplicable longings. Your sensitivity feeds your fears, but their roots are in your early childhood, as you have probably already figured out. Or perhaps you are like Elise, who was too afraid of closeness even to admit to her fear.

ELISE OF THE HUNGRY SELF

Elise was an intelligent, successful HSW, married for twelve years to Chet, an intelligent, successful HSM. Her "only" problem was the emptiness in her life. She came to me for psychotherapy because she knew I specialized in HSPs and thought I might find some clue about this overlooked by other therapists.

Elise and Chet seemed to have an excellent marriage, full of understanding and thoughtfulness. Yet Elise doubted that she loved her husband and suspected this had something to do with her emptiness. It seemed to her that others, including Chet, were feeling something about other people that she was not.

To me, the more puzzling matter was Elise's tense reserve, session after session. She professed to feel more comfortable with me than with the past therapists, even though they had declared her to be exceptionally healthy. My not sending her away with this assurance was both pleasing and frightening to her. But to me, a sense of emptiness and disconnection is a serious symptom, no matter how well adjusted a person seems. Further, Elise had recurring bad dreams. And there was her childhood.

Elise's father, unable to cope with "two infants," had left her young mother when Elise was one. Elise's mother had been a much-applauded concert violinist as a child, a true prodigy. The year before Elise's birth, her mother suffered several scathing reviews by

critics, and due to "nerves," she was unable to perform or even practice and was quite unable to mother a child. This was all handled
"gracefully," according to Elise, by her father's extended family,
which sided with her mother. When her mother was incapacitated,
various relatives took care of Elise, happy to have "such a good girl."
Life was supposedly normal, even when Mother was "sick."

In fact, of course, Elise's mother was never a happy or healthy
woman; she spent her adult life quite out of touch with reality, trying to recover the brief, hollow comfort of childhood fame. From
birth, Elise must have lived in fear of disturbing her mother and
causing one of her "nerve episodes." Sensitive infants especially can
adapt like this. Yet in spite of her effort to adapt, Elise had believed
herself to be the cause of both her mother's inability to perform and
her father's departure.

When Elise was twelve, her mother's brother stepped in and
taught her to be "self-sufficient," encouraging her in her studies and
helping her go to college and professional school. She loved him
dearly for this, but even her new independence and success were
achieved to please someone else, in this case her cherished uncle,
whom she secretly believed would abandon her if she did not do
exactly what he wanted.

ELISE'S "WORKING MODEL": TRUST NO ONE

In the first days of life, infants appear to develop a simple but useful "working model" of themselves and others. In the case of Elise,
hers was that (1) she was bad, the cause of all problems, and
(2) others cannot be counted on.

It may seem surprising that infants can have such a set of operat-
ing assumptions about themselves and others, but there is good evidence for it, and it makes sense that infants would need this in
order to adapt to those on whom they depend for survival.

However, as Elise developed more awareness, around two, it was
probably too terrifying to emphasize the part of her working model
that assumed her parents could not be counted on. It was less distressing to emphasize that she was the problem—at least that gave
her some sense of being in control.

Other patients have told me of similar, almost conscious decisions
about their working models. One abused child gave up quickly on

adults as caretakers but had some hopes left regarding God. He decided that a just, powerful God had allowed bad things to happen to him because he was bad, which was something he could try to change—a far better assumption than that there was a bad God or no God at all looking out for him. As a child, Elise had not quite given up on the adults around her, so she had hoped she could win their favor by being very good—by being whatever they wanted her to be.

Working on these sad but superficially useful assumptions, Elise had developed what is sometimes called a "false self," a seemingly very mature personality that was too perfectly adapted to the outer world, with no connection to her real desires, temperament, or interests. As in her childhood, so in her adulthood: with Chet she was the perfect wife, and with me, the perfect patient.

Except something in Elise warned her that pleasing me was not the way to please me, or to "do therapy" correctly. She also sensed that her emptiness was coming to the fore, could not be ignored, and was not the way an adult should feel. More frightening still was what was behind the emptiness—the desperate, preverbal, almost primitive need for holding and connection, a dread of imminent abandonment, and anger about her mother and father's abandoning her.

HOW THE CHANGES BEGIN

These feelings, along with Elise's nightmares, were all signs to me that her psyche was ready to heal, to change her devastating internal working model. Her identification with being an HSP was where we began. It was the first aspect of herself that she knew to be true, not created to please others. It gave her a foundation. For example, in her sexual life with Chet, she did what he wanted, but without pleasure. When she thought about what an HSP might like and not like about sex, she began to discuss more precisely at least what she did not like, first with me and then with him. The other side of what you don't like is what you like, and so she discovered her authentic sexual self through her sensitive self.

One day she told me that she looked forward to dying and would have taken her life if it were not for Chet and her children. I commented that I supposed she had imagined how terrible they would feel if she died. She looked at me blankly. No, she had not. Then she added that she was ashamed to say it, but she wasn't sure she would mind if they died. She didn't know; she couldn't tell. For the first time, she began to cry, confessing that, to her surprise, *my* death might bother her. In fact, the thought of losing me was terrifying. But she did not want to care about anyone, ever.

And so our work took hold as she began to have her first true connection with anyone. That is, she was increasingly open and intimate with me in spite of her fears and without having to sacrifice her basic, instinctual needs. Instead, ours was a relationship that helped her discover her own feelings. And in time she discovered authentic feelings for Chet and her children too. Her working model had begun to change—she was someone others could love, she was someone who could love them.

A Self-Test of "Attachment Style"

If you like, read the following four statements and then *circle the star beside the one statement* that best describes your attitude about being in a *love* relationship in general (that is, not just your attitude in your current relationship or some past relationship, but rather your overall relationship attitude). More than one statement may fit, depending on circumstances, but circle one and keep the others in mind as you read further.

- It is easy for me to be emotionally close to others. I am comfortable depending on others and having others depend on me. I don't worry much about being alone or rejected.
- I want to be as emotionally close to others as possible, but I often find that others are reluctant to get as close as I would like. I am uncomfortable being without close relationships, but I sometimes worry that others don't love me as much as I love them.
- I am more comfortable not being in very close relationships. It is more important to me to feel independent and self-sufficient. I prefer not to depend on others or have others depend on me.
- It's very hard for me to be emotionally close to others. I want to be, but I find it difficult to trust or depend on them. I worry that I will be hurt—that they will leave me, betray me, or be cruel.

Attachment Theory Rediscovers the Obvious, But with Hard Data

An important breakthrough in understanding relationships came with Freud and those who followed him, who all acknowledged in various ways that our current relationships are conscious or unconscious repetitions of the past. But it is only recently that there has been solid research on this repetition, in the form of the study of what is called attachment theory.

Attachment theory begins with the obvious: A newborn infant is helpless and therefore naturally alert to and ready to bond with whoever is there to take care of him or her. This bond means life. The infant not only needs nutrients and warmth, but absolutely must feel safe, well held, well met, and loved. A lack of love not only interferes with being a loving adult, but with the normal development of the psychological/neurological person. This is established fact. A human life is a social life.

When all goes right, in addition to being held, an infant wants to explore the world. Hopefully the caretaker remains reassuringly responsive and available, a safe home base for the child to return to when something out there seems frightening. In sum, this good caretaker (a) creates a sense of safety, (b) does not prevent the child's exploring when it is safe for the child to do so, and (c) does not disappear or become unavailable while the child explores.

As adults, we carry around this sense of an inner home base, provided we had it. It is the memory of safety with Mother or Father or someone else. It allows us to continue to count on others to be that safe home base. And when others are not available, there's an inner sense of security that remains as our fallback position. We can recall that people were glad to be available to us in the past, are usually available now, and if they are temporarily unavailable, will be back to supporting us shortly.

When caretakers do not provide this security, infants seem to have alternate working models almost "wired in," as these models are easy to identify and are consistent all over the world.

The Four Attachment Styles

Turning back to the four descriptive paragraphs, you can probably see that they are intended as a very rough measure of "attachment style," in order to give you some feeling for which you might be. (Typically children are assessed by being observed with their parents; adults, through a lengthy interview.) Two or more of them may have seemed almost equally true of you, or true at different times in your life. Still, reading more about your first choice among the four should stir your unconscious and help you to recognize if we are getting close to your deeper reasons for fearing intimacy.

1. *The secure style* (the first statement on the test above, adopted by about 50 percent of people): You feel secure that you will be loved and not abandoned by those you are close to. You feel good about yourself and good about others.

2. *The preoccupied style* (the second item, adopted by about 10 percent): You want very much to be in an intimate relationship but fear the other will not reciprocate. This is because, typically, your caretaker was very inconsistent—completely unavailable at some times, intrusively overinvolved at other times. The person may have wanted you to stay a needy child (except when this was inconvenient for him or her), even when you were ready to be independent. In other words, this person was responding to his or her own needs, not yours, and so was never really available. This inconsistency and lack of responsiveness to you, real love, left you anxious about what to do to keep the consistent attention you needed for survival. As an adult, you may keep trying out different ways to attract and keep someone's love, generally suspecting that the other person is about to lose interest. In sum, you feel good about others—they seem wonderful, better than you—but insecure about your own worthiness.

3. *The dismissive avoidant style* (third item, about 25 percent): You have decided it is better to avoid closeness. To deal with the fear and emptiness this can create, you have developed a tough defense that goes something like this: "I'm busy, going places, doing great—I just don't really need a close relationship." You may be a person of few feelings, perhaps very "analytical," but you or others may also detect a telltale underlying preoccupa-

tion with the whole issue of being taken care of—for example, not liking people who are "needy" or "self-pitying," vehemently claiming that you definitely do *not* need to be taken care of by anybody, and meanwhile tending to see people in terms of how they can help you get where you want to be. (This attachment style is more common among men, with their Boy Code instructions not to need anyone or show feelings.) Your parents were probably unresponsive to your emotional needs to be seen and loved, and perhaps to your physical needs too. Nothing was talked about, and much was blocked, so that you have few childhood memories, and fewer feelings about people, then or now. But laboratory studies have found, as you would expect, that dismissive avoidant children show signs of dissociation— that is, when placed in an upsetting situation, their physiology shows a strong reaction, but they say they aren't upset in the least. By adulthood, these physical reactions seem to dwindle, as though a part of the brain gives up on trying to register certain emotions.

The concept of a dismissive avoidant is much like that of the narcissist, described in the last chapter. The negative-sounding label of "narcissist" is no help, is it? The narcissist does not intend to be this way—it is a defense against some pretty bad feelings. Dismissive avoidants at least superficially feel good about themselves, but not that good about others, and deep down, not that good about themselves either—like the fearful avoidant.

4. *The fearful avoidant style* (the fourth item, 15 percent; not described in *The Highly Sensitive Person,* this category is now better established): You are chronically shy, anxious, depressed, and lonely (non-HSPs especially may be passively or overtly hostile as well). You want to be with others but fear rejection, so you are highly conflicted, highly aroused, and your reactions to chances to be close to others tend to be "disorganized" (another term for this type). Your caretakers were probably seriously neglectful or dangerous, emotionally or physically. They were frightening or frightened themselves (depressed, anxious). Again, you were constantly in conflict, wanting to be close but fearing it, which disorganized your behavior, often creating dissociation or trancelike "spaciness" because the whole attachment issue was an unending source of distress.

Unlike the dismissive avoidant, who as a child tried to assume that he or she was okay and the fault was with the other, you felt safer assuming, as Elise did, that there must be something terribly wrong with you. As an adult you may be in a relationship, but going through the motions in a disorganized way, not very present or true to yourself, and like Elise, not truly intimate. Alas, you feel bad about yourself and others.

Your Sensitivity and Your Attachment Style

Being a secure or insecure type has nothing to do with being an HSP or not; about the same percentage of HSPs and non-HSPs are secure. Our experience of our caretakers, not our temperament, gives us our working model of the kind of help we can count on when we explore our world and encounter danger. But our attachment style impacts us more because we are HSPs.

Our extra sensitivity to our caretakers is well demonstrated by a study of eighteen-month-olds, who were exposed to arousing, unfamiliar events while alone with their mothers. As expected, all the sensitive children responded initially to these situations with motionless, heart-pounding vigilance (and adrenaline in their bloodstream)—the pause-to-check response typical of HSPs. (In the same situation, the nonsensitive children dashed into the situation without a pause.) But the sensitive children who were securely attached to their mothers only paused to check. Having decided the new situation was safe, they were soon exploring it like the nonsensitive children.

In contrast, the initial caution of the sensitive children who were in insecure relationships evolved into a true fear response, as indicated by their rising cortisol levels. Cortisol is a hormone secreted when we feel threatened, preparing us for "fight or flight," and is easily measured in the saliva, urine, or blood. Since children are constantly faced with new situations like those in this experiment, the study suggests that insecure sensitive children are going to be chronically fearful and chronically flooded with cortisol. Chronically high cortisol creates chronic daily anxiety, insomnia, a lower immune response, and a still greater tendency to pause to check in new situations. So for HSPs especially, an insecure attachment affects everything else in life.

You probably can't even remember back to being eighteen months old, but like the toddlers in this experiment, your attachment experiences were already designing your personality and physiology.

Attachment Style and Adult Relationships— It Really Matters

Recently, interest in research on attachment has blossomed, mainly because researchers have found objective ways to study it. The attachment styles of infants and children with their parents have been carefully observed in laboratory and home settings. The styles clearly differ, are usually established early in infancy, and strongly affect how children behave away from their parents—their confidence at play, their treatment of other children, their ability to share and be intimate.

Most important, when infants are followed into adulthood in longitudinal studies for twenty years or more, their attachment style usually does not change and predicts all kinds of adult behaviors. In comparing the "secures" to all three types of "insecures," the following differences have been found:

- Secures have a greater sense of general well-being. They are more self-confident and more balanced and realistic in their expectations of themselves.
- Under stress, secures stick to the task better, not becoming either highly emotional or denying the problem.
- Secures are less likely to use alcohol for coping or to have an eating disorder.
- Not surprisingly, most people would prefer to have secure partners. Secures are happier in relationships and are less distant, defensive, or distressed by feeling vulnerable.
- Secures are less frustrated with their partners, less ambivalent about their relationships, and less jealous, clinging, or fearful of abandonment.
- Secures become angry less often, but they see anger as more constructive, feel better during arguments, see less hostility in their partners' intentions, and expect more positive outcomes.
- Secures are more likely to see their partners as trustworthy friends and to accept their faults.

- When anxious, secures are more likely to turn to their partners for support, and if their partners are anxious, they are more likely to give support.
- Secures have more positive emotions and are less likely to control all of their emotions, but especially their positive emotions; these emotional characteristics are strongly associated with relationship satisfaction.
- Secures are less likely to show physiological arousal when separated from their partners.
- Finally, secures are less likely to engage in sex without feeling love for their sexual partners.

How do you recognize secure types? Ask how it was for them growing up in their family and at school. Secures will answer in a straightforward way, admitting some problems but nothing that any reasonable outsider would consider major. They have many happy memories, and they do not speak compulsively about any of their memories. Dismissive avoidants will say that they have no memories of their childhood, or say things like, "Oh, Mom tried to kill herself a few times, but it didn't bother me much." Or "Childhood? Fine." And nothing more. Feelings are minimized. Preoccupieds will tell you the equivalent of a book about their childhood when you only asked a one-sentence question. Fearful avoidants would do the same if they believed you would listen, so a few more caring questions will get the same response from them as the preoccupieds.

Beware, however, that secures prefer other secures and insecures tend to be attracted to each other, even though they can also make each other miserable (imagine the increased insecurity an avoidant dismissive would create in a preoccupied or fearful avoidant). So obviously it helps enormously to be, or become, secure yourself.

On Becoming Secure

While most insecure children grow up to be insecure adults, there are so many exceptions that researchers have a name for them: "earned secures." Indeed, there are good reasons to believe HSPs are unusually well suited to change their insecurity to security. But it takes time and considerable work and reflection; and unfortunately, direct advice on how to do this is scarce, except that "insecures need psychotherapy." I think there are more ways than that, but here I can only give you a list of approaches, like reading off the signs at a crossroads, and tell you that you must eventually explore every one of them, probably in therapy but also outside of therapy. Here are the signs for the roads you must travel:

1. *Gentle patience.* It took years to make you insecure, and it will take some time to undo it. Attachment style resists change because the best chance of survival rests on assuming that the future repeats the past, and HSPs are especially designed to operate on that assumption. So ignore all those comments about "just put the past behind you." Also, the gentle kindness of your patience is essential. Try to stop blaming, punishing, and neglecting yourself. This is terribly difficult, but it repeats what happened to you and so maintains the insecure attachment—not only do you continue to treat yourself badly, but you expect others to because somehow you deserve what happened. You did not deserve it.

2. *Have a better experience.* You have almost surely already had some secure relationships—a few people who responded to your needs too, not just theirs, and thus made you feel you were worth attention and that they would respond if you needed help. But you need more such relationships. Ideally, you have a romantic partner and a same-sex friend and one or two relatives who are secure themselves. You need several because an insecure person can be difficult to make secure—you will tend to test them often. For this reason, psychotherapy is usually the best place to have your first long-term secure relationship. The psychotherapy you undertake, however, must be designed for this purpose, skillfully performed, and long-term (expensive—think of it like a college education). In the *Highly Sensitive Person's Workbook* I suggested ways to find an affordable therapist.

3. *Grieve.* You need to grieve about how bad it was in childhood, that you can never go back and have what you missed in those early years, and that the damage done interfered during your insecure years with you living your life as fully as you might have. This grieving is not about "getting over it and growing up," but the opposite—living with this grief your entire life. It is part of

your story, although you will learn not to bring it up around those who will not understand. Interestingly, earned secures have a residue of sadness, like a scar after surgery, that is not found in other secures.

4. *Individuate.* Individuation means finding out who you are, especially by opening to your unconscious mind. Finding this inner core creates a kind of mature security unlike any other. Individuation is facilitated most by understanding your dreams, which often requires the help of a Jungian therapist or books and seminars on dreams. You'll find that the healing process unfolds in a precise if organic way, bringing up what is needed when it is needed as if it were guided by some higher, kind intelligence, which has to add greatly to your inner security. So even if the first images that come from this core bring dark feelings of anger or hopelessness, you can trust that you need to feel these in order to heal. The idea of individuation can make an HSP feel guiltily self-centered, but individuation is not "small self"-centered at all, because it also reveals the purpose of your life in relation to your ancestors and the world—a destiny that may be very demanding of you and eventually shifts your attention completely from your past and small concerns to the world's future. But all in good time. The point is, the unconscious contains more than specific fearful assumptions to be changed. It has wisdom that will be revealed as the individuation process unfolds.

5. *Revise your assumptions.* Periodically reflect on your fears of intimacy as realistically as possible, because as you progress, it will be easier to talk yourself out of them. Sometimes a "gut fear" established in infancy will never go away, but it can be overridden by thinking to yourself: "I know this fear is meant to protect me, but it's like a false alarm—I do not need to act on it. I appreciate the warning very much, but I think I will ignore it."

6. *Suit your approach to your attachment style.* If you are a fearful avoidant, work on just meeting people and not assuming they will reject you; yours is a substantial task. If you are a preoccupied, your task is letting go of people a little and trusting they will come back when you do ask for attention, not merely when they feel like it. But start to notice that you don't really need or want attention every second, even though it feels that way. If

you are an avoidant dismissive, admit that you have given up on others, as if your heart has turned to stone. For any chance at love, you must let your heart melt. When you have broken through your defense of not caring, you will feel more like a fearful avoidant or a preoccupied. It hurts more, but for you it is fine progress; it just means the anesthetic is wearing off.

7. *Experience pure consciousness.* Like individuation, meditation gives a solid sense of one's core, one's inner being. The form of meditation should be effortless and lead you to a state of pure consciousness, at least sometimes—moments of pure awareness, deep restfulness, without thoughts, perceptions, or emotions (except a peaceful bliss). It is a deeply satisfying state, a feeling that "Mother and Father are at home." But this is the Great Mother/Father. What could provide more security?

TAKING THE BIG STEP

To learn to sail, reading about it will not suffice—you must finally find some water and launch a boat. To overcome fears of intimacy, you must finally enter a close relationship and risk being honest, authentic, and vulnerable. Many people afraid of intimacy say to me, "I'm constantly telling people about myself" or "I always tell my wife what I feel." But "what I feel" turns out to be "what I think," and the whole truth of what they are feeling they have seldom told, out of fear—fear of exposure, angry attacks, abandonment, and all the rest. Particularly for the HSP, losing a chance to be intimate seems much less dangerous than rejection, overarousal, engulfment, and so on. But chances for intimacy are not infinite. Do try.

Let's revisit Max, the HSM I described at the start of the chapter. Recently he told me about this incident: He spent a day at art galleries with a friend he hoped might become an intimate with time, and afterward she wanted to go dancing. Max was feeling overwhelmed by overstimulation but feared being seen as uninteresting and too sensitive, so he claimed he had other plans.

When they met a week later, Max let slip that in fact he had stayed home that night. He was embarrassed and hoped the woman had overlooked his slip, for he could not imagine admitting that he had lied. All evening he felt nervous and distracted, alternating disgust with himself and anger with her for "forcing" him into this situation.

Meanwhile, she had turned cool—she probably did notice his slip and also his different mood. She may well have concluded he was no longer interested. But Max assumed she was withdrawing due to his generally lame personality that could neither tell the truth nor enjoy nightlife.

All of us can see what Max needed to do, even if we'd do what he did. He needed to own up to his exhaustion—and to his sensitivity—on the very first night. Or failing that, which is certainly easy to empathize with, own up the next week as to why he could not be honest with her before. I did point out that he still could call her and discuss what had happened between them. Hard to do, but if the woman was worth any further effort at all, I thought she would be grateful for the honesty. Max did call her and confess, by the way, and she was angry about his lie and could not forgive him. Since she probably has not yet met her own "shadow," she could not sympathize. Or else she had too many other experiences of lying and betrayal. Honesty does not always work at the start of a relationship in the sense of keeping it going, but it does in the sense of exploring whether it is worth keeping.

Being open about certain emotions will be easier than others. Get to know how you feel about owning up to fear, sadness, affection, anger, optimism, curiosity, dishonesty, sexual desire, guilt, and pride, to name a few. Think about how these were handled in your family. Were some of them "against the law"? What would happen to a member of your family who violated that law? As you become more intimate with someone, it is important to discuss which emotions are "touchy" for each of you, so that both of you can watch out for those you are likely to feel you need to hide.

WHEN THE OTHER FEARS INTIMACY

Although I have implied throughout this chapter that HSPs are especially afraid of intimacy, I think that on the average we are far more likely to want intimacy than others and lead others toward it, especially if we are secures, either "earned" or by good parenting. What do you do when a friend or partner seems to fear intimacy more than you—for example, when there is every indication that you and the relationship are important to this other person, but the two of you are not close?

Obviously it does not help to harangue the other about being more trusting. Rather, your best strategy is to be even more intimate, honest, and vulnerable yourself—whatever the results. This is *not* easy. People who fear intimacy can be very prickly and critical—as a cactus would attest, it's the best defense. But be open anyway, if you can. Being more separate and individuated will help enormously so that you feel secure within yourself no matter what response you get back. That way, in a sense, you have less to lose.

Peter Kramer in *Should You Leave?* gives the same sort of advice about getting partners to change: Forget about changing your partner—change yourself, dramatically and consistently. Build the bridge from your side. In this case, be as honest and intimate as you can, as often as you can. If it doesn't help this relationship, it will develop you for the next one.

A LAST LOOK AT YOUR CONCERNS
ABOUT INTIMACY

I hope I have conveyed that I think HSPs have good reason to be cautious as well as skilled regarding intimacy. I respect your concerns about closeness and hope you will not be too hard on yourself about your moments of fear and withdrawal and your omissions of intimate details, even your occasional outright cover-ups.

At the same time, you are so aware of your own feelings and those of others that if you begin to experiment with revealing these insights, you may find there is nothing to fear. The kinds of people who will be attracted to you then are often the very ones you will especially like. And if you explain your sensitivity to them, they are usually happy to respect your needs. So the others be damned. Having settled that, let's move on—let's talk about falling in love.

4

Falling in Love: Sensitivity and the Big Plunge

Falling in love: HSPs do fall harder than non-HSPs, according to my research. This may seem like a contradiction, given the last chapter's discussion of our greater potential to fear intimacy. But most HSPs can grasp the reason for the paradox: We fall in love harder and fear it more because we are drawn to the depth and complexity of the emotions we are going to unleash, but we also know that the consequences of such deep love are unforeseeable, a situation we never relish.

This chapter is about surveying those complex depths a bit, so that we can be reassured by some understanding of what happens when we are in so deep, so lost in a world of mystery and unearthly beauty. Then, from the safety of land, we will discuss how to get out to those deep waters. Yes, unmysterious as it makes love seem, we will discuss how to fall in love. There's nothing like practical tips to keep HSPs grounded. But first, here's a practical, grounded definition of love—with quite the opposite story behind it.

WHAT IS LOVE?

"Love is a set of attitudes, feelings, and behaviors associated with the desire to enter and maintain an intimate relationship with a particular other person." That's how my husband and I define love academically. But personally, it remains the greatest mystery of our lives.

104

We fell in love in 1967, when we were both twenty-four. It was Berkeley in the sixties, a passionate time. We met in an "encounter group." Art was a graduate student, a teaching assistant, the group's facilitator; I was an undergraduate, a mere member. But it was his first time facilitating groups, while I had been in that role in another setting a dozen times. For the whole semester, I critiqued his leadership style and he said nothing. When it was all over, he told me "he felt some affection for me," we kissed, and the fireworks went off.

This experience was so transformative that besides creating a relationship that has lasted over thirty years, it gave rise to a lifelong shared research career studying what happens when two people fall in love, and how love relates to everything else—the spiritual, social, physical, and personal.

That first year we read everything there was written about love at the time and talked about it endlessly. The next year Art focused his doctoral dissertation on love, performing several creative experiments to see how much falling in love could be affected by the excitement, mystery, and power inherent in the social situation where love happens. Being a social psychologist, he took this approach rather than the popular question of "personal chemistry," or why certain personalities are attracted to each other. Actually, at that time no research psychologists were studying falling in love from any perspective, and it was seen as quite audacious, even arrogant, to tackle such a conundrum. But one of his studies in particular, "the bridge study," which I will soon describe, has become one of the most cited experiments in the history of social psychology.

Since then we have written an academic book on falling in love and a series of articles for scholarly journals. We, along with our graduate students and colleagues, have performed dozens of experiments, and now Art is working on locating which parts of the brain are involved in passionate love. Others have joined the field, and psychologists now know many things about love and falling in love that they did not know in 1967. I can honestly say, however, that sudden love still remains a numinous confusion, at least to me. It seems important to our souls that it be just that—a way of transcending the mundane world and making contact with something rare, wonderful, and beyond words. But I will still share the best of the research with you, focusing on those aspects especially relevant to HSPs.

THE INTENSITY OF AN HSP'S LOVE, FIRSTHAND

Can I provide an example of an HSP falling in love? All too easily. On the self-test, I score 23. Art scores 9. When Art and I fell in love, we were both joyful, but I was also tearful, confused, sleepless, transported. It was a surprise to him, and quite unlike him, that he suddenly knew that I was the one with whom he wanted to have children; I suddenly knew nothing at all about myself anymore, and it was no surprise at all to me, because this was not the first time I had been overwhelmed by my own emotions. Clearly my experience was different.

Given this beginning, it was natural that when I later studied HSPs, one of the first questions I asked of them was whether they thought they fell in love with unusual intensity, and sure enough, they said they did. This intensity is greater for HSPs who have had a troubled childhood and an insecure attachment style, but it is true even for those with fine childhoods. The purpose of the first half of this chapter is to understand this intensity, but first I'll relate another example of it—Gary's story.

A CHAMELEON BECOMES A DRAGON

When I interviewed Gary, he was fifty-four and had had five or six careers and as many relationships. Like Elise, whom you met in chapter 3, Gary was an HSP who had the type of troubled childhood—in his case, long illnesses and unavailable parents—that set him on a course of using his sensitivity to observe exactly how to adapt and please others for the sake of his own survival. With the added concern of having to prove his manhood after years of illness, as a young man he became a star athlete and freshman class president in his high school, although he felt no pleasure from any of it. After high school he joined the air force, traveled, then became a salesman in order to "force myself to communicate better." In all of this he was always popular and successful, but he felt like a chameleon, trying to be whatever others wanted, whatever the situation required. He told me that he picked demanding situations deliberately, to prove to himself that he was alive, not numb and dead. "But I never experienced my life as me."

Then came Mika. Gary was teaching at a tennis club (professional tennis being one of his many careers) when a woman strolled in, wanting lessons. She was "physical, direct, earthy, warm-spirited—a Mediterranean type." It was as though his whole world shifted. He fell in love completely. Very hard.

In Gary's words, when he saw Mika, he "came alive." It seemed to him to be one of his first authentic reactions to life, not designed to please anyone else. Indeed, he has always felt alive and himself with Mika. She was "attracted" to him as well. But she was married, so he tried to contain his feelings, to be compliant once again. They did not see each other for a long time. But they could not stay apart. Eventually she divorced to be with him, and they started a new life together.

Becoming a couple brought a crisis upon them. In his view, "her personality changed—she became demanding." They separated, and she married again and had a child.

We can be fairly certain that Gary's insecure attachment style and fears of intimacy played some role in the downfall of their relationship. But what matters here is that, according to Gary, the passion remains. Mika still wants to have a child with him; it is still the case that he "can look in her eyes and disappear." He may not know how to live with her, but he will always know he loves her—it is something very certain about him, a core more like a fiery, demanding dragon than a chameleon.

FOUR VIEWS OF FALLING IN LOVE, FOCUSED ON HSPS

As we look at the reasons humans are thought to fall in love, we will see that HSPs are bound to have especially strong experiences of the same conditions.

Falling for Our Soul Mate

Love happens when the right person comes along—this is the view most of us have. When in the course of our research my husband and I have asked people to tell the story of what happened when they fell in love, their initial admiration for the person who became their lover is always prominent, of course. She was beautiful, he was handsome, her personality was so special; or there were little quirks or specific features that were peculiarly endearing. People also reported that they often felt love the moment they found out they were being loved or admired by the other—another important reason to be honest about your feelings in a close relationship.

The Theories About Who We Choose

Theories abound about why we love the persons we love. One set is based on the unconscious—that we fall in love with people who remind us of someone else long forgotten, or with whom we hope to work out painful, unresolved issues. Or we fall for someone we sense can help us grow in a certain direction, either by teaching us or forcing us to grow through our reaction to them. A woman longs to be at home in the woods, at home with her own instinctive self, but is scared of bugs, darkness, bears, and lightning. A man comes along who loves camping and who actually goes *outside* to watch the lightning. Of course she falls in love with her nature guide. Or a man drinks a bit too much, then falls in love with an alcoholic and confronts his own drinking problem as he reacts to his lover's.

Those interested in the biology of falling in love think there is a special system in the brain that governs this specific choosing—in the words of Helen Fisher, this system allows "individuals to focus their mating effort on preferred partners" who presumably have some genetic advantage for the individuals choosing them. In animals, the system increases the energy directed toward a particular mate; in humans, where attractions can last a lifetime and exist even without mating, there is also exhilaration, the desire for union, and constant thinking about the beloved. As for how we choose the one to focus upon, some biologists have suggested pheromones, odorless molecules used by many species to signal an aggressive or sexually receptive state. But that does not explain why people fall in love by e-mail or letter, or why if the chemistry is so right they can fall out of love so quickly.

From our own research, it is our impression that most people have a fairly clear, broad idea of what a good partner would be like. They are eager to fall in love if they meet someone who fits it at all, at the right time of their life, in the right circumstances, and believe the other likes them. HSPs, with our tendency to reflect, probably have a more elaborate idea of what we are looking for, and being designed to notice the subtle, we probably notice more of the outer and inner qualities of people, so that we really know when we have found it—and fall hard.

How Temperament Leads to Attractions

Everyone's attracted to certain personalities and temperaments more than others, but I have no doubt that for HSPs temperament is an additional, highly charged aspect of attraction, through at least two processes. One would be the potentially special attraction to another HSP. You could be wildly relieved, as if you are meeting your twin. Instant attraction. There is plenty of research showing that humans are attracted to those who are similar—one study even found that people with the most basic similarity, similar DNA, are more likely to love each other.

But a second reason for a powerful attraction could be the opposite, meeting a non-HSP. He or she might seem wonderfully "normal" (like the majority and not like yourself) and laden with extraordinary abilities. These abilities—not being yours—may seem even magical, such as the non-HSP's staying power in the face of high levels of stimulation. You may want to be like this, or at least have it in your life. This, you feel, will make you whole. You may also feel deeply flattered that such a person could love you. The non-HSP can find you similarly magical, intensifying the attraction from both sides. Each of you is overjoyed that such an amazing person would love *you*.

Of course some of the most intense falling in love can occur after leaving another relationship, or as it is ending. Whatever the temperament of your last partner, especially if things did not work out, I predict you will be attracted next to the opposite type. You could say this is because humans are always seeking to integrate differences and achieve wholeness, or to put it more mundanely, the grass always looks greener on the other side. This is undoubtedly stronger for HSPs because if your last partner was another HSP, you now long not only for the wholeness of being with someone different from yourself, a non-HSP, with all the advantages of possessing that difference, but you may also long to be associated for a change with someone whom the culture considers normal, the ideal—something the non-HSP does not feel when longing to be with an HSP.

And if you were last with a non-HSP, not only do you long to enjoy an HSP's depth, as a non-HSP would in being attracted to an HSP, but you may long to be with someone like yourself for a change.

So in all these ways, the particular qualities that make a person "right" will be more salient to you as an HSP.

Falling After Dwelling on the Other's Virtues

By virtues, I mean of course the beauty of the body, mind, soul, and spirit. Research shows that the longer you contemplate an object in an emotional way, the more intense the emotions toward that object will become. Assuming you are not going to contemplate for long somebody who creates unpleasant emotions, the simple message here is that the more you contemplate someone you feel you could love, the more you will indeed love that person. Of course once you get to know all your lover's faults and frailties, your love may change or even disappear. But for the moment we are talking about falling in love—reflecting on a person you have just met, just begun to like, to admire, to love.

By now, you can probably guess what I will say about HSPs on this one: We are specialists at being aware of subtleties by processing information more deeply and reflecting longer than others do, so of course it would be true that when we dwell on the wonders of a person we have begun to like, we begin to feel even more affection than a non-HSP would.

I suppose we have to add that if we are insecure, or even if we are not, part of our thinking may be, "what if he or she doesn't love me as much?" Or "what if we must be separated?" Fears bring up especially intense emotions about the other person, but so does joy, and HSPs report feeling more of all emotions—joys as well as fears. More emotion and more processing of it equals more intense falling in love.

Falling in Emotionally Evocative Situations

The importance of the setting in which two people meet is a rather surprising idea to most of us, who assume we fall in love when we meet the right person. But as I said before, it actually seems that humans are quite ready for love if the situation is right and the person is just slightly right. Why else do we cherish moonlit nights, wind-swept beaches, and other romantic settings?

My husband was among the first to observe this, in his famous "bridge study." In this experiment, men met, individually, the same attractive woman, either on a swaying suspension bridge high over a canyon or on a sturdy footbridge a few feet above a rivulet. The men were far more attracted to the woman if they met her on the swaying suspension bridge. Since then, many studies in other situations have found the same effect. Somehow an exciting situation makes any person present with you seem attractive—perhaps by seeming exciting as well.

Arousal Plus HSP Equals Love

Some of the research that followed the bridge study found that almost any kind of arousal—watching a movie, even riding a stationary bike—could produce attraction. If arousal is the key to falling in love, and you as an HSP are more likely to be excited or aroused by any novel situation, you ought to be in more situations per month, say, that could lead to falling in love with an appropriate person if one happened to be with you in the situation. You don't need to be stuck in an elevator or lost on a desert island. Meeting someone at your first pottery class could suffice.

What Do We Learn from People Who Fall for Their Therapist?

Psychotherapy is another example that demonstrates the effect of the situation on falling in love, regardless of the person. Freud was the first to note that patients often fall in love with their psychotherapists—called an "idealizing transference"—even though patients do not usually have falling in love in mind when they select therapists and may feel equally intense love for the next therapist they see. In my work with HSPs, I believe that their transference can be much stronger, and that there is more here than the resurrection of old loves or needs transferred onto someone else, as the term *transference* was meant to imply. Psychotherapy can provide a rare depth of attention, acceptance, intimacy, and opportunity to explore the most numinous aspects of the psyche. Of course any person offering a situation like that is likely to be appealing, or as psychotherapist Ethel Person expresses it in *Dreams of Love and Fateful*

Encounters, given this situation, "love appears to be a perpetual possibility waiting to be born."

Person also points out, however, that the strong initial feelings can last longer in therapy or in any other situation in which we love from afar but are not rejected either. That is, as discussed before, love flourishes while we can reflect on the other's good qualities without being disturbed by any additional mundane "facts." The bridge study demonstrates initial attraction; psychotherapy demonstrates how long it can be maintained, given circumstances that provide—in Person's words—"both some guarantee of safety from rejection and some hope (or illusion) of reciprocation, while allowing enough structured separation that the imaginative work of falling in love can take place."

Evocative Situation Plus Imaginative HSP Equals Love
Since HSPs are highly imaginative, the role of imagination in falling in love is stronger for us. And the more evocative the situation, the more the imagination is stirred. What you can't see clearly in the moonlight or hear on the windswept beach, you are freer to imagine. For example, there's more to imagine about a woman on a swaying bridge over a wooded canyon (why is she there and what happens if a cable breaks?). Besides the suspension-bridge experiment, Art also tried situations in which men, one at a time, were in a role-playing situation in which a woman tortured him with drops of acid on his forehead (water, actually) versus her role-playing something boring; or a situation in which he overcame her in a physical contest after she put up a slight or a great struggle. The suspension bridge, the torture drama, the overcoming of a strong woman were all our rather crude attempts to create a more evocative, "archetypal" situation, and whether we quite did that or not, they all led to greater attraction than the more mundane comparison conditions.

When you as an HSP are out in the world—walking down a street, watching two dogs play, buying a book—you are more likely to imagine things and to be aware of a deeper, more archetypal level behind the surfaces of things. Or one could say, you are more likely to process the situation to that deepest level. Or you can stick to the explanation that just being out in the world is a bit more arousing than being at home. The point is, the specialness of the situation for falling in love matters to everyone, and more to HSPs. Whether it is physically arousing, utterly romantic, profoundly accepting, emotionally evocative, or deeply archetypal, you are more likely to feel it and to fall in love.

Falling because of Powerful Unconscious Forces

I already mentioned the possible role of unconscious reasons for choosing a particular lover, but the unconscious can also shove us into love for its own reasons. And I think HSPs are shoved more easily. As I said in chapter 3, HSPs are more open to the unconscious— more attuned to that realm of memories, symbols, and ideas, both personal and collective, both of traumas repressed out of fear and wisdom lost through modern living that removes our instincts. The degree of susceptibility to falling in love and to sensing the unconscious often seem linked, again probably because falling in love is so much an uncontrollable force arising from within the unconscious. Some are more open to it than others. One moment Gary was just a normal, well-socialized guy; the next minute Gary was ready to do anything to be with his beloved, and the social rules be damned.

The love-unconscious link is not new—Freudians said people fall because of a wish to regress to infancy and to fulfill infantile wishes for unlimited sexual gratification. Attachment researchers, even more interested in infancy but with a kinder view of human nature, say we wish to regain that secure attachment we had, or should have had, in infancy. The Jungians would say yes to all of these but would add that humans also sense in love a chance to connect with God, Creation, the Beloved.

The Return to the Paradise of Essential Spirit

All of these views would fit with saying that when we fall in love, we are imagining paradise. Again, HSPs are especially good at imagining. Rationally we know paradise does not exist, but to imagine it and seek it makes life seem so much bigger. Falling in love is wonderful in part just because it is so expanding, unwilling to conform to the prevailing rational view, and beyond human control—like the unconscious. It is wild like the forest outside the city walls, where the wolves prowl.

Love restores in us what John Desteian in *Coming Together— Coming Apart* calls essential spirit—the rich, instinctual level of life always longed for but gradually lost as we conform more and more to what Desteian calls prevailing spirit.

Prevailing spirit is our culture's teaching about what works for the majority. In the case of love, it says that infatuation is not the best guide for choosing a life partner, marriage requires compromise and accepting disappointments, and falling in love outside of marriage leads to impulsive actions that damage a lasting commitment. Prevailing spirit becomes our personal view for most of our lives, especially for most HSPs, and it is a fine and necessary perspective. But so is essential spirit, the deeper, juicier, bodily-instinct level that nourishes the drier, more practical prevailing spirit. HSPs intuit the critical need for essential spirit as well. And we sense that one of the openings through which essential spirit reaches the surface of life to revive ourselves and society is through falling in love.

Deeply loyal to both of these two spirits, no wonder HSPs fall in love so hard when we finally do. The higher the dam—the prevailing-spirit resistance to falling in love and behaving irrationally or irresponsibly—the bigger the flood when it breaks and we HSPs finally love, whatever the price. It is as though HSPs and falling in love generally are both conduits of essential spirit. We were made for each other.

Can Essential and Prevailing Spirit Be Wed?

From the viewpoint of essential spirit, falling in love involves a marriage that HSPs in particular long for. It is a marriage between the deep instincts, or essential spirit, and our everyday feelings, desires, and values, which are usually tamed by prevailing spirit. To wed these two, our deep instincts and surface feelings, is to create a state of wholeness that humans have lost as they have become more rational and civilized. In lovers, especially if they are HSPs, essential and prevailing spirit could be said to be married and procreating, or so one hopes. And if they really are creating new life, everyone notices. The lovers lose all interest in the things that once seemed important and find fresh meaning in life where there was none.

Often the meaning in life that is conceived and born by falling in love, again especially for an HSP, is the instinct/desire to see the end of one's isolated individual ego with its determined-to-adapt, prevailing-spirit attitude. The ego wants to sacrifice itself to something larger—not just one's beloved, but to the relationship, to the new child it has created, to love itself, the Beloved, Universal Being.

If the Spirits Wed, What of the Child That Is Born?

John Haule, a Jungian analyst, explains in his book *Divine Madness* that the Sufis believed that deep love could give birth to a "next generation" of feelings, a new kind of love, called *fana. Fana* means ecstatic contemplation of the divine. Christian and Jewish mystics describe the same state of bliss, achieved through love of God, but the romantic troubadours and the Arabic Sufis emphasized that one can achieve *fana* equally well by vanishing into the divine in another person.

Maybe I've lost some of you here, but I also know many of you are still with me. I am confident that HSPs have always been more likely to have such experiences when falling in love and to have been at the forefront of explaining them to others as not irrational foolishness but a potential paradise that does exist, inside and all around us, all the time.

Of course *fana* can lead an HSP astray, into a dead-end infatuation or the worship of an illusion, perhaps even more easily than the non-HSP. But if it is true *fana,* according to the Sufis, you will pass to *baqa,* yet another "generation" of love and even more real from the perspective of many HSPs. In *baqa* you are encompassed by a greater personality within yourself or a higher power within the world. There is no other—there is just the One. So according to this view, you know true love by its spiritual fruits: it leads to knowledge of your deepest, most transcendental self (more on this in chapter 9).

LOVE FROM AFAR, UNREQUITED LOVE, IMPOSSIBLE LOVE

HSPs are also prone to more "impossible" loves, for the same reasons we can fall in love so intensely. In particular, the unconscious does not always respect conscious, practical problems like who is available or interested in you. And if you are noticing subtle cues, you may expect interest from a person showing unconscious signs of interest when in fact they are not conscious of any interest. Plus, as you learned in chapter 3, you may consciously want to be in love but unconsciously fear intimacy, so that an impossible love is the perfect solution, especially for the fearful-avoidant or dismissing-avoidant attachment styles.

What do you do if you find yourself in love with someone who cannot or will not reciprocate? You must learn to ride this tiger of impossible love, to make it transformative, not humiliating, permanently damaging, or a means to avoid a closer relationship. In particular, you'll need the strength to subdue your determination to have an outer relationship with an unavailable person. The most important realization in this is that you always have the option to relate to the person on an inner level (which will be discussed more in chapter 9).

You also need to believe that you deserve real commitment, attention, and caring from an outer lover. From your inner lover, you can expect both more and less. The less is the lack of physical presence and connection. The more is that *fana* and *baqa* are perhaps easier to achieve when the lover is an inner figure. On balance, however, most of us will gain more wisdom and feel more security and pleasure with a flesh-and-blood lover in addition to an inner lover.

Perhaps the best brief course in transforming an impossible love into what you need comes from Carl Jung. He was fond of saying that the unconscious creates just such terrible situations "in order to force the individual to bring out his very best . . . to renounce one's will and one's own wit and do nothing but wait and trust to the impersonal power of growth and development." So when up against a wall, Jung would always say that to see over the wall you must not struggle and climb, but put down roots like a tree and wait for clarity to come from deeper sources. When up against an impossible love, go inside and down into your depths, then wait for the psyche to reveal the purpose of this passion.

YOU'VE THOUGHT IT OVER AND YOU WANT TO FALL IN LOVE

As I promised at the start of this chapter, we will now switch from contemplating the divine to explicating the practical—what might be done to facilitate the moment of falling in love, if you wish that to happen to you, and also how to deepen a new relationship so that it moves in the direction of love. Can such a mystery be reduced to a list of suggestions? We may as well try and see.

All of what follows is said succinctly, without much acknowledgment of how complicated and difficult these matters can be—except my acknowledgment here. (For more about love-shyness, see chapter 2, and about shyness in general, *The Highly Sensitive Person*.) Doing even a little can bring more love into your life—you do not have to build Shangri-la in a day, or even build it at all. Some affection between you and someone else would do, and it is the rare person who does not desire affection.

I will begin with my own list of how to tell a "good bet," so that you don't use the tips I give you to romance the wrong person. Next I will discuss how to meet another HSP, then how to meet non-HSPs—you do have a choice. The benefits and drawbacks of a relationship with each will be clearer after 5 and 6. I will end with how to deepen a new relationship.

Choose Well, or People Not to Fall in Love with

None of what follows are reasons by themselves to have or avoid a relationship with someone, but they are surprisingly good predictors, in my experience. I believe HSPs can especially benefit from a few guidelines, because we have such sympathy for everyone, such gratitude for any kindness shown, and sometimes such a readiness to "settle for what we can get," being unsure that we will ever find anyone who will love such an "overly" sensitive soul. Meanwhile, someone who could really appreciate you is waiting just around the bend.

- Elaine's number-one rule: See how the person treats his or her mother. Never mind if Mother seems to richly deserve poor treatment, because that still probably means that the first intimate relationship experienced by the person you are getting to know was not so hot.
- The corollary: Try to find a person with a secure attachment style, whatever your own. (I described how to spot "secures" in chapter 3.)
- A close friendship with a person of a different culture can be wonderful, but think long and hard about a lifelong, exclusive partnership. There will be disagreements and strains you never imagined.
- Listen to the person's work history. HSPs often have more job changes than others, but a dozen stories of being fired or having

to quit because of feeling victimized does not suggest good work relationships. Romantic partnerships involve working together, too.

- Beware of those who only talk about themselves and show little empathy for you.
- Also beware of those hopelessly obsessed with their body and appearance.
- Avoid addicts of all sorts. Let them recover for a few years—*then* fall in love.
- Do not stay around someone who has violently angry outbursts, even if they are rare. They probably will become much less rare.

Meeting HSPs

1. *Go where they go, do what they do.* To do that, you must think how they think—easy for you, since you are one of them. Assuming that when you go out you want deep, interesting experiences that are not too stimulating, where would you go? Try attending seminars (seminars long enough to have breaks when you can meet people), religious retreats, and art and historical events; but avoid crowds (by going early, late, or to events that are off-beat). Head out into nature, engaging in loner activities like hiking, jogging, swimming, cycling, or kayaking, and strike up conversations in the parking lot, at rest stops, or in stores geared to such sports. Remember, you must go out alone in order to have conversations with other HSPs. The list of places to try is long once you stop telling yourself there's no place to meet HSPs because they don't go to happy hours and singles clubs.
2. *Learn to recognize them.* For you, this won't be difficult, once you start noticing. HSPs often have a feel or look about them. This is hard to put into words, but personality (including temperament) does show in bodies and faces—the muscles settle into habitual gestures and expressions. HSPs usually look more thoughtful, subtle, perhaps a bit delicate, guarded, or wistful. They will be at the edges, hopefully showing a deep calm as they observe and reflect whatever is going on, but possibly looking rattled or dazed by overstimulation. If they are in a group, they will usually be saying less, and what they do say is either

startlingly to the point or incredibly mundane because they are overaroused or evading attention.

3. *Ask others to introduce you to the HSPs they know.* If your friends don't speak "HSP," you can ask to meet other "sensitive types like me" whom they know or even "introverts" or "quiet types" if that fits you. Ask your most outgoing, sociable friends especially—they tend to collect a few HSPs as interesting oddities but may not have thought to introduce you.

4. *Approach HSPs carefully and be persistent.* You are at a gathering and you spot another HSP, are introduced to one, or hear one speaking to someone else. Let's face it—most likely this person is already thinking about leaving, not about meeting another stranger, HSP or not. You know what you need to do—unless you are so anxious at the thought of speaking to a stranger that you stop thinking about the needs of the other person; and we *can* become that shy. But if you can, approach the other as you would like to be approached—with consideration, gentle directness, and leaving plenty of room for the HSP to observe and think about you. Perhaps make a comment about what you are both looking at—the kind of observation an HSP is likely to make, such as noticing the subtle beauty in a scene or what's really going on in the group. Think of yourself as trying to offer a respite, a sanctuary, some deeper conversation. The topic depends on the sort of gathering, which hints at the kind of HSP you are talking to. But I can imagine being lured into a conversation at an art exhibit by being asked something like, "What do you think—is there really a link between creativity and madness?" Or at a party, "I try to understand why complete strangers will introduce themselves here, when six yards away, out on that street, they would never even glance in each other's eyes."

But suppose you have done your best and you still see that I'm-out-of-here expression. You might try observing to the HSP how noisy it is and that you are thinking of going and you suppose he or she is too, but maybe you could find a quieter spot. Maybe step outside. Or if you are very brave, say that you rarely do this sort of thing, but your intuition tells you that you both *might* enjoy meeting some time in a quieter place, just for a conversation—could you exchange phone numbers?

In getting to know an HSP, persistence is important, provided you are not a nuisance. If you get neutral or distracted responses, but not an outright rejection, try again. I know this goes against your natural HSP tendency not to take a risk when the indicators are less than promising, but you will have to overcome this if you seriously want to get to know another HSP. HSPs will always pause to check you over and need time to decide about you. They may change their minds several times in the course of getting to know you better, but they may not get to know you at all if you leave it up to them.

Meeting Non-HSPs

1. *Go where they go, but on your own terms*. You can go almost anywhere to meet non-HSPs, including all the places I mentioned for finding HSPs. In fact, looking for a non-HSP at an HSP-sort-of-place like the symphony or a Sierra Club hike, if you enjoy these, might be a good idea. You will then have something in common with the non-HSP you meet.

   Be sure to converse with non-HSPs in situations that are nonarousing for you, if possible. If you do not feel comfortable in groups or meeting strangers, do not try to get to know a stranger while in a group. You will not be at your best. Move out of the group in some way. On a hike, for example, try to see that the two of you fall behind or walk ahead. Or invite the non-HSP you meet in a class, at a party, or in some other group to go alone with you on a walk or for a meal.

2. *When you are feeling aroused or nervous, ask questions and listen*. In the first moments of meeting or at any other time when the arousal is going up for you, switch the attention from you to the non-HSP. Ask questions—you can think of these in advance—that can't be easily answered with a yes or no, like "Where did you grow up?" or "Where do you like to travel?" Your non-HSP will be less anxious than you and will start to talk freely. As you become absorbed in what you are hearing, you'll forget your concerns about yourself, plus you are probably a good listener and will be appreciated for your interest.

3. *Let the non-HSP get to know you, especially your deeper aspects*. Do not listen so much that you do not speak up yourself. Again,

think in advance about your most interesting aspects and how to mention them so that others will be curious. It is my experience that HSPs make better second impressions than first impressions. We may not have ready wits, but we do have deep thoughts of the sort not spoken in the first moments of meeting.

Not all non-HSPs, however, will appreciate your deeper thoughts, and it helps to know whether yours does, so you can know whether to bother to keep talking with him or her. If you only listen, the non-HSP may decide this is so gratifying that you are soon receiving his or her professions of affection (professions you reciprocate out of gratitude for being appreciated), only to find later that you are in a one-sided relationship in which you are always the audience, reflecting deeply on the performance of your non-HSP partner—*not* a good situation for you.

4. *Be ready for the differences between you.* Sooner or later the differences between the two of you will surface. From the start you will want to be ready to do the work described in the next chapter, standing up for who you are, seeing that you both respect your sensitivity, your gender, your roots—all that is you. At the same time, you'll be respecting the other's right to his or her temperament, gender, roots, and all the rest. You do not have to like all the consequences for you of these differences. If some irritate you, you respect that feeling in yourself by acknowledging it openly. But that does not mean the other person is obliged to change.

Do not forget that the non-HSP may be intimidated by your intuition, your quick insights. Praise his or her abilities as they surface, pointing out your differences and how they can complement each other.

Deepening the Relationship

Whether you have met an HSP or non-HSP, if you want to be in love, you will want to deepen the relationship. Is it manipulative to plan for closeness? Not if you make these gestures because you are genuinely interested in the other person. Is planning unromantic—shouldn't love just happen? This all depends on how impatient you are, but as a social psychologist I am heartily convinced that the situation and what you do in it, which you can control, has much to do with falling in love. Compared to meeting each other, whether the relationship deepens and lasts is far more up to you—now the two of you.

1. *If you like the person, for heaven's sake, say so.* Telling the other person your feelings is the most important risk you can take to make love happen. You do not want to come on too strong and definitely do not want to exaggerate your affections. But when feelings are growing, one of you will eventually acknowledge it; to be sure of this, acknowledge it yourself. You don't have to swear everlasting devotion. Just be honest about how you feel now and maybe how you would like to feel in the future.

2. *Spend time together in creative or emotionally meaningful situations.* You are probably thinking, "next she'll tell me to *arrange* to be stuck in an elevator with somebody," or on a swaying suspension bridge. Yes, choosing the site for falling in love sounds very manipulative. But whenever we are going out with someone, we make plans. Romantic plans. Why not be creative? A picnic, even indoors, is more interesting than lunch at the local, pseudoromantic chain restaurant. How about a box lunch at the zoo, perhaps in front of the lions? Creativity and vision are the gifts HSPs bring to a relationship, or can with a little reflection.

   Relationships deepen most when you go through intense times together. Students know this from studying for finals together, teammates from playing in play-offs together, parents from their friendships with other parents during pregnancies and childbirths. You bond. In contrast, going to the movies or watching videos of other people bonding during their intense times is not quite the same. So, next time you are in a bit of a crisis and the person you have met seems right for it, ask this person to come wait with you before your root canal or for the news about your mother's surgery. Say you could use someone to talk to about your dog's death. Or if he or she is in a crisis—perhaps too busy to see you for a date—ask what you can do to help. You don't have to agree to more than you want to, but coming over and doing the laundry or cleaning the cat's litter box is a surprisingly intimate, life-relevant act compared to choosing a restaurant together.

3. *Apply the lessons from transference in psychotherapy.* Be enormously accepting, which should be easy if you are in love. Add

nurturance—allow the other to be dependent, playful, childlike. Don't forget seclusion—a private world of the two of you. Touch on the archetypal realm, perhaps reading to each other, maybe poetry or love stories from mythology. Above all, nourish the intimacy between the two of you, the revelations, the trust, the authenticity (but authenticity deserves its own point, which follows).

4. *Be honest.* You may be tired of hearing me say it, but the more you can be authentic about your feelings, the closer the two of you will be. Of course there are limits, mainly to do with the stages of a relationship. Intimate self-disclosure proceeds in stages, and most of us have a good sense of what is appropriate for which stage. But taking the lead in moving to the next stage when it is time is like taking the lead in saying you love the other person. It can stir a deep response.

   What else can you be honest about besides your love? You can talk about your fears of the other person's reaction to you or for the future of your relationship. You can confess when you have been disappointed or annoyed by the other person—sorting it out often greatly deepens your connection. You can talk about your perceptions of the two of you as a pair, or of your "history" (even if it is only hours long), or the habits you two have developed—the things both of you are starting to always say or not say. If the relationship is ready, the other person will share similar feelings and observations.

5. *Beware of jumping to the wrong conclusions.* It is a well-established psychological fact that, for example, if we or someone close to us lied, we assume that the situation called for it or this was an exceptional event, but if someone we don't know well has told a lie, we attribute it to personality. The person is dishonest. How does this apply to getting to know someone? Suppose you leave a message for someone and get no call back. You would figure that a friend was too busy or his or her answering machine didn't work—the situation explains it. However, if you called a relative stranger for a date and get no call back, you assume he or she is too wonderful to be interested in the likes of you, or too rude, or too indifferent—his or her personality explains it. But think about it: the odds are equal with friends and strangers that their lives will become too hectic to call back or their answering machines will fail to record a call. Call again.

People who have low self-esteem, which includes many HSPs, can reverse this error in the conclusions they draw about themselves and others. When we do something wrong, it's our flawed personality; when someone else does, it was an accident—the situation. If we don't call a relative stranger back, we may decide it's our cowardly, shy personality. When people do not call us back, we decide they didn't like us in particular or were too busy to bother with us. It's the situation—it's the fact that *we* were the one calling. But consider your own situation—maybe you would not be hesitating if the person you were trying to call had been friendlier when you met. Both self-love and other-love increases when we don't make too many personality attributions about ourselves or others, when we recognize that people cannot be completely explained with a label such as shy, rude, or even highly sensitive, and that situations are complex, rich, often unpredictable, and infinitely interesting.

6. *Give it time.* Contrary to popular opinion, only about 11 percent of people say they fell in love at first sight. More often, a familiar face gradually becomes a loved one. HSPs in particular need time to decide about others—you need time, and if the other is an HSP, that person does too. You need time together and you need time between to think it over. Feelings definitely change—think of how your own do. If you persist, love may grow, or it may die. But time is on your side, in that the more you know each other, the more it will be that whatever happens will be for the best.

PREVENTING THE FALL

There are also times in life when we definitely do not want to fall in love. Perhaps we wish to stay in a committed relationship through all of its ups and downs, ignoring the alternatives, all our exits closed. In order *not* to fall in love:

1. *Do not express any romantic feelings you have.* These could well be reciprocated.
2. *Avoid exciting, intimate, or arousing situations in the company of attractive others.* If you do feel an attraction in such a situation or afterward, understand it for what it is—just due to the situation.

3. *Acknowledge your infatuation with certain temperaments.* In particular, if your partner is an HSP, I can almost guarantee that your wayward romantic impulses will be directed toward a non-HSP; and if your partner is a non-HSP, toward an HSP like yourself. But since you can't have everything, appreciate what you have and don't act on your attractions. Or better, develop a close but nonromantic friendship with someone with the temperament your partner lacks.

4. *Do not be intimate with anyone who makes it clear he or she is available for a romantic relationship.* Reserve your intimacy for your partner or for friendships that are clearly not going to become romantic. Being intimate includes sharing very private thoughts; building trust through high levels of honesty, acceptance, and kindness; and also simply being alone together a lot. In particular, do not "play therapist"! You may bring on an idealizing transference.

5. *But do not throw out the baby with the bath water.* Your impulses to fall in love are always important signs from the psyche. They are your imaginings, your yearnings. Ignore them at your peril, for they will come back with extra force the next time. Rather, try to postpone any action while feeling the feelings fully in order to understand why you have so much love in this situation, at this time in your life, for this particular type of person. What imbalance is trying to be redressed? There's nothing to fear here. The more you understand the feelings, the less likely you are to act on them.

AFTER THE FALL

For many of you, the time of falling in love seems long past. You want to understand what followed. Perhaps you want to know why the love faded and how to revive it. Were those intense months of joy some mean biological trick of nature to get everybody paired off?

In the next three chapters we will discuss "after the fall," first when the tumble into love was with a non-HSP, then with an HSP. In chapter 7 we will look at some points HSPs need to keep in mind, no matter what our partners' temperament.

5

HSPs with Non-HSPs: Making Love Last When Temperaments Clash

Mismatches in temperament and the resultant misunderstandings are certainly the greatest problem that temperament poses for those in close relationships. And according to my data, about half of all HSPs have partners who are not HSPs. Also, interestingly, even more than 50 percent of us *think* we are with non-HSPs when we actually aren't. Further, just as no two people are *exactly* the same height, in every couple one person is more sensitive, the other at least a little less—or one HSP's sensitivity is stronger in some ways, the HSP partner's in other ways. Thus, I recommend that everyone read this chapter and the next (on two HSPs getting along, as many of our relative-to-us non-HSP partners are still at least moderately sensitive). But first, meet Patrick and Connie.

PATRICK AND CONNIE

Patrick, an HSP, and Connie, a non-HSP, have been married thirty years and love each other deeply. They have excellent communication skills, patience, and respect for each other. They take time to be alone together. They have supported each other through every crisis and against all comers. Still, it has been a relationship with many strains (although few fights), especially since their two daughters have become teenagers.

A new complication is that they now teach in the same high school, so they can readily compare themselves. For Patrick teaching high school is rewarding but requires significant effort. He is a conscientious teacher; respected by the administration, parents, and students; quick to be asked for professional advice; and is exhausted every night. In contrast, Connie is often chided by the administration for not attending to her official responsibilities, but she is elected favorite teacher every year by the students. They love her energy, and she loves to teach. She adds special activities to every class—sometimes ideas that Patrick suggested but was too overwhelmed to do himself.

On the weekends, Patrick catches up on his teaching duties while taking equal or more responsibility around the home. But as soon as he can do so with good conscience, he withdraws to his studio to paint, his real passion, or to his garden to weed and think. Connie has always used the weekends to work on craft projects with her daughters. A few years ago she settled on making stuffed animals, which she gave away to relatives and worthy causes during the holidays. Then one of her giraffes was seen by an executive of a high-end catalog gift company, and he bought everything she had and wants as much more as he can get. Most of the work is now done by local women Connie has hired—in addition to teaching, she is now managing a highly successful small business.

One decision Connie and Patrick have made is to use some of this extra income to have more getaway weekends together. Also, Patrick can now consider an early retirement. But the pros and cons of their differences have never been more striking. This is common as couples mature—each person wants to be more true to his own nature, and the strains for HSP/non-HSP couples require greater and greater creativity, respect, and grace.

We'll keep Patrick and Connie in mind as we discuss the blessings and challenges of the HSP/non-HSP couple.

THE GOOD NEWS

How the Two of You Benefit from Your Differences

1. *You have flexibility and, between you, a wide range of abilities— you can accomplish more, handle more, enjoy more than other couples.* You have "hybrid vigor." When functioning as a team,

you will notice the subtleties and your partner will act on that information. You can press on to your limit, knowing your partner will take over and protect you when overarousal and fatigue strike. Patrick, for example, will be aware that their daughters are needing some reining in, but Connie is usually the one to put their decisions into action.

2. *Your relationship is interesting and exciting—for both of you.* The "marriage of opposites" is never dull. You take each other on adventures and live vicarious lives not available to those who are similar. Connie experiences through Patrick the subtle vision of an artist; Patrick experiences through Connie the excitement of an entrepreneur.

3. *Coping with your differences builds character.* It stretches you. Differences are the biggest problem on the planet. As you learn to live with each other's, you add to the collective knowledge of how to acknowledge difference without undue judgment, resentment, and disappointment.

4. *You will change each other.* You will teach each other. You will include the other into yourself. Research shows that two dissimilar partners will each change their personalities over their lifetime, becoming more similar and thus adding new dimensions to themselves, while the personalities of two similar partners tend to stay the same.

5. *You will learn more about your "shadow."* In Jungian terms, the shadow is the disowned, disliked part of yourself (discussed more in chapter 7). Two people who are very similar may ignore the shadow parts they share. For example, two non-HSPs who both fly long distances several times a week for their work might never complain about each other's lack of balance in life; two HSPs who are easily moved by the pleas of manipulative relatives, salesmen, or fake charities will never complain about the other's gullibility. But your partner, being different, will have a very different sort of shadow and will be much more likely to be aware of yours.

Patrick is quick to comment on Connie's tendency to take on too much and then not meet her commitments—it's Connie's shadow, and one that another husband, especially a non-HSP, might not notice, or even have in common with her. And Connie points out to Patrick how he clings to a kind of naivete about "politics" at school rather than standing up for himself, something another HSP might not notice.

How You, the HSP, Personally Benefit

1. *You are protected from what upsets you, helped with what you don't like to do.* This can be such an advantage that HSPs can feel guilty about it, but usually what's hard for you is relatively easy for your partner and he or she is truly glad to be needed—it reassures your partner that you are not going to completely disappear into your own thoughts. And doing these tasks often keeps your partner at his or her right level of stimulation. When Art and I travel, he actually prefers to dash about checking train schedules and buying tickets; I would rather wait quietly for him to do that. No need for either of us to feel guilty.

2. *Given that your non-HSP loves you, you have the very healing experience of being respected.* HSPs can have a long history of feeling second-best or not respected by non-HSPs. How good for you to find one who loves you—probably in large part because you *are* sensitive.

3. *You are going to have more adventures.* Because your partner is not as hesitant before plunging into an activity, you are bound to have more adventures than an HSP with another HSP.

    My favorite example of this is how much I always wanted to own a horse but somehow imagined it to be impossible. When I met Art and we were living in the country for a while, he asked, "Why don't you buy a horse?" I explained that I had never had one, didn't know how to take care of one, horses are big and complicated, we had no fenced pasture, we were too busy to add this to our lives, and so forth. He said, "Get some books from the library about it, buy what you need, get someone to help you pick out a good one, bring it home, and that will force me to take time to build a fence around it!" And so I finally owned a horse.

    In a less dramatic way, Art coaxes me out to more theater, ballet, and concerts than I ever would go to alone—he enjoys these more with me, so I make myself go "for his sake." But I am so very glad that he does get me to go out. When I am alone, I go out very little (when he is alone, he goes out more often than with me).

4. *You will become more flexible because, while staying yourself, you will also become more like your partner.* After years of going out with Art, when I am alone I actually do occasionally arrange to go to the theater or ballet. I miss it more than I think I will. The non-HSP models spontaneity in particular and, by not allowing you to become a slave to your precious routines, makes you more able to break free on your own.

How Your Non-HSP Partner Benefits

1. *HSPs notice subtleties, enjoying the good ones and changing the bothersome ones, so that life is better, the environment nicer.* Art and I recently moved into a new apartment, and from the first day I was bothered by the windows being dirty. Art never noticed, but when I mentioned it, he was the one to find out how to get them cleaned. Once they were cleaned, he raved about how much more he enjoyed our new home. Decorating the apartment was a similar story—I had to say no to many ideas of his that for me would have created an overstimulating environment, but he is now delighted with the serene look of the place. Similarly, I will point things out to him on walks that he enjoys enormously, although he was too busy talking to notice these on his own.

2. *HSPs take their partners on HSP-type adventures.* Art and I like to take walking trips in France. The maps we use are quite detailed. On our most recent trip, several times I noticed tiny crosses on the map, marking chapels or hermitages. At my behest, we hiked several miles into out-of-the-way spots to see these; Art loved them. Similarly, Patrick is extremely concerned by certain political injustices and discusses them often. Connie, the non-HSP, also has these interests now, thanks to Patrick, and is actually more the adventurous activist than Patrick, but only because he first pointed out the issues to her.

I also was the one to start us both meditating, something Art has particularly enjoyed for almost thirty years.

3. *HSPs prevent trouble, giving warning before the non-HSP would ever notice.* Both Connie and Art say their partners think ahead, watching for problems. We HSPs notice first when someone is becoming annoyed. We see the thing that needs to be fixed before it completely breaks. Patrick and I are the ones in each couple who have insisted on retirement plans. Art and Connie—more optimistic, oblivious, and impulsive—can get tired of all the "doom and gloom" about what can go wrong. Sometimes Patrick and I are right, sometimes wrong. But Art and Connie are deeply grateful for those early warnings that did prove accurate and prevented costly troubles.

4. *HSPs create a healthier lifestyle for their non-HSP partners.* While the non-HSP may be able to ignore signs of needing to sleep, eat, exercise, or stop for a break, the HSP cannot. Since couples find it easier to stay somewhat in synch about these things, the non-HSP automatically lives a more sensible, sensitive life. For example, I absolutely have to have a day off once a week. When Art is alone he never takes time off, but when with me he agrees that we benefit greatly from our days off.

THE CHALLENGES

My data on the satisfaction of HSPs in relationships indicates a slight tendency for HSPs with non-HSPs to be less happy. Still, these are all only slight differences, and *many* HSP/non-HSP couples are as happy or happier than HSP/HSP couples. That is, your chances of having a wonderful relationship with a non-HSP are very good, and are even better if you are reading this book.

I want you to be realistic, however, about the challenge, and to appreciate why you have had certain difficulties. Psychiatrist Burton Appleford, in *Sensitivity—Agony or Ecstasy?,* holds that problems in marriages between people quite different in their sensitivity have some similarity in their seriousness to the problems in marriages between people with very different IQs. For example, just as those of high intelligence have certain experiences that their partners of less intelligence can't grasp or share, so do HSPs with non-HSPs. However, unlike having a partner of lower overall intelligence, you have a partner with a *different* kind of "intelligence" and assets. This is something to remember as we explore the challenges for HSP/non-HSP couples.

The Problems Due to Differences in Optimal Level of Arousal

There is a strong drive in all humans and other animals to maintain an optimal level of arousal. In couples of similar temperaments, when there is a large difference in what's optimal, it is only temporary—for example, one is working overtime for a while and the other is staying home all day. When a situation is temporary, it is easy to compromise or even for one partner to adapt entirely to the other's needs, as when the one staying home lets the one working overtime rest at home as much as possible, going out alone if need be. But when the difference in optimal level is built-in and permanent due to temperament, things are rougher. Compromises are even more important—one person always adapting to the other will not work. At the same time, a compromise that leads to overarousal for the HSP and boredom for the non-HSP simply means both are dissatisfied. The solutions (discussed later in this chapter) require genuine creativity.

Looking back at Patrick and Connie, Patrick has great stories of trying to take up scuba diving to please Connie—especially the expensive package tour that included one day of deep-sea diving, a day on which Connie was ill. Patrick conscientiously went alone, not wanting to waste the money or avoid a challenge, but he ended up in constant fear and wondering rather bitterly how he had gotten himself into the situation. After that he gave up trying to enjoy what he could not enjoy. But they still go as a family to exotic places with great scuba diving—Connie arranges the travel plans so that Patrick has time to relax on the beach while she goes diving with her daughters.

The problem is that as an HSP/non-HSP couple agrees to live more separate lives, in accord with the degree of stimulation each enjoys, this can lead to estrangement if taken too far. Connie's kitchen-table corporation has made Patrick proud of her, and the money has certainly made life easier. But their lives are lived far more separately now, which for them has led to a sense that they are not just separate but are often somehow working in opposition to each other. Some of the other problems that arise around the difference between the HSP and non-HSP in optimal level of arousal are as follows:

1. *Non-HSPs seem to want more intimacy, HSPs to want more time alone.* Even if fears of intimacy are low and attachment styles are similar in a couple, HSPs still may want less intimacy than non-HSPs. Intimacy is highly arousing, and especially after a hard day, an HSP may simply prefer to be alone. Forget a "romantic evening" (from the non-HSP's point of view) of dining on rich food in a noisy restaurant, followed by dancing in an even noisier nightclub. Besides probably feeling rejected, the non-HSP is just plain disappointed—here is a person ready to connect with all of his or her heart and soul, paired with a person who comes home and wants to sit and stare at the wall.

2. *Both of you have to deal with your (the HSP's) times of overarousal.* If a couple does not understand the natural limits of an HSP, both people are likely to be constantly overarousing the HSP. Then you both have to deal with the consequences, such as irritability, blowups, bouts of depression, frequent infections and injuries, absentminded mistakes, insomnia, or obsessive worrying. You, the HSP, may also use food, alcohol, or substances to numb your overaroused system. The above-mentioned consequences can become chronic when the overarousal becomes chronic.

   Often both of you understand your HSP limits intellectually but deny the extent to which each of you is still violating them. You may feel like a mental case or hypochondriac and your partner like the doctor or therapist, always expected to contain his or her own feelings, calm things down, be the rescuer.

3. *Both of you have to deal with spillover from vicariously living the other's very different experience.* When you are highly stressed by a deadline, a criticism at work, or an overarousing day, your non-HSP partner cannot help but become a bit anxious, too. You wouldn't want it to be otherwise. Yet the non-HSP also gets tired of what, from his or her perspective, is much ado about nothing.

   When the non-HSP is the one taking on a lot and coming close to a state of overarousal, as Connie is while juggling her home, teaching, and thriving new business, an HSP like Patrick cannot help but feel especially affected. He wants to give her her freedom, so he tries not to complain, uncomfortable as it is just to watch such frenetic activity. But when even she complains that it's too much—*dares* to complain—he feels like bursting out with "You created it! How can you expect me to help? Stop doing it if you're so miserable!"

4. *The HSP will have more difficulties at work,* with many ramifications in the relationship. For example, let's face it, most HSPs do not do a forty-hour week well, especially if you add a commute or children waiting for you at home. You may have all sorts of other problems around work that non-HSPs may not understand. Your work has to have meaning. You have trouble finding a congenial social and physical work environment, since workplaces are better suited to the other 80 percent of the population. So you may move from job to job, or even from career to career, suffering over each change—and your partner suffering with you.

Most of all, you may not earn as much as non-HSPs, which can be particularly trying if you are a man. And this situation is not at all unusual—I can think of at least five HSP/non-HSP couples in which the HSM is earning less or even nothing. In each case the couples have enough money, but both partners struggle with their gender-stereotyped feelings about it—sometimes successfully, sometimes not.

The problem is not limited to HSMs, however. Today women are expected to work, and most couples enjoy two incomes. A woman not working may be acceptable when her children are small, but generally HSWs who do not work feel as "wrong" as men do, inferior to their working partners, or not justified in spending anything on themselves. Their husband may envy the couples they see all around them with more wealth and less pressure on the men because their wives work.

Some Solutions

1. *Remind your non-HSP partner that intimacy takes many forms.* As I will say repeatedly, you each must believe the other's experi-

ence. For you, the HSP, downtime is essential after a busy period. This is physiology and has nothing to do with love. You may not even necessarily want to be totally alone. In fact, often you can relax more with your partner—if you can just be quiet together. But after a period of high stimulation, you have to have the downtime before the intimate time. That's reality.

Be sure to tell your partner when you do feel intimate. To your partner, it may seem that you are both "just reading." If you mention being happy reading silently together, he or she may feel the intimacy too.

Whenever possible, adapt to your partner's idea of intimacy too. If that's enjoying a rock concert or the auto races together, well, quietly pack your earplugs. Going along is a fine way to show your love if you don't make it a case of martyrdom.

Partners should not be too angry, by the way, if the other misses the fact that this is an act of love—just point it out, with good humor. It truly is important that each appreciates how much love is being expressed by these acts of adaptation. Probably your experience of the rock concert will *not* be the joy it is to your partner; and your partner's experience of silently reading together will not give the pleasure it gives to you.

2. *Accept and plan for your difference in optimal level of arousal.* Accepting requires that both of you end your denial about these limits. Why the denial? To adapt to you, the HSP, something has to be given up. Arousal comes from many sources, and if one is added, others must go. A new baby? You'll have to cut back at work or quit if you are going to be part of the child-raising, which means a loss of income. Starting a new job? For a few months you will need to be excused from most work around the house and from the leisure activities the two of you share, to be made up later if possible. But that's hard on your partner.

Once you truly accept these limits, planning for them is relatively easy. Here are just a few suggestions that *both* of you should agree need to be applied to you.

• Decide your priorities and let some dreams go. For you, having a highly successful career may require having only one or even no children.

• You need a room of your own, or at least a corner of your own, to decorate in a calming way, to retreat to when your partner is being happily or unhappily frenetic.

• If possible, live someplace quiet, or decrease the sound through soundproofing in at least one room.

• Get yourself out into nature regularly.

• Avoid unnecessary decisions and choices. Stick with decisions once made. Accept that some decisions turn out to be wrong— you can't know some things beforehand, and you can't always be right.

• Your partner should let you have your routines, especially if these do not bother him or her.

• Stick to a budget or financial plan. HSPs often suffer when in debt. Have some financial margin—expect economic ups and downs, so that they minimize their influence on your life.

• Have time margins—leave extra time to get to places like airline flights and weddings. Most HSPs truly suffer when they must rush or be late.

• Keep holidays simple and meaningful. Don't let them escalate into overstimulating extravaganzas you cannot enjoy.

• Be sure you balance the rest of your life with sufficient sleep, exercise, downtime, and opportunities for spiritual experiences— for HSPs these are the foundations of everything else and therefore your first priorities, not frills.

3. *The two of you must also arrange to keep the non-HSP in his or her optimal level of arousal.* Although this is not as pressing a need, since the world will naturally give the non-HSP plenty to do, underarousal in the non-HSP should not be overlooked. He or she may also need a room to retreat to—to play the radio, keep messy piles of paper that you can't stand to see, work late or early, and generally fool around. He or she may need to go out to a cafe to read awhile before bed rather than simply retiring after another of the same kind of evening at home. By the way, the non-HSP/non-HSS who is underaroused is not necessarily looking for a radically new experience. He or she just needs a bit more stimulation. The non-HSP/HSS will need considerably more novel adventures.

4. *Be creative in planning time together.* This is essential, because you must have happy times together to keep your love alive and

appealing to you. How can you be creative? For example, I have never enjoyed exploring big cities very much, but Art loves cities. Fortunately, I can enjoy art museums and good restaurants for a day or two. But what I love is to be in a forest, by the ocean, or wandering through a lovely landscape, which Art enjoys too, as long as we keep moving. So when we travel, we generally spend a few days in a European city (not too exotic for me or too familiar for him) doing activities we both find meaningful. Art keeps it simple and does all the arranging. Then we head for the wide open spaces for a walking trip through the countryside.

5. *Appreciate that everything you do together is affected by your difference—often in ways you do not suspect.* How you argue, what you argue about, how you make love—it's all affected by your having quite different nervous systems. When there's a problem, try seeing if it can be explained by your temperament differences. This explanation really helps to stop the blaming and defensiveness, the biggest problem when couples have conflicts.

6. *Be careful how you use your temperament differences "in combat."* Once you are aware of your differences, it can be tempting to use these to your advantage in a power struggle—and all couples have them. Do not use this basic aspect of yourselves as a weapon or easy target. It is not fair, for example, for your non-HSP partner to use the strategy of making such a highly stimulating fuss that you back down in order to avoid the overarousal required simply to state your case. Nor is it fair for you to threaten a complete collapse or explosion due to overarousal if your partner mentions some need, irritation, or complaint about which you do not want to compromise. Often these strategies slip into our behavior without our being conscious of it, so do a little self-examination now and then if your behavior during a conflict seems to "smell fishy" to you.

The Problems Due to Your Greater Awareness of Subtleties

The next set of problems, those resulting from being sensitive to subtleties, are well illustrated by Linda and Mark.

LINDA AND MARK

Linda had a good relationship with her mother as a child, but her father divorced her mother when she was six in order to marry her mother's cousin. Linda's family moved often after that, and at the new schools Linda was quiet, slow to make friends, and felt she never fit in. Around eight she decided she was "high strung," different, and to some degree accepted this about herself. In college she met Mark, who was her first and only romantic interest. She instantly liked his loving nature, that he was comforting and affectionate with her, "had courtly manners, but was also lots of fun."

Fun was important to Linda, because she is easily bored—definitely an HSP/HSS. As a young adult she sought out "adventure seekers" for friends, until she realized being close to them was "too much of a drain." Mark is her opposite, one of those interesting cases of someone who is neither an HSP nor an HSS. As she says "he's never dull; things always come up—but compared to me, he can tolerate more boredom *and* take more stimulation." Armed with a solid, almost stolid nervous system, plus a good mind and education, Mark has been a good provider.

Linda always felt that Mark respected her sensitivity "almost too much," because in contrast, she eventually discovered that she did not respect his nonsensitivity. In the beginning she avoided all confrontation with Mark, adopting his values and ways of thinking, never admitting to disagreeing. Then in 1973 she began meditating, something Mark did not care for. His indifference about spiritual matters led to considerable soul-searching for Linda. Meditation was becoming very important to her, and his lack of interest was frankly distressing. She did not like him any more—the crisis was upon them.

Linda began falling in love from afar with men who were more spiritual; then she had an affair. She and Mark separated three times. "Clearly I was judgmental about his not being spiritual." But she felt powerless to stop the wasting away of her love for him.

Then she met her present spiritual teacher, a wise and gentle swami. She was filled with love, but not exactly toward Mark. Mark resented this intrusion into his marriage. He still wanted them to return to their old ways, which was doing everything together (that is, her agreeing with him about everything). But he could not share this spiritual quest.

Linda's teacher told her simply to meditate and see Mark as part of her path. "What we're given, we're supposed to have." Mark visited the swami and as a result, softened considerably toward Linda's spiritual interest. And she began to see that her intense attachment to her teacher was in part due to her father's leaving her behind when she was six. The attachment to the teacher remained, even strengthened, but it was not so unconscious and devouring.

Change was needed, however—in herself. Encouraged by her teacher to respect herself, Linda insisted that she and Mark enter marital therapy, and she began "talking back." She still does not become angry with him "but gets hurt, steps back, and eventually says firmly, 'that's your way, not mine.' " The resentment and disappointment with him has dwindled. She is still sad that he will never share this important part of her life. But she finds great comfort in being with those who gather to see her spiritual teacher. Most are HSPs, she believes, and "the atmosphere there helps."

Most important, Linda sees now how much she and Mark actually complement each other. "I've grown a lot—he's taught me a lot." She's also more aware of their similarities now. "My weak points are his, and I hate him for them. Our good points are alike too. I might not have chosen him, yet he's just right."

Differences—How Reasons for Love Become Reasons for Contempt

Linda and Mark are a classic HSP/non-HSP story of being attracted to each other by the difference in their processing of subtleties, which gave her subtle spiritual experiences and him a clear, practical vision of the surface realities of life. This difference, which caused each to love and admire the other so much at first, became the greatest source of disappointment and irritation with each other later. Indeed, at their relationship's worst, I think they held each other in utter contempt for this same difference.

Both marital researchers and practicing marital counselors find that differences often work like this, especially when they involve aspects of personality that are almost inaccessible to the other, such as temperament differences. Initially A likes B for being so successful (B is not at all ambitious), and B likes A for wanting to make a nice home (A has no talent for it). Later B is tired of A always working, and A feels B is boring. In the case of differences in the awareness of subtleties versus practicalities, the potential for contempt seems huge because of the vast distance between the opposing talents—the distance between heaven and earth.

Let's consider other issues that can arise from your having such keen awareness of subtleties while your partner does not.

1. *As more realism sets in for both of you, your sensitivity becomes judgmental and your non-HSP partner can easily become defensive.* Maybe you are disappointed with your partner's "shallowness." He or she is "clueless," "totally unconscious." Once this observation sets in, you will process it to the hilt. Every possible lifetime consequence of this and every other of your partner's "flaws" (flaws from your point of view, at least) will be considered. Your partner may feel you must be right about all these flaws, given your intuition, and feel ashamed. Yet it also seems all wrong and terribly unfair, which it is.

   I agree with Peter Kramer's suggestions in *Should You Leave?* that sensitive people are overwhelmed by the myriad of cues we receive about the other person when we become very close. Everyone has foibles, and the HSP is suddenly experiencing another's idiosyncrasies in greater detail than we may have ever received in previous, less intimate relationships. It becomes difficult to distinguish a solid person with a few problems (since you are picking up on *every* problem) from a true problem person.

   On top of that, as the HSP, you notice many more flaws in your partner than your partner may notice in you. You will be even more prone to look for flaws and feel disappointment if you were also disappointed in childhood by a parent, as Linda was by her father. To some degree she was unconsciously oriented to watch for potential disappointing qualities in Mark.

   It's not hard to imagine the impact on your partner as you silently or not so silently catalog his or her "bad points." Your partner's core sense of self-worth will be threatened—after all, you are so sensitive and know him or her too well to be wrong. So watch out—no one can manage under such an attack for long without coming up with a strong defense, including a counteroffensive.

2. *You may also go to the other extreme and avoid any comment about the shortcomings you are noticing.* Why? Being prone to process everything deeply, it hurts to deeply process another's

criticism of us too. To avoid being criticized, you may decide never to criticize your partner, and to be above all criticism yourself. From your viewpoint there may even be an unspoken agreement never to criticize each other. The trouble is, in any long-term relationship, both partners are bound to begin to be dissatisfied and need to speak about it; otherwise, resentment builds. The suppressed anger inevitably undermines real intimacy. If you are lucky, eventually the anger explodes out and intimacy is restored, but with a lot of unnecessary pain because of the delay.

A slightly different scenario involves partners avoiding making any criticism of the other so well that they create for one (or both) an overly accepting, infantilizing atmosphere—a situation that can turn reasonable adults into childishly entitled people who rarely think of others. This might delay the explosions, but they still must come.

Everyone knows all of this intellectually, but the problem can arise anyway with an HSP in a relationship. Even those of us with the best childhoods seem to be sensitive to being criticized, so we can readily decide to prevent it. When the mutual non-criticism has gone on for years, and then the dam breaks, the outcome can easily be either the end of the relationship or a vitally renewed one. You can almost plan on one of them.

3. *You seem able to read your non-HSP partner's mind, while your partner cannot read yours—leading to all sorts of communication problems.* One consequence is that your non-HSP partner may come to expect to be fully understood, when in fact there will always be large gaps in your understanding of him or her. You also may make the mistake of thinking your partner has realized something about you that he or she did not, because in your partner's place you would have. When you see you have not been intuitively understood, you may be quite disappointed. Or you may be just plain tired of having to say what would have been obvious to you if it had been your partner sending the cue.

4. *Especially in conversations with more than one other person, you may speak less, trying to think deeply about topics, while your partner fills these vacuums with "shallow" chatter.* Or the whole subject changes: Someone was discussing their back trouble, and you were thinking about what you know about spinal pain. Meanwhile the topic switches to diet, so you think about nutri-

tion. Then to restaurants, travel, foreign affairs, politics. You've said almost nothing—and heard little worth responding to, in your opinion, because non-HSPs seem to speak without much reflection. Your silence can be interpreted as shyness or disinterest—but whatever others think, they fill the vacuum you leave, assuming you don't mind. In fact, you had a lot you wanted to say and feel very left out or angry.

5. *When you are upset, you probably tend to contain your feelings and reflect on them; your partner eases tension by expressing every little concern or upset.* Your preference when packing for a trip, for example, may be to be quiet and concentrate. Your partner probably does a play-by-play running commentary with all sorts of rhetorical questions like, "I wonder what the weather will be?" and "Where are the tickets?" Your behaviors during a crisis reflect the same conflicting styles. You try to stay calm, quiet; your partner wonders out loud if the two of you are making the right responses and how badly things will turn out. Being conscientious, you feel you have to respond to any and all questions or worries, but your partner doesn't really expect answers—he or she just wants the comfort of speaking to you as you struggle side by side. But the constant talking adds stimulation, wrecking your concentration, leading to irritation, conflict.

6. *When your disillusionment leads to judgment, and your judgments lead to your partner feeling defensive, the two of you will do more "splitting."* Splitting is a defense used first and most in childhood. It allows us to see ourselves or others at a given moment as completely terrific or completely terrible, without our having to deal with those aspects, good or bad, that we are having trouble accepting. Life is so easy this way, at first. When we first fall in love, we may "split off" any bad traits in the other, seeing only the terrific. When we become disillusioned or feel attacked, if this feels very bad, we may "split off" any good traits in the other, seeing only the horrific instead.

The same kind of splitting can happen inside ourselves, of course, when we *have* to feel we ourselves are all perfect or all terrible, denying any awareness of experiences that do not validate that. To maintain this blindness, we often "get rid of" the denied half by projecting it onto someone else—and who is handier than our so-different partner?

Theoretically HSPs would not use the defenses of splitting and projecting very much, as we are not good at any of the denying, rationalizing defenses. The unconscious seeps through in more noticeable ways for us, as in dissociation, diffuse anxiety, and physical symptoms. But we can be very distressed by finding fault in ourselves or in people we have idealized. The fault seems to have so many implications—too many. So we may "split" at first, while we adjust to the new reality.

For example, suppose a conscientious HSM is told by his non HSP wife that she feels neglected because he is so unavailable. He may see some truth in this for a moment but then be flooded by the implications—he's already spending all the time he can with her, he feels overwhelmed at work, and now it seems he's failing as a husband too. This view of himself is pretty unbearable, so he defends himself. He decides she's the one at fault—she's demanding, controlling, or too needy. Why did he marry this awful person? Now she's all bad, and he's all good. What a relief. After thinking it over, he may decide that in fact they are both okay. She has a justifiable complaint. He sees she's not even that upset with him. He just has to schedule more time with her, maintain balance in his life. (We will talk more about splitting in chapter 7.)

Close relationships almost always involve one interesting form of splitting—a kind of extreme specialization. Sometimes it is harmless, as when the pair decides that one of them is a genius at reading maps and following directions, the other terrible at it. Sometimes the split is more crippling, as when one is seen as good with money and the other as hopeless, so that the latter never develops a sense of financial independence. Since HSP/non-HSP couples already have numerous differences, this specialization kind of splitting will happen more easily for you. In fact, in regard to sensitivity, the less sensitive person begins to be seen by both as the very insensitive person. Watch for this in your relationship.

Some Solutions

1. *Rein in your awareness of every flaw.* As psychiatrist Peter Kramer put it, for you as an HSP to enter a relationship "requires a conscious effort to ignore what is perceived with great accu-

racy"—that is, your partner's faults, which loom large and numerous. As you process them deeply, they seem to have implications for all parts of your life. Once you know, however, that your sensitivity may inflate the number and seriousness of your partner's flaws, you can compensate for this. Focus on your partner's strengths, processing those deeply as well. Remember that every partner is a package deal. As for the faults, reflect on this fact: When you choose a partner, you choose a set of problems. Look around you. Is there really any person you know well who would be easier to live with than your partner? If you think it might be an HSP, be sure to read about the problems two HSPs can have, in the next chapter.

It is easy to idealize someone you hardly know. As Ethel Person said, infatuation requires enough separation so that "the imaginative work of falling in love can take place." So fight fire with fire: Use your HSP imagination to imagine what it would really be like living with another HSP. Imagine what you would miss about your sweet non-HSP.

2. *Separate yourself a bit from your partner—his or her foibles are not yours.* In a close relationship, we can include our partners into ourselves to such a degree that we can confuse ourselves with them. That's good if you are deciding whether to rescue your partner from a burning building or share one of your kidneys. It is not so helpful when you worry not only about what you may be doing to bother others, but also about what your non-HSP partner may be doing. Add a bout of low self-esteem that has spread to become low self-esteem for both of you, and you are sure to think you are with the biggest insensitive bore or troublemaker on the planet.

Try thinking a new way when, just as an example, you feel your non-HSP partner is being "totally unconscious," impulsively talking away without noticing how others seem (to you) to be bored or annoyed. You might not talk on like that, but if he or she does, so what? Is it really bothering anyone? Could other people even be enjoying your partner? Can you trust others to put your partner in line if needed? Do you judge your friends for what their partners do? Do you even judge their partners all that much when they talk too much? Probably not.

3. *To reduce splitting, reclaim your disowned self.* The psyche uses

splitting to protect the ego from unbearable truths, but the psyche doesn't really seem to like this solution very much—sooner or later it will press for what was split off to come back into consciousness. Hopefully, like Linda, you will still be in your relationship. So when things seem very "black and white," that's a good time to sit tight rather than make decisions. And it is a crucial time to consider whether the faults you are most upset with in your partner, or the idealized virtues, might be just as true of you.

4. *Also to reduce splitting, try thinking about the negatives and the positives at the same time.* Instead of processing an attribute of your partner so that it brings up everything negative about him or her, try thinking about that attribute in terms of its many positive, negative, and neutral implications, depending on the setting. (We will discuss this more in chapter 7.)

5. *Ask your partner to invite you into conversations when there are more than the two of you,* rather than filling the vacuum you leave. Perhaps he or she can ask your opinion or bring the conversation around to one of your specialties or deep interests. Also ask your partner to encourage the breakdown of a foursome into twosomes, since one-on-one is usually more enjoyable for an HSP.

6. *Ask for silence when you truly need it; tolerate the "running commentary" whenever you can.* Above all, discuss your differences in needing silence or talking as equally valid ways of behaving, but with consequences for both of you. When your partner talks at a time you really need quiet, he or she will eventually pay the consequences in your fatigue and irritability or his or her feeling foolish for chattering on when you disliked it. On the other hand, if your partner must always stay silent for you, I'll wager that you actually would miss the talking—it's familiar, reassuring. Also, when people are silent, we HSPs have to worry about what they are really thinking—a less common worry with a non-HSP partner.

7. *Learn to increase your volume to a level the non-HSP can hear.* It is very important to realize that the way you like to be addressed—subtly, softly, indirectly—will not always be heard by a non-HSP. My husband often jokes that on a scale of one to ten, I'll ask him to do something at a level of one or two, then if I'm not heard, I'll turn it up to ten and sound to him angry and critical. A five the first time would have been perfect, even though it seems to an HSP to

be too much. By volume I mean literally how loud you speak and also how directly and assertively. Not, "Gee, I'm getting cold," but, "Would you please turn up the heat?" HSPs can "take hints" all too well, but non-HSPs often miss them. (This suggestion is also essential with non-HSPs in the workplace, by the way.)

The Problems Due to Low HSP-Esteem

For all the reasons discussed in chapter 1, HSPs are not considered ideal in our culture. When even those who loved you most were gently hinting that for your own sake you should try to be less sensitive, of course you grew up feeling there was something wrong with you—something you could not change because it was your basic, apparently *ab*normal nervous system. So you probably developed a deeply rooted lack of self-esteem, no matter how well you have compensated for it since with all sorts of achievements.

It can be difficult at first to grasp how much low self-esteem is an obstacle to real love. Feeling fundamentally flawed is a dangerous place for an ego, putting you perilously close to depression and self-destructiveness. So the psyche must place the protection of your fragile ego ahead of everything else. Whom you love, how intimate you become, how you respond to a flirtation or rejection are all determined by whether it will bolster or further weaken the ego's self-esteem. Never mind the effect on your partner of how you respond to him or her or to others; that has to come second.

Further, you dare not merge your fish tank with another's while you feel your own few fish are small and drab (as we discussed in chapter 3). Yet you may pick others whose tanks seem full of brilliant fish, for no one else would make you feel good enough about yourself or compensate for what you think you lack. If the other's fish turn out to be a bit drab too, you may be secretly delighted, but you may also be forced by your low self-esteem to look for yet another aquarium.

Or you may pick someone with an almost empty fish tank, making you feel better, or at least safe that you have *someone,* but leaving you dissatisfied as well.

In short, low self-esteem can cause you to choose the wrong partner, be dishonest, or betray someone you say you love—hardly increasing your good opinion of yourself. For HSPs with non-HSPs specifically, however, low self-esteem can create special problems.

1. *Being with a non-HSP can take on additional, dangerous meanings for you.* As I already described, at least unconsciously you probably tend to see non-HSPs as normal, good, fortunate, and as deserving of esteem as you are not. With this black-and-white thinking, at first you may split off all of your good traits and project them onto your non-HSP partner, making it harder to see your virtues and his or her faults and ceding your partner far too much power over you. Power corrupts, and too much submission by you can turn even a nice person into someone who feels justified in controlling or criticizing you constantly. Even if a partner hesitates at first, it is awfully tempting to play the role of know-it-all if you unconsciously invite your partner to dance that dance with poor stupid you. If he or she does not know the steps, you lead until the steps are clear.

   Underneath all this idealizing of non-HSPs, we HSPs with low self-esteem can also feel terrible envy. Envy usually operates in the unconscious, but this makes it all the more destructive. Like Cinderella's stepsisters and stepmother, envious people want to possess the Good, which seems to reside entirely in those around them. They want to enslave the Good, or failing that, they will seek to destroy it along with those who have it. They will do this literally, or symbolically, or over and over in imagination. If you are aware of such envy in yourself, rest assured that you are not alone.

2. *The comments of friends and relatives take on too much weight.* When you are unsure of yourself, you may look to others for advice or insights about your relationship. Not only do others not know the two of you well enough to make such comments, but they are likely to reinforce the kinds of stereotypes and prejudices that have already made you feel bad about yourself or your partner.

   Art has always been an energetic person. When he was an infant, his crib had to have a second set of crib rails above it to keep him in. When he was six months old, his mother's doctor insisted she take a vacation from him—he was running her ragged. While she was gone, legend has it that it required five other family members to tend him. He was not a bad child, just an energetic one.

   Most people find it exhausting just to watch Art live an hour of his life, and they interpret his rushing around and intense pursuit of each goal as neurotic in origin. Not having his temperament, I can fall into seeing it that way, too—perhaps they are right and all his projects are just a defense against his existential angst. When other people ask me how I can live with him, if I am feeling unsure of myself and Art that day, I may say I am not sure how I do and even begin to feel truly sorry for myself.

Yet this is just his temperament. He lives with mine, I live with his. He benefits from our differences, and I do too. He does so much for me, thanks to that same energy. But all of this is easy to forget when people are expressing their prejudices and misunderstandings about his temperament.

In turn, Art has had people ask him how he lives with someone so absorbed in her inner life, so fussy and delicate, so much less eager than he is to join the group, to have fun. These are all prejudices about HSPs that ignore the good points. He admits, however, that he has to be careful not to be caught up in them, especially when he is not feeling very good about himself and therefore doubts his ongoing choice to share his life with mine.

3. *HSPs are also more affected by the larger culture's prejudices about temperament, especially those regarding the relative worth of the four genders.* Since this was the topic of chapter 2, I will only remind you that we are all thoroughly imbued with the idea that the non-HSM is the tough ideal, the non-HSW is probably almost as tough and ideal, and the HSW and HSM are something else. Believe all of this and you are in trouble. If you accept your non-HSP partner as the ideal, you will see yourself as second-rate—bad for both of you. Your partner will be forced to feel he or she chose poorly by taking an HSP—and have to live up to an image that will interfere with being authentic with you.

Some Solutions

1. *Work on your low self-esteem* in the ways suggested in *The Highly Sensitive Person* and *The Highly Sensitive Person's Workbook,* through reframing your "failures" and appreciating your trait.
2. *Be conscious of your internal prejudices regarding your own temperament.* Examine who in your past reinforced your feeling flawed for being sensitive and try to listen and talk back to that

internalized voice. Look at the impact of your parents, your school years, the media, and other self-help books you may have used. *The HSP's Workbook* can help with this too. Believe it: Everything you do to increase your appreciation of your sensitivity is also an act of love toward your non-HSP partner.

3. *Replace envy with realism.* Try not to lose sight of your good points—you *do* possess a great deal of the Good—and note the difficulties others have, your partner included. Their lives are not as grand or good as they appear to be—what's to envy, really?

4. *Be careful about the influences of others.* Read critically anything you come upon about temperament, shyness, introversion, and so forth. Speak up when you hear temperament prejudices so that your passive response does not allow these prejudices to seep into your belief system.

5. *Be conscious of your prejudices regarding your partner's temperament.* As you become happier about being an HSP, you may find more fault with your non-HSP partner. But this splitting is not necessary for you to respect yourself. In fact, in the long run you will be back to criticizing yourself, this time for your choice of a partner. The two of you are *separate* people, and maybe you are *both* okay, in different ways. Remember, for your partner to have loved you in spite of the culture's prejudices about HSPs, he or she has probably learned how to ignore these prejudices and see you as a package deal, wonderful in spite of the flaws that have been pointed out to him or her by everyone else. Therefore your partner may be an excellent person to imitate as you learn to appreciate him or her as a package deal, too.

A WORD TO HSWS WITH SUPPOSEDLY NON-HSM PARTNERS

As I mentioned in the first paragraph of this chapter, more HSPs think they are with non-HSPs than actually are. This seems especially true of HSWs. The classic gender-war issue is that a woman is all too sensitive to a man's feelings and sick of his inability to reciprocate. But suppose your supposedly non-HSM partner is actually an HSM who has carefully covered up his sensitivity due to early and intense indoctrination into the Boy Code (see chapter 2). On top of this, suppose he has had a difficult early childhood? Being a man, he is more likely to have adopted an avoidant-dismissive attachment style and to seem disinterested in having or showing feelings, especially feelings of need or of caring for others.

It can be very threatening to such a man that you as an HSW are so interested in deep feelings. He fears being lured into that dangerous area where he will be exposed as vulnerable and not a "real man." Would you leave him if he cried or needed you desperately? Or because it seems he never will? Or could you instead use your own sensitivity to attune yourself to his defenses and coax his sensitivity and vulnerability out into the open? And if not completely out into the open with you, could you help him accept his need for psychotherapy? If you think about the problems on this planet, there are so many men who need the help of an HSW. It's not your duty to help them all, or even this one, if it isn't right for you. But perhaps if he can appreciate your efforts to help, listen to your own struggles without too much judgment, and give even a little back, it would indeed be right for you.

CHANGE WHAT YOU CANNOT ACCEPT, ACCEPT WHAT YOU CANNOT CHANGE

Above all, gain the wisdom to know the difference between what you can and can't change. Yes, you want to grow and change, and hopefully your partner does too. You want to help each other in this by urging change. But one of the greatest steps in growth is to accept each other—to accept the inevitable disappointment of your partner's inherited limits, to appreciate that every person is a "package deal" and "when you choose a partner, you choose a set of problems."

It is almost the essence of wisdom to accept the limits of life and mortality, to be thrilled by what you do have for as many moments of the day as you can be aware and in love.

So now that the HSP/non-HSP couples have pondered their joys and problems, it is time for the HSP/HSP couples to go under the lights.

6

When Both of You Are Highly
Sensitive: Keeping the Peace
Between Two Peas in a Pod

A chapter on the problems of people with similar temperaments might seem unneeded. After all, I have been emphasizing the impact of temperament differences, not similarities, on the success of close relationships. But even if it sounds like HSP/HSP couples would suffer only from an abundance of riches, they do have their own problems, thanks precisely to their double dose of sensitivity.

Further, as I've said, my research indicates that many HSPs are in relationships with partners they think of as non-HSPs but who are actually also quite sensitive, even HSPs themselves, but just less sensitive than the one feeling very sensitive. This illusion of difference often comes from the splitting I described in the last chapter: If both are sensitive, but one is even a little more so, the two may decide that one is sensitive and the other is not. This is unfortunate, because there will be times when the less-sensitive partner is actually being more affected by the trait and the always-seen-as-more-sensitive person could step in and be extremely helpful, knowing just what to do. But all of this requires that the more-sensitive HSP recognize how sensitive his or her partner may actually be.

So even if you seem not to be in an HSP/HSP couple, you may be more like one than you think, or it may be good for you to at least consider this possibility. Besides, you may be in one in the future, and you surely have relationships with HSP friends or relatives. So read on.

THE GOOD NEWS

The good news, of course, I already announced: The odds are slightly better than fifty-fifty that if you are with another HSP, you are more satisfied with your relationship than if you were with a non-HSP. This is especially true for HSMs. People in HSP/HSP couples also tend to say they are closer to their partners.

We might call it good news, too, that so many HSPs have found one another, given their greater likelihood of being introverted, shy, or simply happy to stay home alone on Saturday nights. To make my point, I am going to introduce three HSP/HSP couples by telling how they met and fell in love. Their stories make you think there's a special cupid or guardian angel assigned just to the task of getting HSPs together.

THE MEETING OF COMMON MINDS AND HEARTS

Kate and Alex, both in their twenties, found each other by e-mail, but connecting took a long time. They read about each other, exchanged pictures, started writing, and met in person much later. When they did meet, Kate confessed to not liking Alex's high voice. And he liked her from the start almost too much for Kate's tastes. Being liked was something she was not used to: Kate had been in five or six relationships, all with non-HSPs, and when they had not worked out, she or her partners had tended to see it as her fault. It seems like her subconscious was saying, "Real men (non-HSMs were the only ones she had known) don't like me." Alex saw her as perfect for him. For that she thought he was a bit odd.

In fact, according to Kate, everything with Alex has been different. Her feelings for him at first were not nearly as intense as with her past boyfriends, but their pleasure in each other has grown steadily over several years. And while her family had liked her previous boyfriends, this time around both she and Alex have had to ignore their own families, who can't understand what the two see in each other. But Kate, who realized in high school that she was an HSP because she didn't like loud music and nightclubs, is now very certain of her choice. She cannot imagine being with anyone but an HSP.

Teresa and Juan, in their thirties, met in college. Teresa had been in several intense romantic relationships that had ended badly, each leaving her more guarded than the last. She saw herself as in love with the idea of love, almost addicted to the euphoria and the crises. But by the time she met Juan in one of her classes, she had suffered so much that she did not want to be in a relationship at all. Yet she truly wanted a lifetime partner and children.

Teresa was taking a psychology course and decided she might try one more time by looking in a scientific, rational way for someone who could best meet her needs. After a few dates with Juan, he seemed to be the one who fit, although he was not someone with all the right words, physical features, or romantic moves. But he was thoughtful. There was a calm between them. She sees now that he is, like her, a definite HSP.

Seven years later, Teresa sometimes worries that she cheated herself, not experiencing the euphoria she had wanted from love, but Juan "is always there for me. If I ask him to change, he tries. He is a good father. He is emotionally healthy. Our relationship gets better every year."

You met Diane and Stan in chapter 2. Mostly I described Diane's unhappy marriage to Ron, a non-HSP, which was motivated purely by her need after college to find shelter for a sensitive self that was unprepared to live an independent life. After her divorce, Diane eventually met Stan at a seminar. A year and a half later they met again at a yoga retreat. Like most other HSP/HSP couples, they have come together slowly. Very protective of their time alone, they do not live together; they spend Sundays together plus Monday and Tuesday evenings, but no other times.

In fact, this need for solitude was the issue that almost kept them from becoming a couple. Soon after they started dating, Diane found out that Stan had been lying to her about his days off. He would tell her he was working rather than admit he was choosing not to spend his days off with her. She was of course distressed that he would lie to her. But he had been in a long relationship in which his non-HSP partner had vehemently resented his taking time off without her. He had simply gotten into the habit of lying in order to avoid these battles. Realizing Diane was different, he immediately stopped his old habit. In fact he finds that she knows when he needs time alone even before he does, and she is glad to give it to him—and have it for herself.

What I hear in each of these stories is that the couples have had to adjust to the freedom of being with a similar—there's so much less need to pose, explain, struggle. At the same time, their love grows slowly. This is something of a paradox, since generally HSPs tend to fall in love hard—but apparently they do not fall fast, at least not with other HSPs. While the mind (and perhaps the nervous system) knows right away that one has found someone good, the heart's appreciation may grow more slowly with time, especially given the culture's prejudice against HSPs, as Kate and Alex found. Our culture has given us a non-HSP ideal of instant, impulsive, intense love. For whatever reason, two HSPs may not have this love story.

This potentially different love script seems important to appreciate when you are getting to know an HSP—things may need time, and you may be fonder of each other than you realize. So now let's consider some of the reasons why that fondness grows.

How the Two of You Benefit from Your Similarity

1. *You understand each other.* Perhaps the ultimate test of understanding is if you can understand and forgive being lied to. Of course Diane was upset by Stan's lies about his days off without her, but she completely understood. She could still trust him.

   Remember my description in chapter 3 of jumping to the conclusion that a mistake is due to a person's flawed personality rather than a difficult situation? Since Stan was so much like Diane, she could fully empathize with his need for time alone and thus did not attribute his lie to a basically dishonest personality, but to the situation—a reflexive response to past pressure from a non-HSP (like her own ex, Ron) to be constantly available. She might have done the same herself. A non-HSP probably would not—could not—have been so understanding.

2. *You are comfortable together.* You are physically comfortable at much the same level of arousal from stimulation. One isn't turning up the volume, the other turning it down. (Although of course no two people have *exactly* the same level of sensitivity.) You can agree on more values, on more perceptions. One of you says, "Did you see that?" and the other says "Sure did," not "What, are you crazy?" No more "You're just being too sensitive."

What a pleasure. You are also probably in agreement about the importance of social justice, environmental protection, working on your inner life, and pondering the meaning of existence. No fights over these or feelings of being alone in your interests.

3. *You are thorough in your efforts at communication.* Stan and Diane actually had a weekly "check-in" for a while, when they would discuss their "red flags," the potential relationship problems they had noted. Their having this plan and even a term for what they were watching for, "red flags," certainly captures the quality of conscientious attention two HSPs are likely to pay to their relationship. HSPs do not have to convince each other that good relationships take work and good communication is complicated.

How You Personally Benefit from Your Similarity

1. *Your partner will raise your self-esteem.* Although this is not automatic, by loving each other, most HSPs are learning to love themselves more. This can be a lifelong battle in this culture—think of Alex and Kate having to love each other in spite of their families not understanding their choice of partners. Alex must have felt like he had some basic flaw when Kate told him her parents didn't care much for him, and vice versa. But Alex saw that Kate personally preferred him over all the non-HSPs she had known in the past—even though her family liked the non-HSPs more. This has helped him understand his worth, and both of them to see the temperament prejudices they have to keep from internalizing.

2. *You will be able to go deeply into your feelings, especially those that need healing, and usually be thoroughly understood.* Whether your partner has equal problems or not, he or she will probably be able to listen in a deep and healing way.

So given all these blessings, where might you two have trouble?

THE CHALLENGES

As I've said, HSPs seem to be a bit happier with HSPs than non-HSP partners. However, HSPs in general, regardless of their partner's temperaments, are slightly more likely to be unhappy in their relationships than non-HSPs. So two HSPs, although happier than either would be with a non-HSP, may still be less happy, on the average, than would two non-HSPs.

This slightly lower satisfaction, on average, among HSPs may be because HSPs tend to ponder deeply the questions asked on measures of relationship satisfaction. Perhaps HSPs give more multifaceted, ambivalent, serious, and conscientious answers, even though an outsider would say that the relationships of HSPs are as happy or happier than those of non-HSPs.

But the trend to be less satisfied may also reflect the fact that about half of HSPs have had troubled childhoods and report insecure attachment styles as adults, and HSPs are more impacted by all of this. Again, the research on marital satisfaction is very clear: The more insecurity, negative emotion, or "neuroticism" (anxiety and depression) in either partner, the less happy the relationship. These affect the relationship satisfaction of both the one with the distress and the partner, who may or may not be distressed as well.

The obvious implication is that when two HSPs are together, the likelihood of negative emotions interfering with their relationship is higher, and this may explain their slightly lower reports, on the average, of happiness in relationships.

The Problems Due to Your Similarly Low Optimal Level of Arousal

1. *Neither of you is likely to correct small discomforts that involve confronting others.* Two HSPs together are often delighted to find they can agree that their taxi driver is driving oddly or a restaurant is too noisy. But which one is going to risk an arousing, upsetting scene by stopping the driver and insisting on getting out without paying for the ride? Which one is going to ask for a quieter table or, failing that, lead the two of you out without guilt? I don't mean that HSPs do not act boldly when necessary, but these are difficult, arousing, probably minor challenges that two HSPs might let pass, but which a non-HSP partner might take on for an HSP with relish. When these small matters go unresolved, you both may suffer, and both may wish that the other

could act more heroically. HSWs with HSMs might have this feeling even more.

2. *Neither one of you likes to deal with "stuff."* For example, neither of you probably likes "cold calling" strangers about much of anything, even to ask for information. You certainly do not like confrontations. You do not like wildly busy days or big changes in your lives. You probably don't even like running errands and shopping. Guess what? Non-HSPs often actually do, or it isn't hard for them—just kind of fun or challenging. In a relationship with an HSP, you will have to do more of this than with a non-HSP. It's easy to imagine sometimes wishing your partner were someone less sensitive.

3. *Neither one of you can work long hours or revel in a house full of noisy children.* Your lifestyle will be—must be—different from couples in which one or both are non-HSPs, and there will be inevitable comparisons and disappointments because of your limits.

4. *You will tend to avoid dealing with your conflicts.* There are actually people who do enjoy a "good fight," but you two probably do not. You may intellectually believe disagreements are inevitable, criticisms need to be voiced, and an argument can clear the air. But you may put it off indefinitely, even telling yourselves everything is fine.

5. *You are prone to use being together as a safe place to unwind, getting your excitement elsewhere.* There's plenty of excitement out there in the world—at home you say you want to rest. So you rest together, and you like it that way.

When you two met, you were excited about each other. You saw each other as providing new perspectives, opportunities, pleasures. Your life was enriched, your selves expanded. As the excitement of getting to know each other declines with familiarity, you still want to think of your relationship as source of self-expansion. The two of you may achieve this through inner work together—discussing your hopes, fears, insights, and dreams. But both of you also need to be out in midstream sometimes to feel complete. The whole world you, and you know it. Becoming comfortable out there is often the greatest source of self-expansion for HSPs. Your relationship needs to take you there too, not just home or inside.

Some Solutions

1. *If there are certain tasks both of you don't like, use your intuition and creativity to get around them.* Mainly, simplify your life. There are many books on this topic now, probably written by HSPs. Or find creative ways to increase your income slightly, without too much effort, and then hire others to do the things you two don't like to do. A bright high-school or college student can make phone calls, run errands, pay bills, even handle many of your hassles and confrontations, all for a minimum wage. Get a recommendation from a high-school principal or college career counselor—you want an outstanding student needing a job (most of them do). They move on soon, of course, and you have to train someone new, but they are inexpensive and eager to receive their first glowing job reference. (Don't, however, get involved in their lives.)

2. *Don't plan to have many children. If you already do, plan on one of you not working.* And get help for the left at home, so he or she can have daily breaks. In fact it's best for HSP/HSP couples to divide childcare in a way that gives each parent blocks of time with no child-related responsibilities.

3. *Make the most of your differences.* Divide up tasks according your preference. One of you will always find something a little easier than the other. That seems obvious, but HSPs tend to do what is hardest for them rather than what is easiest—they feel guilty making someone else do what they themselves dread, forgetting that the other may feel no dread at all. Also, keep in mind how sometimes a task becomes easy when you are in the right mood. With that in mind, you can agree on how long you can wait for one of you to be in that mood.

4. *Realize that because "worldly," highly arousing tasks are difficult for you, sometimes they are exactly what you need to do.* Besides needing to get them done for their own sake, so that life is less stressful in the long run, the phone calls and errands can be as much a part of your *inner* work of self-development as the tasks you are naturally good at, like artistic self-expression, higher education in your field, psychological reflection, or spiritual practices. So step up to the plate and swing, and let your

partner take the next turn. He or she may groan and procrastinate, but don't rush to feel guilty or intervene. Both of you need the practice.

5. *Discuss how you will handle conflict before it arises and how you did afterward.* Teresa and Juan are particularly uncomfortable with arguments. She told me with obvious shock that one night they had argued for an hour and a half! (Only two HSPs would argue this long just once in seven years of marriage.) She worked hard not to get too aroused, talking herself through the experience, trying not to overreact, "playing therapist" and letting Juan talk, not taking it on as all her fault. Finally they went to separate rooms. She did deep breathing, prayed, thought it all over. "It took months for us to get over it." She and Juan never discussed that particular issue again.

Teresa is like many HSPs—an ounce of prevention would be better than these necessary but almost deadly cures. She and Juan need more, not less, talk about what's troubling them. They also need more talk about how and when they will talk.

Diane and Stan have learned these preventative skills from their past relationships with non-HSPs who did not want to talk at all. They are eager to have weekly check-ins to discuss the week's "red flags."

Without some scheme like Diane and Stan's, HSPs can be so distressed by the inevitable blowups that they avoid arguing more than ever in the future. It's a hard lesson to learn: you two will have fewer fights, not more, if you discuss conflicts openly and consciously, rather than trying to sweep them under the carpet, be nice, and get over disappointments and irritations.

Discuss ways to deal with the problem of both of you dreading arguments. For example, take time-outs (discussed more in the next chapter). Find out which fighting tactics bother each of you most, and don't use them. And definitely consider having a trusted marital therapist to help "contain" you during the big fights.

You also might try bringing up issues without insisting on settling them in one exhausting discussion. This way you take advantage of your shared preference for processing deeply. It means having to live with the tension of a disagreement while you go about your lives and reflect, but learning to do that can also have its benefits.

In the next chapter we will discuss in detail how the usual advice for improving communication and conflict resolution in a close relationship can be adapted for HSPs.

6. *Reserve some of your best energy for doing exciting things with your partner.* This can be reading a book out loud to each other or discussing a movie you've just seen. It means that every single night you do *not* bore each other with the dull news of the day (or overstimulate each other with the bad news), then go to bed and read alone. Planning how to get away together, some easy change of pace, and being sure you do it, is often a very good way to spend an evening. (We'll discuss this more in chapter 7.)

The Problems Due to Your Similar Awareness of Subtleties

Decisions are maddeningly slow when you are aware of every little detail and implication of a situation, and that's how it is for HSPs. On the other hand, just because of all this sensitivity to subtleties, when HSPs are overstimulated by too many details and subtleties, we can miss the obvious altogether. We become the most absent-minded of professors, always without keys or umbrellas because we are immersed in reflection. When two of you process everything thoroughly, both the benefits and problems seem to be multiplied.

1. *You have trouble making decisions.* You might think all couples have trouble making decisions. Nope. Most couples let just one of the pair make a decision. An HSP often can't bear all that responsibility or bear to risk delegating it. Most couples also impulsively jump into things sometimes. The only thing HSP/HSP couples might jump into would be a very warm swimming pool.

HSP/HSP couples can begin to dread decisions, which means dreading an important part of their lives together. Couple-esteem can be reduced as you begin to think you are a pair of losers who can't even choose a restaurant, ruining an evening thinking about how much better it might have been eating Italian instead of Chinese. An HSW may wish her HSM were more the bold leader. An HSM may wish his HSW were more of a princess/movie star who knew her own mind. In fact neither would enjoy having the other deciding for him or her before having had a chance to reflect.

2. *Sensitivity to your partner's smallest needs and trying to meet them can exhaust you both, keep you both feeling guilty for the other's slightest discomfort, and reduce your sense of personal responsibility.* Teresa brought this home to me when she told me about having to learn to balance how much she gave, how much she took, and how much she and Juan, two HSPs, kept their needs independent. All couples have to strike this balance according to their own tastes regarding separateness-interdependence. But two HSPs can become tightly interdependent so quickly they never have the chance to choose the balance they might prefer. As I discussed in chapter 2, being ever attuned to the other's slightest need, the HSP naturally tries to fill it unless he or she makes a conscious effort not to.

For example, Teresa thought she always ought to cook dinner for Juan. Her mother had cooked for her father, and she had noticed Juan was hungry when he came home, liked to eat at a regular time each day, and was a fussy eater. Meanwhile, Juan was aware that Teresa disliked cooking meals and as a result hardly enjoyed them. Yet for years neither spoke of it. Once they did, they quickly agreed that she should cook when she felt like it, and at other times he would enjoy cooking for both of them or making his own meals whenever he was hungry.

Similarly, Teresa enjoys an occasional social gathering; Juan does not. When they must both go, Teresa is constantly aware of Juan's discomfort, trying to introduce him to people and leaving before she would like to. Juan goes and stays longer than he would like because he knows it is important to Teresa. They still have not discussed and resolved this issue.

There is a fine line between generosity and martyrdom. Every person must decide where this is and take responsibility for the decision, negotiating it if necessary. Always complying is sure to build resentment over time. Yes, it is kind of you to meet your partner's needs, and is convenient for your partner, but it is *not* your obligation. He or she is an adult, not an infant in arms. Keep it that way.

3. *The two of you can have trouble being practical, grounded, realistic about what's out there in the world.* Although HSPs are highly intuitive and therefore prefer to use their intuition, intuition is not infallible. It is just one way of knowing things, by carefully processing, consciously or unconsciously, the information you have and arriving at a sense of how things are or what will happen. There's another way to know things: get more information. But as HSPs, you two probably prefer to intuit. Asking or going to look is less your nature; it is more arousing and requires more effort—probably it seems less elegant and clever too. But an intuition that is not grounded in *some* experience amounts to guessing.

How does the overuse of intuition affect an HSP/HSP couple? In part, it puts stress on you both when intuition does not make up for information and experience, so that, for example, your business fails or you can't get a job in the field you trained in for several years. Or you just drive across town assuming a store will be open without calling to find out it closes early on Sunday. It is also the source of miscommunications, both between the two of you and with others. And it is another reason for low couple-esteem, for thinking the two of you are losers after you've gotten lost once again, physically, financially, professionally, or socially.

4. *You can both be too touchy, too easily hurt or criticized, too quick to apologize.* "I'm sorry, it's all my fault." "No, it's mine—please, let's do whatever you want." "No, I want to do what *you* want."

By processing subtleties to their fullest, you can take small matters just a little too seriously. You see more possible consequences for yourself and others than are really likely. And the more you process anything with emotional content, including criticism or another's discomfort, the more emotion you will feel about it. For example, Kate described to me how much it bothered her when Alex was overly (for her tastes) apologetic for any error of his that she pointed out. It made it difficult for her to bring up even the slightest complaint or source of irritation.

Some Solutions

1. *When making decisions, first be sure that the information you have is well based on fact, not the result of ungrounded intuition.*

Get help with decisions. If it is a life decision, go to a counselor. If it's a business decision, hire a consultant. A travel decision? Ask someone who has been there, done that. If it's about a purchase, read *Consumer Reports*. It makes a couple of HSPs like you feel so much better about a decision. Just be sure the person you ask has no reason to benefit from how you decide. And take into account temperament—don't ask the I-just-dive-right-in types how cold the water is.

2. *Take your time, if you can, in arriving at your final choice.* HSPs often make their decisions unconsciously or spontaneously. You don't know what to do, then one day you both wake up and know. In between you have probably subconsciously been trying out living with one decision for a day or two, then living with another, all of which feels so "indecisive" and worrisome. But usually we do finally know. The long tension of uncertainty has to be borne if we want to come to that final place of being intuitively sure.

If you can't avoid hurrying a choice, try to think of a way you could undo it or lessen its impact if it goes wrong, and think through together what you would do if your worst fear about the result of your hurried decision came true. It may not be that bad. Otherwise, decision-stress can be very hard on an HSP/HSP couple.

3. *If you don't arrive at a place of certainty after a good amount of time, it may be time to go ahead anyway with the best information you have.* Sometimes a sense of certainty never comes, because of some fear, especially the fear of change and novelty. If you suspect fear is influencing your intuition, "switch functions" (see below). You may have to help each other override this fear if all the data, logic, and feeling about it says go ahead.

When the pair of you—or if it is a personal decision, one of you—finally arrives at a decision, try to stop all further processing of it. Help your partner to stop too by not bringing it up over and over. Leave it be. Yes, it may turn out to be wrong, but with difficult decisions you never have all the information and know how they will turn out ahead of time. If later you learn you chose wrong, that's how it goes. Imagining all the ways you could be wrong without more information to know for sure is just too hard on you.

By the way, HSPs usually make excellent decisions. Don't just take for granted your good history of this as individuals and as a couple—remember your past successes.

If the decision you must make now seems momentous, give yourselves permission to treat it as hard work, but work you are an expert at. I often say that our culture admires more a fast decision that's wrong over a right decision that took a while. HSPs like to make the latter kind and usually do. At the same time, as experts, maybe you don't need to process quite as long as you used to.

4. *Rein in each other's processing when it's excessive.* It's strange to think of trying to process subtleties less, but sometimes that is your task, in a sense. For example, you need to be able to hear a criticism as just that, a complaint about one thing, without processing it to the point that you decide you are terrible. It may not even be your fault; but if it is, let yourself make a mistake. I know it's hard to do, but it is extremely important. You'll make mistakes every single day. And if you can avoid being defensive or plunging into self-loathing, it will be much better for your partner and your relationship. If you do slip into one of these states, when you come out of it, apologize and vow to keep your perspective better next time.

It also helps to take your time digesting criticism and "failures." Use your partner to help. Often these turn out to be minor, or perfectly excusable, or reversible, or even no mistake at all. I learned this a very hard way. Three weeks after I took my written exams for my doctorate, I came home one night, opened my mail, and found a letter telling me I had failed—me, one of the best students in my class according to everyone. What an awful, awful night I had. By morning, however, I saw it had to be a mistake. And it was. It turned out I had not failed at all.

5. *To expand the flexibility of each other's subtle processing, think in terms of Jung's four functions.* According to Jung, there are four functions of the conscious mind, four ways of approaching the world. Each function is one kind of intelligence, and everyone has a specialty or dominant function. Most but not all HSPs are intuitive types. Intuitive types listen and look, process all the subtleties unconsciously, then start making intuitive leaps beyond the information given. The opposite of intuition is sens-

ing—processing the "surface" of information by simply seeing and hearing attentively. Compared to intuitive types, sensing types spend less time reflecting on what they see or hear and more time noticing what's actually present. They don't intuit additional possibilities. What they see is what is. Magicians rely on them—they don't wonder so much how a trick was done. They prefer to read directions, follow recipes, want "just the facts," and can even take some pleasure in neatly filling out a form.

The other two functions, thinking and feeling—also opposites—have more to do with the reasons for our decisions than how we process information. I find HSPs fairly evenly split on which of these is stronger. The thinking function uses abstract principles or theories as rules for decision making. The feeling function is *not* about deciding emotionally, but about evaluating the human, personal impact, which includes the emotional impact. "Thinkers" and "feelers" can be equally compassionate (or selfish), but how they help can differ: A feeling type might first pick up an injured child and comfort it; a thinking type might first review the rules of first aid and decide whether to call 911. We need both types of responses in the world.

There are tests to determine your dominant function. You can also just identify your weakest function—which, when you have to use it, makes you feel really helpless, frustrated, touchy, and ashamed. Your dominant one is its opposite. If your dominant function is intuition, developing sensing will be a lifelong task. You can use your thinking and feeling, probably more balanced in you, to augment your intuition. For example, thinking or feeling about the consequences of a decision will often tell you when it is time to gather more information—like a sensing type would do—rather than use intuition.

In a close relationship, it is useful to know where each of you stands on the four functions, as you can compensate for each other's weaknesses and take advantage of each other's strengths. For two HSPs, it is even more useful because intuition may be the dominant function for both of you. And when you both have the same dominant function, you will reinforce it in each other, reduce your practice with the other functions, and collude to ignore your mutual inferior function until it snags you both.

Treat your inferior function as a developmental task, your psychological project, or even as a spiritual path, your meaning in life. HSPs are generally motivated by framing things in this way, and it is the right way, I believe. Jung saw the inferior function as a doorway to the unconscious. For example, if you are an intuitive type and become immersed in sensuality—music, sex, food—at these times you are most open to the unconscious. (The sensing type will be less easily transported by the senses, being "used to them.") Jung saw the inferior function's development as an important route to greater wholeness. To be able to look and nothing more, to stay present and mindful, to listen without exploring the meaning—this sensing way of being practically defines enlightenment for an intuitive type.

You can help each other best by not rescuing your partner when he or she is working with the inferior function. Let an intuitive partner struggle with the map without you; when he or she is going off into wild possibilities and making unwarranted assumptions, suggest that your partner just be present. If your partner is a feeling type, he or she needs to think through the logic of a situation without your help. If a thinking type, to feel what he or she would *like,* regardless of its practicality. If a sensing type, to look beyond the surface to the infinite other possibilities.

The Problems Due to Low HSP-Esteem

Two HSPs can boost each other's self-esteem if even one is aware of and combating his or her internalized prejudice against sensitivity. Otherwise, two HSPs can spiral each other into still lower self-esteem. In this case, the following problems may occur:

1. *You lack respect for each other.* I have already discussed the importance of self-love for loving someone else, especially since we all tend to see our partners almost as parts of ourselves, even mixing up their traits with our own. This is even more possible when someone is very similar to you. So the more you see yourself as "too" sensitive (inferior, a loser, whatever), the more you will see your HSP partner the same way. You come to devalue your own choice of a partner, both because it was your choice and because you chose someone like yourself.

   Low self-esteem can also lead to projecting what you dislike about yourself, but can't face, onto your partner, as I described in chapter 5. If you unconsciously feel that your sensitivity makes you weak, neurotic, or not a "real man" or a "competent woman," you may try to get rid of this feeling by seeing your so-similar partner as weak, neurotic, or failing as a man or woman. If you complain that your partner is wallowing in self-pity, for example, you probably have a history of ignoring your own suffering and choking down your tears. You have no patience with someone indulging in what you do not allow yourself.

Even if there's a sizable "hook" or objective truth to your projection, you need to have sympathy for both of you. If you or your partner is "weak" or "neurotic," it's probably due to a troubled childhood or too much stress throughout life, in combination with a sensitive nervous system that needed something else. As you accept yourself, your tolerance of your partner will probably grow too.

2. *One or both of you is prone to anxiety or depression, which will affect the other.* Low self-esteem typically leads to negative feelings in general—fear or hopelessness regarding how you expect the world to treat you and how you expect to be able to cope. I have seen depressed, anxious, insecure HSPs carry on almost normally at work and with friends, but no one can hide these low feelings from a partner, especially from another HSP. Even quiet withdrawal will be noticed. The other may manage okay when you are troubled, or may feel that his or her anchor is gone, in which case you may both spiral downward.

Some Solutions

I have already enjoined enough about the importance of respecting your sensitivity. I would add only the following for HSP/HSP couples especially.

1. *Be sure to value sensitivity in your partner as well as yourself.* It may seem sometimes that you are dissatisfied with only your own sensitivity, or only with your partner's. But at a less conscious level you have to be judging both of you. Your appreciation of your trait will rise and fall according to all kinds of events—something you see on TV, remember from the past, hear from an acquaintance. Kate does not enjoy nightclubs and loud music, but

she wishes she did. Alex doesn't mind not enjoying them. So I can imagine Kate hearing about a couple's exciting evenings on the town and beginning to blame Alex for their not going out more. It is so easy to assign the other HSP your sensitivity and then rail against it. Then you don't have to feel bad about yourself. But the real solution is to remember the package deal—value the benefits of your sensitivity that go along with the drawbacks, like not enjoying what others consider an exciting evening, and feel good about both of you.

2. *Heal your wounds as much as you can.* Psychotherapy and inner work of all sorts is an act of love and a moral duty if you are troubled and have a very sensitive partner. He or she cannot help but be very vulnerable to your moods. Make it your life's goal to increase your security and hopefulness. If it's your partner who is depressed or anxious, it will help if you separate just a bit, allow the other some room to do his or her inner work. Don't take his or her moods personally or let the moments of fear and hopelessness spread to you. To maintain this separate stability, this calm in the face of depression, will require your own healing and diligent inner work. It is not a matter of simple willpower. But as you stand firm for your partner, and your partner does this for you, the two of you become co-seekers in the search for reasons for joy and meaning in life.

3. *Consider medication.* If you or your partner is depressed or anxious, and you have been advised that medication would help, this may be the decision that saves your relationship. This is not about sensitivity being an illness or syndrome, and if a doctor tries to tell you that, refuse to work with him or her. Most HSPs feel their sensitivity is actually able to be more fully experienced by taking an antidepressant (which is usually the treatment of choice for HSPs who are depressed or anxious). So you may find that with medication, probably in combination with some psychotherapy or good counseling, you will not only feel better about yourself and your partner, but also about your sensitivity. Yes, there are other ways to treat depression and anxiety, and you should be well informed about your options. But choose one and take action. Every episode of two or three weeks of persistent depression or anxiety adds to the risk of another episode like it later, so again, do *something*.

Kate, of Kate and Alex, is a good role model. She fell into a deep depression while in college. She finally listened to her body, which couldn't sleep or eat, and began taking antidepressants. Whenever she stops, the depression returns, so she takes medication and there's no problem. It may be that she has inherited some vulnerability from her mother—a "high-strung, anxious person"—or that certain extreme stresses during Kate's childhood, due to her mother's deep depressions, has affected Kate's neurophysiological flexibility. Or it may be that, when the time is right, Kate needs to explore her feelings about her mother's unavailability during those years. Whatever the reason for her own depression, I think her straightforward handling of the matter makes a lot of sense.

There's one caution, however, offered by Peter Kramer in Should You Leave? (he's also the author of Listening to Prozac and is very experienced on the subject). Sometimes couples have founded their entire relationship on coping with each other's depression and anxiety. If one begins to improve, the other may follow, and there is a happy ending. But the other may refuse or be unable to follow, for many reasons. This leaves the one improving with a hard choice. He or she will have an almost unbearable urge to move out of this depression-based life. But abandoning the other will also seem unbearable. So if both of you have been anxious or depressed, do try to seek treatment at the same time.

A FINAL WORD TO YOU BOTH

In conclusion, rejoice in having found someone so like yourself. If this also means more healing work for you and your partner, due to your past and your culture's treatment of this trait, then that is part of your particular "package deal," just as the HSP with a non-HSP partner has a difficult assortment of blessings and problems. Fortunately you two are well designed to help each other by becoming true experts in each other's subtle psychology and in the psychology of relationships. To nurture that expertise is our next chapter's goal.

7

Creating a Satisfying, Sensitive Partnership: Relationship Advice Revised for HSPs

Let's begin with the story of an HSP about to be married. In typical HSP fashion, he wanted to get started right, so he was reading "seven or eight of the best books" about relationships, recommended by his premarital counselor, friends, and a search of the internet. He was also sharing the work of planning the wedding, and he was of course still deepening his relationship with his fiance. He had called me because he had seen me in the past for psychotherapy around his sensitivity, and he now wanted my opinion of him as a prospective husband. He was beginning to fear he was not going to be a good one. He could see all the signs mentioned in the books—all sorts of troubles in his family when he was growing up, indications of unconscious problems, plus his increasing irritability, anxiety, depression, and sudden mood swings—sure signs of neuroticism, that bane of the happy marriage.

Standing outside of this maelstrom, I could see a far more serious but simple and immediate problem: he was overstimulated, overaroused, overwhelmed by the approach of the biggest initiation of his life. The overarousal was making him miserable, and probably miserable to be with. Miserable people do not have happy engagements or marriages, no matter how much good advice they get from outside. So I asked him if he had any doubts about his choice of a partner. He said not really—only doubts about her choice of him. I told him that no one can say for sure how a marriage will fare, and that his uncertainty was creating much of his nervousness, but it is just part of life. Maybe he could wait to read the books—he would have years for them—and make his highest priority just staying within his optimal level of arousal during this inevitably stimulating time. He and his fiance could work on this goal together—I heard signs from him that she was as overwhelmed as he, and probably more so with his new apprehensions. Indeed, I said that among all the things they could learn to do for each other, this might be the most important.

I have told you this story because I do not want you to be overwhelmed like him, so this chapter offers only six of the many good ideas to be found on maintaining happy relationships—the six that I thought were most pertinent to HSPs. These are suggestions that apply whether you and your partner are matched in temperaments or not—they are just important points for HSPs to remember.

After discussing these, I will suggest how to find a good relationship counselor—a professional every couple probably needs as much as a good family doctor, but especially if you are an HSP trying to learn to think deeply about your love. And we will consider when to stop trying to repair a relationship and just leave, something HSPs find especially difficult to do.

We will begin with a suggestion you probably have not heard before, as it is the result of new research by my husband and myself.

THE IMPORTANCE OF DOING EXCITING THINGS TOGETHER

In the last chapter I mentioned that a pair of HSPs must be careful not to make their relationship such a calming refuge that it becomes boring. But this is actually a common problem in all HSP relationships. While two HSPs may allow their relationship to become dull by both staying home too much, if you are in an HSP/non-HSP couple, you may send the non-HSP out without you too frequently, so that your partner is in his or her optimal level of arousal, but the relationship itself ceases to feel expanding and exciting for either of you.

One way of understanding your feelings when you fell in love is that you were both feeling excited, energized by essential spirit (as described in chapter 4), expanded by this person you were including into your life. You were probably staying up all night, talking for hours, enchanted with stories about the other's life and new insights about your own. (To capture through research some of this self-expanding effect of love, Art and I gathered weekly self-descriptions from young single people over several months, during which time some fell in love. Those freshly in love described themselves at greater length and with more diversity of concepts. They seemed literally expanded.)

After you got to know each other, of course, the sense of excitement and expansion slowed down. And, indeed, most couples, HSPs or not, report a steady decline in relationship satisfaction over time. Almost instinctively, people start trying to correct this by doing some things together that are exciting—traveling, going out to new places, meeting one another's friends. Building a life together can be exciting in itself—decorating a home, having children, working on projects together. But couples who avoid doing most of these activities, or anything else very exciting, are especially likely to find themselves dissatisfied with the relationship. They may not think of boredom as a relationship problem, but it is—even if outside the relationship, in their careers or friendships, they are having all sorts of interesting experiences.

Groundbreaking Research on the Need to Break New Ground

None of this discussion about boredom is just speculation. About ten years ago Art and I carried out some initial surveys in which we found boredom in relationships to be a strong indicator of more general relationship dissatisfaction. Thus, one of Art's doctoral students, Charlotte Reissman, did an experiment to test it more carefully. She asked married couples to go over a list of possible activities and indicate which ones would be "pleasant" or "exciting" for them to do together. Then one-third were randomly assigned to do some of their self-chosen exciting activities together for an hour and a half every week for ten weeks. Another third of the couples were assigned to do their self-chosen pleasant activities for the same amount of time. A third group did nothing special. At the end of the ten weeks, those doing exciting activities together indicated a significant increase in their marital satisfaction. Those couples spending the same amount of time together doing simply pleasant activities, and those doing no special extra activities, did not show any increase at all in marital satisfaction over the ten weeks. That is, simply spending extra time together, if it did not involve exciting activities, was no better than not spending extra time together.

In another experiment, couples came into our laboratory and were randomly assigned to take part in either a very exciting, challenging task together or a monotonous one, or to do nothing at all together. Afterward, each couple was videotaped while planning a trip, and their discussions were rated later by trained observers who did not know that the couples had done any kind of special activity beforehand. The discussions of those who had done the exciting, challenging task together were significantly more positive and less hostile. Also, when couples in this experiment were tested before and after the task on their marital satisfaction and the love felt for each other, couples doing the exciting, challenging tasks showed significantly greater increases than the others in their satisfaction and love.

This research has made quite a stir among those who study close relationships, as relationship quality has always been seen as the result of the personalities or histories of each of the partners plus their communication skills. Yet it seems very possible that much of the trouble couples have could be due to boredom. Like doggies who haven't had a long walk in awhile, bored people can stir up all sorts of personal and interpersonal trouble to keep a relationship interesting.

Apply Excitement to HSPs with Care

Of course, as an HSP you need to be reassured that doing exciting things together does not mean doing overexciting, overarousing things together. It means both of you being in your *optimal* level of arousal, together, rather than always using your time together for quiet rest, to gather strength for the next time you each go off alone into the world. This way you associate your relationship with excitement as well as repose.

Choose activities that are interesting and exciting for both of you. If your partner is also an HSP, this should be easy, as you have about the same optimal level of arousal. With a non-HSP, you might want to choose something that is familiar enough to you that it is exciting but not highly arousing, and unfamiliar enough for your partner that he or she finds it quite exciting. For example, I am comfortable on horseback, but being up on a horse is pretty exciting for Art! María, an HSP, and Dan, a non-HSP (you will know them better soon), often travel in María's homeland, Peru, and in other Latin American countries because she feels at home there, but she still is excited by going back home and by traveling to new locales. Dan, who speaks no Spanish, always finds any part of Latin America quite exciting.

Doing exciting activities together as a means of improving your relationship is especially helpful if either of you is not inclined to talk much—or if it seems like that's all you do! It can also be a way to increase the general positive feelings so that you can then tackle, or retackle, your conflicts. How do you handle conflicts? That's our next topic.

DIALOGUE TO APPRECIATE EACH OTHER'S PERSPECTIVE

I have already mentioned dialogue as important for dealing with gender and temperament differences, but I want to emphasize it here. Some human differences are so fundamental that they create quite different feelings and responses to the world, and two people who differ in any of these major ways—such as gender, temperament, ethnicity, religion, or experiences with poverty or racism— may find it very hard to believe that their beloved partner, or anyone, could hold such crazy views. But even ordinary conflicts like how to spend money or raise children can sometimes make you feel like you must be from different universes. The solution is the same—begin with a determination to hear the other's perspective as valid simply because it is held by a person you respect. And dialogue.

Listen Empathically, Speak Emphatically

Those who advise couples, myself included, used to put their emphasis on reflective, empathic listening. But that has not proven to be quite sufficient, because sometimes one partner is quite skilled at listening but does not express his or her own perspective with enough force to have it honored, or else just gives in too easily. This was first observed about women, but in my experience HSPs, men or women, are even more prone to lay low, let their partners speak and speak and speak, then fear it will be too overarousing to try to marshall sufficient evidence to counter their partners' viewpoint. So the HSPs just go along with the others' plans. But it won't work, HSPs. There's plenty of research indicating that neither partner is happy in the long run if all the power and influence resides with one person in the relationship. So you better learn to hold up your end in a dialogue.

In dialogue, empathic listening is half of what is required—the listener attends to the feelings as well as the content and does not interrupt, interpret, advise, or even offer his or her own experience or ask questions. (This is described in both *The Highly Sensitive Person* and *The Highly Sensitive Person's Workbook*.) But here's the other half of dialogue: When your partner is doing the listening, you give your own perspective without flinching from your authentic truth. You speak plainly, honestly, without blaming, using "I statements": "I need that" or "I see it this way." Then you listen to your partner's reply or defense, following the usual rules—no interruptions, advice, or interpretations of what your partner is "really doing."

Dialogue—A Matter of Honor and Trust

To dialogue, each of you must trust the other not only to listen without making hasty judgments or interrupting, but to speak the full truth about what is going on. Each person's view of the situation is equally valid and should be honored. It should not be edited, criticized, or invalidated in any way—by your partner *or* by your own inner critical voice or fear of overarousal.

If you have a partner who chooses not to dialogue, but to just have his or her way, you need to explain why this will be a serious mistake in the long run. Simply put, if he or she wants the two of you to be intimate, you must trust each other, and trust requires neither person feeling dominated, and this requires that both of you listen respectfully to each other and have equal influence over final outcomes.

Of course there are topics on which you will never agree, and for these it is even more important that you adhere to the fundamental principle of dialogue: On issues of values and feelings (not issues like which way is north), both views could be right and are equally valid as viewpoints. By hearing each other out, you understand the underlying issues better and exactly why your partner cannot concede. After a good dialogue, you may even feel that if you were your partner, you would have to hold the same view of the matter as he or she does. But you are not your partner, so maybe you do not and cannot hold the same view. That's important too.

DAN AND MARÍA

I was privileged to watch a fine use of dialogue brought to me by Dan and María, whom I already mentioned. Dan, the non-HSP, was Jewish, a lawyer in environmental law. María, the HSP, was Peruvian and raised Catholic. She was a talented dancer. When they met, they were not practicing their religions. When they decided to marry, they discussed, for about two minutes, how they would raise their children. Daniel felt strongly that even partly Jewish children should be raised as Jews. María was in a period of deep doubt about her faith and also wanted to avoid a conflict she thought she would lose, so she agreed to this plan.

By the time María was an expectant mother, however, she had refound her faith and returned to her Peruvian roots. Still, to Dan, an agreement was an agreement—not only did he not want to raise his child Catholic, but he did not want María to think she could just change her mind on something so important. For María, this was a situation she had encountered before—she would agree with something to make Dan happy and to avoid an argument because she usually lost anyway, but later she would find she just could not comply. Once she had even lied to him to hide the fact that she had done what she had wanted to do after saying she would not, which made her very ashamed and which Dan of course discovered. After that episode, he proclaimed her a bit lax about keeping her word and was even more determined not to let her break her agreement on the religion issue. Those were their two positions when they came to see me, most of it told by Dan.

It was obviously time for Dan to sit and listen, without interrupting to criticize María or defend himself, while María told of her newfound passionate feelings about Christianity as the way of life she wanted for her children. He also needed to hear how she had agreed not only on the occasion of their deciding on their children's religious upbringing, but on many others, always in order to avoid arguments with a skilled lawyer who never stopped until he had won his case, no matter how exhausted or upset she was. As for lying to him once, she felt she had apologized enough and certainly had never done it again. Had he really never, ever lied to her in any way? It especially hurt her that she thought she had heard him hint more than once that she might not be the best one to teach their children religious values, given her lying. But what she remembered best was a fight before their marriage, this one over where they would live, when she was so frustrated and angry by his relentless logic that she finally exploded and screamed that she hated him. He calmly called her an emotional Latin, as if that were final proof that he was right, she was wrong, and then walked out. Later she apologized, they lived where Dan thought was best, and María promised never to behave that way again. And she never had. But I could tell that Dan was finally beginning to realize that it might have been better to explore what had brought her to that state or, even better, to have listened to her viewpoint from the outset, rather than have her live in fear of him, hiding her resentment.

Then it was Dan's turn, and María had to listen to her husband's feelings about his Jewish roots, the loss of most of his extended family in the Holocaust, his anger that Christians and the Pope in particular did so little to help the Jews, and his wish that his children see themselves as Jews, with all that meant to him. And he had his own memory of that early fight over where they'd live, when her anger conjured up his father's drunken rages when he was a boy. There was also his deep horror that she would ever lie to him, perhaps betray him in other ways, too—a distressing fear that even he had not fully acknowledged until this dialogue.

María was deeply moved to hear the heated feelings underlying Dan's coolly logical positions. She could also see that if she had stood up for herself, she could have spared him what for him was a major betrayal—the one lie she had told him.

I think you can readily see the necessity of dialogue in this example. While Dan and María's ongoing dialogues have not, probably cannot, lead them to a solution about their child's religious upbringing that will be optimal for both of them, it definitely can lead to the feeling that whatever they do, their process of arriving at this and all future decisions will honor both of their perspectives equally. That's what dialogue can do.

CONTAIN STATES OF OVERAROUSAL DURING CONFLICTS

My third suggestion is seen by marital researchers as increasingly critical, whatever one's temperament, but it is probably the most important single point for HSPs. María's overarousal during her arguments with Dan were so aversive for her that in order to avoid it she was willing to appease him, ignore her own views and needs, and even lie—something she definitely did not feel was her usual or authentic self. HSPs can dread overarousal that much, as you probably know. This dread can truly keep you from doing what you know you ought to do—express your opinion in a dialogue, for example— no matter how sensitive you are to what needs to be done.

Non-HSPs also dread overarousal. Although Dan was less aware of his discomfort with it, he must have been very overaroused when María lost her temper and screamed at him. Perhaps it was so aversive to him that he had been controlling her emotional expressions with rational arguments ever since. In Dan's case, emotional arguments quickly led to overarousal because of his half-conscious fear that one of them would lose control, as his father used to do. The point is that once overaroused, whatever the reason or process, the state is equally unpleasant for non-HSPs and equally likely to lead to errors in relationship judgment. But HSPs are more likely to become overaroused and to reach that point first.

The Signs of Overarousal

Psychologist John Gottman of the University of Washington, Seattle—author of *Why Marriages Succeed or Fail, The Seven Principles for Making Marriage Work,* and numerous research papers—studies what makes the difference between marriages that work and those that don't (a smart approach, since most books are written by relationship therapists who routinely observe only distressed relationships). He studies couples as they interact in his laboratory, and he is so keenly aware of the bad effects of overarousal on couples' dialogues that he has the partners wired up in his lab so he can detect it and train them to reduce it.

Although Gottman does not discuss temperament differences, I will: HSPs are more likely to experience overarousal, so it is even more essential for you to become adept in dealing with it in your relationships. You know very well how it feels to be overaroused, but let's review the outer signs, specified by Gottman and others, so that you can watch for them in each other.

If you take the pulses of people who are overaroused, they will probably be racing at about 95 to 100 beats a minute (precisely what's high for each person depends on the resting pulse rate). They will keep their eyes closed more (trying to reduce the stimulation) or their eyelids may flutter. They may fold their arms across their chest or swivel their hips away from their partner. They may play with their hair or with a prop like a pencil or tissue, or cover their faces with their hands. The facial muscles look overcontrolled—chin tight, lips pressed together so the red part of the upper lip isn't seen. The "grief muscle" is tensed: The corners of the brows are drawn up and together with a furrow in the middle of the brows, or the brows are straight across. The voice gets higher and the breath is shallow—coming from the throat, not the chest. There are sighs or speech disturbances such as unfinished sentences, repetitions, slips of the tongue, omissions, stuttering, or many "ahs."

In a more global sense, overaroused people show little humor, interest, or brightening of their expressions in response to anything. They are hypervigilant for threat, and when a negative train of thought begins, it persists far longer. New information and insights are not processed, so everything said is pretty much wasted on the overaroused. If you are hoping to see them employ some new behavior, forget it—overaroused people won't apply new learning unless it has become almost automatic through many rehearsals.

Mostly, overaroused people want to get out of the discussion, as María desired, or totally control it, as Dan did. If you keep them in it, they are more likely to complain about all sorts of things and engage in what Gottman calls the "four horsemen"—criticism, defensiveness, contempt, and stonewalling or emotional withdrawal (the last being most typical of HSPs).

Preventing Overarousal

Obviously you want to prevent episodes of overarousal. Here are some ways:

- Don't get into a likely-to-arouse discussion when either of you is tired, overstimulated, or already stressed about something else.
- Retire to a protected, calming environment for your discussion, like in the woods or by the ocean.
- Bring up a tense topic gently, with tact and whatever appreciation you can have about what the other has already done to minimize the problem.
- When things go wrong or you feel in error, try to correct things and receive well the other's attempts to do the same.
- Look for every place where you can compromise or give in without feeling you have violated your own needs.
- Check pulses when overarousal threatens. I'm serious. This is a very objective way to agree that one of you needs a time-out.
- Make the time-out at least twenty minutes—that's how long it takes to return to normal.
- Agree about when you will resume your discussion, and don't put it off too long.
- Both partners should agree to do everything possible individually to maintain an optimal level of arousal, recover from past bouts of chronic overarousal, and heal past emotional wounds.
- As a further preventative, see to it in any way you can that the positive events and feelings associated with your relationship greatly outnumber the negatives ones.

About correcting your errors in how you have argued: A good example of an error would be insulting or labeling your partner ("you're a jerk" or "you're neurotic") rather than sticking to the issue—definitely against the rules of good fighting. Saying right away "I shouldn't have said that—I'm sorry" is the exact opposite of defensiveness. According to Gottman, 83 percent of marriages last if the partners show this repair skill, so learn it, and when your partner admits an error, praise him or her so both of you learn it.

Recovering from overarousal through meditation retreats, massages, special diets, or psychotherapy can help a person maintain a broader, calmer perspective during conflicts (the opposite of the constricted, threatened state one feels when overaroused). Thus, such self-care is not self-centered. It is simply needed, especially by an HSP; it is an investment.

When an HSP keeps things positive—when the HSP's nervous system is humming right—he or she will be a big depositor in what John Gottman calls the marital bank account. Every time something positive happens to either of you, you have made a deposit, whether it is good sex, a kind exchange, a nice chat over lunch, or a satisfying vacation. A withdrawal occurs every time something negative happens, whether it is a minor argument or the death of a child. When the bank account is empty, just one episode of overarousal may be enough to end the relationship, because there's just no more reason to stay. Because HSPs seem to have the potential to be more overaroused over less, and to have episodes of intense joy or gloom, you could say that this makes us the big tycoons in the relationship world—easy come, easy go; that is, easy to add good feelings to the bank account, easy to go bankrupt. (HSPs may be the last to actually go—to leave a relationship.) Chronic overarousal or chronic fear of it, so that dialogue is avoided, are sure ways to end up in a marital economic depression.

ENGAGE: DO IT YOUR WAY, BUT DO NOT DISENGAGE

Conflict and anger do not predict divorce. In fact, happy and unhappy couples have the same number and type of issues over which they disagree. How you behave during conflicts is what predicts divorce. HSPs are likely to avoid conflicts or withdraw during them—one of the worst strategies. Most relationships end due to this kind of disengagement—fully 80 percent of couples divorcing say they were simply "growing apart," whereas only 40 percent give fighting or conflicts of opinion as the reason. Fighting might lead to a resolution; not talking about a conflict can only lead to this "growing apart," as it did for María. Or Jack.

JACK AND RAVEN

In this couple, Jack was the HSP, a young father raising triplets with the help of a full-time nanny, while Raven, the mother, worked as a family physician. Jack also had a successful business working from home as a practice consultant for doctors. Having a bright and sensitive mind, it had been easy for him to do this after dropping out of medical school, where he and Raven had met. But his business only gave him a superficial sense of achievement. What he really wanted to do with his life he still did not know.

The arrival of the triplets had been a blow to Jack, who had not been so certain their two-year relationship was ready for one child, much less three. At least *he* was not ready. All of his adult life he had been under the pressure of either getting into medical school, being there, or making the agonizing decision to quit. But Raven, seven years older, had heard the ticking of her biological clock, so Jack had agreed that she would use fertility drugs when she did not conceive easily.

When they first learned Raven was carrying triplets, Jack had hinted at his unhappiness. Raven blew up; she felt he blamed her and obviously did not love her or the expected babies. He never forgot her shouting, "Do you want me to have an abortion? Is that it?" He felt ashamed and shocked, and never again discussed any of his deeper feelings with her. She seemed not to notice or mind. Feeling sick about what life had dealt him, Jack decided to give all his love to the triplets, to sacrifice everything for them. His life seemed over. He tried not to think about his marriage at all.

The Signs of Disengagement

Jack and probably Raven are experiencing the classic signs of disengagement:

- You think your relationship's problems are too severe to be resolved and decide it is best to come to some solution on your own rather than have any more episodes of intense over-arousal.
- You try to adjust, lower your expectations. But you aren't feeling true acceptance and love—Gottman could tell if he had you in his lab, because he would see chronic physiological arousal,

even if you seemed calm and resigned. On the average, the pulse is seventeen beats per minute higher in married persons who are eventually going to divorce.

- The two of you begin to lead parallel lives.
- You feel lonely. At this point, unless there are other reasons you would not end the relationship—such as your religious beliefs, financial situation, or newborn triplets—this step will seem inevitable.

Disengagement is not always so extreme. It can occur in just one area—perhaps you have given up on spending leisure time together, discussing your situation at work, or having sex. It seems tolerable. But while even one area of life is too distressing to discuss, your relationship is on precarious ground.

Reengagement

The best solution for disengagement is to prevent it by noticing signs of trouble before they have gone this far. As an HSP, you can notice these while they are still quite subtle: feelings of irritation, anger, futility, distance, or worry about the relationship; knowing that your partner doesn't know what you are thinking and vice versa; overarousal at the thought of what would happen if you discussed certain subjects together; lack of a desire to touch or show physical affection.

To overcome disengagement, both of you must admit that it is a serious problem and work to change it. Changing it requires, first, that the disengaged person, often an HSP, discuss what first began to shut him or her down. Often it was a particular discussion, where the HSP was highly overaroused or heard a comment that he or she has since processed in such a way that the topic now seems too dangerous, painful, finished, or ruined. Whatever went wrong in that discussion must be revisited and not go wrong again. Next time there must be dialogue, not blaming or defensiveness, and there must be time-outs when overarousal gets too high.

Second, the disengaged person must, for a change, dialogue openly and argue vehemently for his or her position. If this is you, in a sense you must do the opposite of reflective listening or being tuned into the other. You must be completely tuned into yourself, expressing your own needs, feelings, and perspectives, rather than keeping all of that to yourself and assuming it's useless to discuss things.

In Jack's case, he would need to begin by expressing, late though it is, all the reasons why he wishes they had not had children so early in their relationship and all his hopelessness about his future. Raven would have to listen—as Dan listened to María—without judgment or defensiveness. Then they would reverse the roles.

On some issues, however, a calm attitude of listening can be very difficult for even the most loving spouse to achieve without some further inner work on why he or she is being so touchy. For example, Raven may need to face the possibility that her wounding outburst about an abortion may have reflected her own secret thoughts, which were totally unacceptable to her but certainly quick to come to mind when Jack merely hinted at some concerns. This brings us to our next topic.

UNCOVERING UNACKNOWLEDGED LIFELONG HOPES AND FEARS

Behind conflicts that seem especially intense and recurring, there often lies a lifelong unfulfilled hope or unresolved fear—in Raven's case, that the lifestyle demanded by triplets and her practice would end her hope for a deeply intimate, private relationship with a partner—how would there be time?—and in Jack's case, his hope for an entire new life after leaving medical school.

HSPs are especially likely to struggle to find meaning in their work and to have lifelong hopes about that. Needing meaning and purpose so much, we will suffer greatly if anything seems to stand in the way, even while we also want to please our partner. And we can have deep-rooted fears, having processed the frightening experiences we have had or heard about in great detail—fears of catastrophes (for example, making us refuse to move to a region that has earthquakes or tornados), fears for our loved ones (making us fight with a spouse over allowing a teenager to learn to drive), fears for our world (giving us a major tizzy when a partner fails to recycle).

We may be embarrassed about the depth of some of these hopes and fears—embarrassed by the "phobias," idealism, or "selfishness" of our private plans.

How Hidden Hopes and Fears Make Mountains from Molehills

Suppose you forgot to keep certain receipts that could be used for a tax deduction. Suddenly your partner is shouting at you about how you are wasting both of your hard-earned salaries. What's behind this? Perhaps it is your partner's fear of poverty after experiencing it in childhood. Or he or she tries to save because of a secret, perhaps half-conscious hope of making some purchase or trip, taking an early retirement, or making a career change. Maybe he or she thinks you don't value this goal very much. And maybe that's true, so you resist saving every last nickel and dime of taxes. Maybe your hope has been to live a life unconcerned with money, a life lived fully each day, before death or illness makes a mockery of all that saving for the future. So you both shout over a stupid little receipt.

Remember Chris and Jordan from chapter 1? Jordan, an HSS, wanted to accept a transfer to the London office of his firm—not exactly a molehill, but not an unreasonable desire either. In response, Chris wanted the two of them to go to counseling so that Jordan would realize he had Attention Deficit Disorder and stay put. If that strategy did not work, Chris intended to refuse to move. Why the stonewalling? In fact, Chris had always secretly hoped to move to a small town, put down roots, and develop a sense of community and place. Meanwhile, Jordan had always planned to live in a variety of places during his life, especially in vibrant foreign cities. Each stands in the way of the other's entire vision of life—they need to start talking about this.

Behind the struggle of Dan and María there was one vision of a family steeped in Jewish heritage that seemed opposed to a hope for a devoutly religious Catholic family. How could there not be nasty fights?

When you have a lifelong hope and your partner's plans appear to be standing in the way of it being fulfilled, you can fight with a vigor neither of you thought possible—although this hope and this standing in the way of it may never have been made explicit or even be fully conscious. Similarly, when you have a lifelong fear that your partner seems to ignore or expects you to overcome, you may refuse to do certain things with unexpected stubbornness. So when one or both of you is fighting, defending, or stonewalling as though possessed, try asking, "Is there a big unnamed hope or fear beneath all this uproar?" There almost always is, if you can only name it.

On the other hand, as an HSP, you may put up too little fight and uproar, as Jack did, and disengage instead.

Beware of the Moments When Essential Spirit Departs

In chapter 4 I described John Desteian's view of love as an up-welling of essential spirit, that rich, instinctual level of life that is overlaid with prevailing spirit—the collective, civilized level of life. I also said that one reason for the tremendous expansion we feel when we fall in love may be that we feel infused with essential spirit, something partially lost during childhood or even before, when humans became more repressed and out of touch with nature. Essential spirit often fuels our deepest hopes and dreams, especially for HSPs. Stifle it, and you risk provoking either excesses of resistance quite uncharacteristic of HSPs or else loveless disengagement.

The trouble is, HSPs in particular also absorb the prevailing spirit through our being so conscientious and easily socialized. We sense the presence of essential spirit deep down in our souls, as those who locate where to dig wells can sense water deep within the earth. And when we risk love, we tap that essential spirit and feel pure delight. Now we will do *anything* to keep it. And because of this very determination, we may lose it again. It happens at certain critical moments, when we turn to prevailing spirit for all of our answers.

Suppose you love classical music and want to hear a particular chamber orchestra tonight—they will be playing two pieces that can always move you to tears, but more so these days, now that you are so in love. Your new beloved, it turns out, has no real interest in classical music and would like to stay home and catch up on some work while you "go if you like."

You had no idea how much you had been enjoying the fantasy of the two of you listening to that music, transported, no words necessary. But there would be words later—a deep discussion at the intermission, a savoring of the afterglow at a cafe. Then there would be a sensual ending, the music embodied in your lovemaking.

But, like a typical HSP, you reflect on your disappointment and try to do what's right, which seems to be whatever the other would want. Yes, that's right. You think back desperately to what your parents would advise, or some book author like me. Don't be self-centered, childish, demanding, caught in a complex. Differences are understandable. In close relationships you must compromise.

You are now looking to prevailing spirit for the right response to preserve your love—exactly the wrong place to look, although you do not know it.

So what do you *do* about your difference—your passion for chamber music, your partner's disinterest? The whole question lies not in whether you adapt or how you do it, but why. Dialogue, for example, can be used to protect essential spirit, as it is intended, or to obey prevailing spirit, as when you silence your most authentic self. Whether you silence yourself depends on whether you feel courageous, in tune with your essential spirit, or you feel like a child giving in to the parental prevailing spirit out of an old fear of abandonment. That child has no choice but to repress his or her own desires and adapt, stifling essential spirit.

In Desteian's words, "A person who is aware of his own power and authority and of his right to be part of a family or group can choose to make a sacrifice" and do what the other wants without harming the essential spirit in the relationship. The same compromise—"okay, we'll skip the concert"—can be the result of working with your mutual differences, with each of you feeling the power, authority, and right to choose to make a conscious sacrifice, or it can be the result of a powerful defense against acknowledging personal boundaries, differences, and the fear of individuality, with all the separateness and fear of loss that these imply. The needed sense of personal power, authority, right, and courage all come with the inner work suggested throughout his book as the first vocational calling of HSPs. But there are some skills involved as well.

Expose the Hope or Fear, Dialogue, and Be Creative

While it will not work to feel obliged to fulfill another's hope or live out another's fear—to stifle one's own essential spirit for the other's—no one should have to entirely give up a hope or deny a fear either. This still strangles essential spirit within the relationship. So wise couples learn to uncover the hopes and fears behind a continuing conflict, then protect and honor them as well as they can. They dialogue about them, to make them the other's as much as possible, or they compromise, but always with an eye to essential spirit. The HSP's job in these situations is to be absurdly creative.

For example, Art and I moved to Long Island in 1994 so that he could take an academic job that was perfect for him. Long Island turned out to be anything but perfect for me. I realized after a few months that I did not want to put down roots in a new place at my age—I might be there the rest of my life. In particular I did not want to start a psychotherapy practice there, which is difficult to leave once begun. I am a native Californian, and I wanted it to stay that way. (By the way, this experience convinced me that HSPs are more affected by where we live than non-HSPs seem to be—our contact with our natural environment is a large part of our contact with essential spirit.)

One day I hit on a brilliant but scary plan. Art could be in California for the six weeks of his winter break and the four months of his summer; I could stay on Long Island for two two-month sojourns in the spring and fall, so we would only be separated for two six-week periods before and after the winter break. It seemed risky—would we grow apart, would Art resent my need for such a radical lifestyle? When we described it to our friends and families, the reactions varied from dire warnings to envy, but they were never mild.

Well, it has turned out to be a creative compromise that has not only worked but has been more pleasurable for both of us than if either of us had had our way completely. That's what I mean by creative solutions.

Every couple has to find their own way on these issues, and this is a place where character can grow as well as creativity as you are stretched to take a larger perspective. Where do your hopes and fears fit into the larger scheme of your life and of human life, of you and your partner this year and twenty years from now? How does a new car balance out with having another baby, buying a new house, getting your doctorate, or sending your partner home to the old country to see aging parents before they die? Tough decisions, when made together, respectfully, strengthen the bond between you.

BECOME SOPHISTICATED ABOUT COMPLEXES

Dialoguing, reducing overarousal during conflict, and combating disengagement are very helpful to many couples, but those who recommend these rather rational sorts of techniques also admit they sometimes don't work. John Gottman, for example, finds that 85 percent of marriages are distressed because one or both of the partners feel bad about themselves or about those they try to be close to (they have low self-esteem, or in chapter 3's terms, they are insecures). People who feel this way have a hard time dialoguing, for example. Their fears of inadequacy get in the way of listening. They immediately feel criticized and criticize back. Thus, as an adjunct to the skills training we have discussed so far, many relationship therapists try to explore the unconscious reasons some people dislike themselves and their partners or generally can't seem to get along in a close relationship. Insecure attachment is one way of expressing those unconscious reasons, but a broader and deeper approach is the Jungian theory of complexes (a theory well supported by clinical experience, including my own).

The Two Sides to Every Complex

Our complexes are the regions in our personality that gobble up our energy and distort our perceptions, very much like black holes in space. A typical, familiar complex is the mother complex—or perhaps a better term for it is the child complex, or mother-child complex. As children we all developed feelings about our mothers, but for some of us our experiences have produced a true complex, a "hot spot" in our personality. Bring up Mother and we get teary, grouchy, silent, touchy, overly talkative, nervous, depressed, angry, dissociated, or fiercely dismissive of the whole topic.

Complexes always seem to have two poles—for example, the positive and negative mother—even though usually only one pole at a time is conscious, active, or uppermost. The other is pressing to appear, however, as the psyche seeks wholeness and an end to one-sidedness. I have seen many clients come in talking incessantly about their wonderful mothers, and before long we are discussing their mothers as all or mostly troubling (the reverse has also happened).

You know you have a complex around an issue when that topic tends to energize or preoccupy you. (A complex is often the focus of one's career.) All of us are to some degree in a complex all of the time. But you know you are fully identified with it, acting out of it, sucked down the black hole, when an issue makes you supertalkative, opinionated, and absolute in your thinking and language. Thinking about it may also make you depressed, anxious, overexcited, or ready to take uncharacteristic risks. You become kind of "wild-eyed" or like a "loose cannon."

Usually, of course, the partner of the person in a complex spots its activation first and is probably quite familiar with its effects. Telling people they are in a complex while they are in one, however, is playing with fire. But it is very helpful to the person to bring it up gingerly at a later time. "Boy, you sure were in a bad mood last night. Didn't it make you wonder what was going on? I've noticed that often happens after your mother calls."

Here are some typical complexes for HSPs: A "star" complex—a driven part that is highly competent, successful, and admired that hides or compensates for a sensitive part that threatens to go quite dramatically mad from the pressure. Or a child-prodigy complex, with a repressed pole that is the orphaned child whom no one would see or love if the child were not a prodigy. There's the hero/scapegoat complex—the group elevates and secretly envies the hero's visions and insights but then can easily turn the hero into the scapegoat, who is symbolically stoned to death when a vision becomes unpopular. A similar fate befalls the HSP who lives out the eccentric-genius/stupid-crank complex—the group admires you one day and rejects or even jails you the next. Then there's the complex that makes you a hardworking, honest, conscientious citizen—until you notice your sly crook or traitor. Or the obedient worker—until you find yourself playing the rebel or union organizer.

Many HSPs have a victim-dominator complex. They identify with the victim pole of the complex, feeling weak and powerless after all those years of being called "too sensitive." They may spend great energy trying to get free of their dominators, be stronger, see some justice done. What they have repressed and ignored is their strength, and also their capacity to dominate others, which others may be all too well aware of. (You may have noticed that all the complexes are linked and overlapping—your feeling tells you which ones are yours, not any rule or description from outside.)

Splitting and Projection Revisited

The repressed half of a complex is usually split off (as described in chapter 6). This leaves it free to cause you trouble, in particular when you project it onto your partner.

When you are projecting, you are excited—you've spotted this terrific or terrible trait in the other. You have a flash of deadly certainty. All this intense love or hate is often a warning that you are engaged in a defense that is vital to your psychological status quo, a defense *against* information about yourself.

If you have projected something wonderful onto the other, all might be fine—you might live in your happy illusion—if it were not for the way the other pole erupts so predictably. It just requires a few disappointments. This is another way to understand how a difference that was loved becomes hated, as in the discussion in chapter 5 of Linda's awareness of spiritual subtleties and Mark's attention to the practical and obvious. A complex was at work in each of them.

What makes all of this more intense is that we often seem to choose partners with matching complexes, their conscious pole being our unconscious one. Someone wanting to be rescued and cared for is attracted to and attractive to someone who is eager to rescue. Once the rescuer reveals any weakness, he or she is not only in trouble with the one wanting always to be the rescued, but is also in trouble with his or her own internalized critic, who believes that the other half of his or her complex—wanting to be rescued—is a terrible sin. Both persons are facing the terror and opportunity of completely revising their habitual identities toward something more whole and realistic.

Looking back on Jack and Raven, Jack had a mother complex. His mother, involved in a successful career, had left him with a series of caretakers almost from birth. Although not entirely conscious of it, Jack had hoped that Raven, being so strong, would take care of him a bit, the way he had wanted his mother to do more often—with Raven he thought he was at last the adored child. So when Jack was expected to do the mothering, of triplets, while Raven was working long days out of the house the way his mother had, his negative mother complex was the pole that came up—he was the abandoned child. Hopeless resignation is a typical emotion when under the spell of the negative mother.

Meanwhile, Raven's own mother complex was present. Her rather unhappy mother had never had her own career and had urged Raven, her only daughter, to live the life she had not. Raven was the strong, achieving parent to her mother, so she had known how to be that for Jack. But she also secretly longed to be taken care of—by Jack. Raven tended to feel she was becoming too much like her unhappy mother, however, if she showed any need for nurturing. But if she had been able to show this need the day she learned she was carrying triplets, she might have broken down too, instead of blasting Jack for his understandable first reaction (actually so like her own). They might have comforted each other about the mixed blessing coming their way so early in their marriage and in their work-filled young lives.

The Shadow Knows

All these split-off halves or poles of your complexes—everything you have stuffed down into the unconscious and rejected about yourself—end up in what Jungians call the shadow. The shadow is an apt term for the dark, unpleasant side of our personalities. (Although people with low self-esteem, such as many HSPs, stuff away their good qualities and have "white shadows.")

Getting to know your shadow—which integrates it into your conscious mind so that it is no longer stuffed into the unconscious—is important for several reasons. It frees up energy, both the energy required to control the shadow qualities and the energy of the parts themselves. The greedy, weak, and bossy parts of you, for example, have knowledge and ways of being in the world that are useful as long as they do not rule you. Also, once you know something about your shadow, you are less likely to act from that pole of your complex unconsciously or to project it onto others. Recognizing your own greed, you take pains to share and not to be so critical when you see another person being a bit greedy. Recognizing your own weakness, you will criticize it less in your partner and be less likely to be in its grip yourself at the wrong time. Recognizing your tendency to be the engulfing, controlling mother, you are tolerantly quiet when others are a bit bossy, and quieter still when others need to find their own solutions.

The shadow with its split-off negative halves of complexes can obviously wreak havoc in a relationship. But much as close relationships suffer from them, they are also the only place you can really learn about them. Casual friends will not bring up such matters—a good reason to deepen your friendships. But your partner, or anyone you live or travel with for awhile, will be able to tolerate your unowned shadow only so long, and you will be forced to mention his or hers as well.

As Jung puts it, "A general and merely academic 'insight into one's mistakes' is ineffectual." We do not feel their impact on others.

> But they show up acutely when a human relationship brings them to the fore and when they are noticed by the other person as well as by oneself. Then and then only can they really be felt and their true nature recognized. Similarly, confessions made to one's secret self generally have little or no effect, whereas confessions made to another are much more promising.

Knowing about your flaws only in an "academic" sense, outside of a relationship, is like dropping bombs from ten thousand feet and flying back to a safe air base. Actually seeing how a partner is devastated by your behavior is like touring the devastation after your bombing run. And telling your partner when he or she has distressed you is giving him or her the tour of the destruction done to you.

When Splitting Is More Serious

We all have complexes and can be totally possessed by a powerful split-off part of a complex now and then, especially when we as HSPs are overwhelmed by fear, need, guilt, shame, or a sense of being unfairly blamed. The question is, will this "possession" last a few minutes, hours, days, or years? Can it be tempered after reflection or after your partner has pointed it out? Can it be kept from oscillating between one extreme and the other?

The extremes typical of a complex mean that you have lost sight of the obvious fact that most people, your partner included, are usually good enough, rather than all good or all bad. This sensible perspective about the human condition is not always so easily arrived at, however. As children mature, parents are supposed to help their children gradually accept the flaws in themselves and those they love. If children are disappointed too deeply or too early by their parents, or feel they have disappointed their parents too much, they develop splitting as a defense against the unbearable truth—another way to understand the insecure-attachment styles.

As we saw in chapter 3, the child decides he or she is all bad and grows up hoping and believing there is some all-good, all-accepting, all-nurturing rescuing other who will supply all that was withheld in childhood. In other cases, the parents themselves see the child as all bad or all good, or prolong their children's worship of them. Children of such parents develop splitting as an early, strong, primitive defense that will require patience and perhaps psychotherapy to reduce. But I will at least sketch out the task before you.

How Splitting Happens—Knowing May Help

Hopefully what you are reading here will help you realize what you are splitting off and projecting (chapter 7 of *The Highly Sensitive Person's Workbook* has a task to help you with this too). If you *do* recognize these defenses, you may be able to contain some of the more obvious projections onto your partner, even if the splitting within yourself and the reasons for it are still in the process of being healed. Your partner can help considerably both by rejecting what you have been projecting, good and bad, and admitting to his or her hook or matching complex. This takes some of the shame and blame off of you, which you certainly don't need more of. More important, it makes your partner own up to how his or her complexes operate in the relationship, because they surely do. Understanding how splitting happens inside your mind can also help.

Research shows that some people store all their negative descriptors of themselves in one memory file, so to speak—"slow at languages," "too serious," "live alone but don't want to." In another memory file, all the positive descriptors are stored—"good at math," "conscientious," "have had some good relationships in the past," and so forth. People who don't regularly use splitting as a defense keep their descriptive terms for themselves in content-related categories—for example, "slow at languages" and "good at math" would go into what we could call the "abilities" category, and "live alone" and "have had some good relationships" go into a "current romantic situation" category.

When faced with negative information about themselves, those who store all their negative self-descriptors together are more upset by the information because it brings up all the other negatives too. For example, when told they are slow at a task, they have stored "slow at a task," with "slow at languages," "too serious," and "live alone but don't want to," and those probably also bring up "stupid," "bad," "unsuccessful," "unpopular," "rejected," and "unhappy" as well. Obviously it would be better if you could re-sort how you store descriptions of yourself, and maybe with conscious effort you can.

In further research, it was found that this phenomenon applies to how people think about their partners as well. So, *try* to re-sort your descriptions of your partner too. Don't put all the negatives together, so that the observation that your partner may have "talked too much tonight" doesn't have to lead to "inconsiderate," "stupid," "unconscious," "bad partner," "stupid me for choosing this person," "bad me who deserves this person," and so forth. It might lead to a more focused category that is both positive and negative: "outgoing," "funny," "likes people," "bores people." Work on seeing the "package deal"—the good and the bad that come together. It is the perfect opposite of splitting, although it requires time to develop.

Mainly I must emphasize that especially if either you or your partner have long-standing, personal-history reasons to split and project, both of you will have to be psychologically astute to have a lasting, intimate, satisfying relationship—or one that is satisfying to an HSP. It will not happen without a great deal of attention and learning. It involves recognizing the insecurity, complexes, and unresolved childhood issues behind all the puzzling current conflicts and emotions. As an HSP, believe me, you can do this sorting out especially well. But you must go on to replace your projections with a thorough understanding of one another. You need to temper the childhood-based complexes that insist that your partner give you what you need or that he or she is a terrible parent who will punish or reject you if you express your needs. If each of you seems to threaten such behavior, the other must insist on better treatment rather than become a frightened or angry child.

Discuss openly what you each may be projecting from your past onto one another. Then promise to try not to do it. Remind one another, gently. Raven could say to Jack, "I'm not your mother—you can ask me to stay home more, and I will." Jack can say to Raven, "I'm not your mother—you do not have to be strong all the time and prove to me how accomplished you are."

SOMETIMES YOU NEED HELP

Couples often need help with their relationships. Yet research has found that only 1 percent of those who divorce have ever sought marital counseling. Don't be one of the 99 percent.

Don't be a naive consumer either. In a survey of those who have used various forms of psychotherapy, marital counseling is reported to be far less helpful than individual therapy. Some reasons are that couples often come when it is too late, or individual problems such as low self-esteem or depression are the crux of the issue. Above all, many therapists are not adequately skilled in working with couples—they learned to do individual therapy and think they can teach themselves whatever else they need to know to work with couples, or they may be pastors or educators with no formal training at all in either individual or couples counseling. But working with couples requires special skills. So choose someone with good training in that work specifically, and probably someone professionally licensed in your state as a psychologist, marital counselor, or whatever would be appropriate.

Of course licenses and training do not guarantee anything. You also want recommendations from other couples, and then you may want to talk to two or three counselors before choosing yours. This is a big decision—this person can strongly influence your life for good or ill. Both of you should like the person and feel you can trust this three-way working relationship. If you see someone you like and your partner does not, you may win that battle but lose the war, so to speak. Also agree ahead of time that if at any point one of you begins to feel strongly sided against, you will discuss it with the therapist. And if the problem continues, you will find someone less biased. (Good therapists usually can adroitly avoid seeming to support one partner more, even if privately they see one as somehow more "right." Of course, if one of you ends up being viewed as the problem by several counselors, then you can begin to ask yourselves and the counselors why.)

I also recommend against seeing someone who is seeing you or your partner in individual therapy—your relationship therapist's "client" is your relationship, the two of you, and should not have his or her loyalties divided between that and one of you.

WHEN TO QUIT

Sometimes one can't see the forest for the trees: You are so absorbed in trying to solve relationship problems that you do not realize you are dealing with a deeply disturbed person whom you cannot possibly change and whom you really do not wish to continue living with. The world is full of extremely troubled people with excellent defenses and ways to cover up their disturbances initially. There are enough for all of us to fall for at least one, once (or over and over, for those in the grip of a victim complex).

Should HSPs be better at detecting and avoiding the deeply troubled? We will be better, yes, with experience. But without experience, we may pick up on their powerful needs and want to help without being able to foresee all the consequences of being in a close relationship with them.

In these cases, the solution is not learning skills so you can do better or withdrawing a projection and being more conscious. Waking up to the other's flaws is not due to you projecting your own shadow. This relationship is just a mistake. You need to become astute enough psychologically to distinguish problems you can work on alone and as a couple from those you can't work on without professional help for one or both of you, and to distinguish those, in turn, from problems that cannot be solved at all at this time, with this person.

To start on learning that distinction, you should know that most of the time a problem that cannot be readily solved within a relationship or relationship counseling is permeating the person's life and other relationships. They can't hold a job for long or keep friends. You will also hear a pretty obvious story, or clues to a story, of serious neglect, abuse, or repeated trauma in childhood.

Being sensitive, you will soon know about these wounds. The trick is not to think you can heal them yourself. People like this require individual professional help. They are also very bad bets as partners, especially if they have done nothing to begin healing. And if such a wounded person does go into therapy, it could be a long haul before he or she is better, and this person may outgrow the need for you before then. If he or she refuses to seek help, at least couples therapy, then you truly do not want to stay.

This is tough talk, but it is not news to you, really. In chapter 3 we talked about the insecure attachment style, and in chapter 4, the signs of "good bets" for lovers. Just think of the extreme worst cases—that's what you can't handle on your own. At one extreme are the people who are "maxing" on attachment—so afraid of abandonment that they are frantic if you need some solitude or want to change in any way. If you try, their response may be either pathological jealousy or utter subservience to your will, in which case they have no essential spirit to offer you at all.

At the other extreme are the minimizers, the extreme dismissive avoidants and narcissists, who have decided they need no one. Being sensitive, you sense they "just need love" and try to draw them into a relationship. But they are far too afraid of intimacy to allow that for long. They often lack what you and I would call normal "human" emotional reactions to events in your life or theirs.

Either of the above two extremes can also be the third type: those who, when under relationship stress (i.e., separations, arguments, illness), become rageful, suicidal, or violent toward you. They will tend to see *everything* in black and white, absolutes. They are splitting *all* the time. "You always" do this and "I always feel" that. But the black can switch to white and white to black in a moment. You were an angel, now you are the embodiment of evil. Such people are exceptionally out of touch with their vulnerable feelings, although they will seem in touch with some emotions, like anger, in order to defend themselves. But any attempt to make changes or suggest the need for healing will feel to them like their core selves are being attacked, and their only choice is to attack back.

Again, discerning what you are dealing with is not easy. Some partners can be very defensive or resistant to change for less prob-

lematic reasons—perhaps simply because they are not very psychologically minded, or they fear their partners "analyzing" them. This
can be a justifiable fear, especially when the "analyzer" is you, an
HSP, and your partner is not. He or she knows from experience how
uncanny you can be about seeing into what seemed private. But
your partner should have enough ego strength to listen when you
declare loud and clear that the relationship is not working for you
and that you need to do something, together, to change it.

If your partner is truly verbally or physically abusive to you or
anyone else, the bottom line is that obviously you must leave, at
least until both of you have received good help. But if your partner
cannot be intimate and honest, and cannot admit that the two of you
are having a problem in which each of you has played a role, and
cannot seek help of some sort, at least from reading some relevant
books, in my opinion you may also have good cause to leave, at
least until your partner comes to his or her senses. You have a duty
to tell your partner why you are unhappy, however, and to give him
or her a chance to change or seek help with you. But if that chance
is refused and the need denied, well, I would consider my alternatives.

A FINAL, SIMPLE SUGGESTION

Like all self-help books, this book gives you many fine opportunities to blame other people or situations—such as your temperament—rather than looking at your own complexes and what you
might need to do about them. With books, there is no relatively objective outsider like a therapist to help you discern when you are
doing that. However, I say the following with all my heart: Please,
please, please try not to use your temperament as an excuse to be
a pain in the neck to your partner.

8

Our Sexuality: Sensitive People in Bed

This chapter is the first exploration that I know of, anywhere, of how inherited temperament affects sexuality. It goes beyond conjecture to interviews and data from 443 persons, both HSPs and non-HSPs (for comparison). It also discusses the effect on sexuality of that other basic trait, high sensation seeking.

As any HSP could have predicted, our sexual experiences and preferences differ from non-HSPs at important points, but they are too similar to be in any sense abnormal. We are being normal for HSPs.

The possibility that inherited temperament broadens what should be considered normal sexuality has been overlooked by sex educators, relationship counselors, and authors of self-help books. This is a rather major oversight, because while most people consciously agree to a liberal definition of "normal" between two consenting adults, at a less conscious level many struggle with a straitjacket of sexual ideas. And of course without better information about us, we HSPs in particular will compare our responses to the norms, reflect, and worry that we are a bit odd. This chapter should help us breathe easier about all that.

But first, below you will find the survey that was used for this research, should you enjoy answering it now and then comparing your answers to the results of the survey.

Temperament and Sexuality Questionnaire

It is important that you answer all questions as truthfully as you can—do not think about how you "ought" to respond.

How "sex" is defined in the questions to follow: To keep wordings simple and consistent with that of other researchers, when a question says "sex" or "having sex," this means "any mutually voluntary activity with another person that involves genital contact and sexual excitement or arousal—that is, feeling really turned on, even if intercourse or orgasm did not occur." So this does not include kissing or close dancing without genital contact and does not include forced sexual activity. Of course sexual activity does not require a partner, and there will be questions about that too. But except where that is clear, sex in these questions will refer to voluntary genital contact, with arousal, with another person.

1. About how often have you had sex in the past twelve months?
   - ☐ Not at all
   - ☐ Once or twice
   - ☐ About once a month
   - ☐ Two or three times a month
   - ☐ About once a week
   - ☐ Two or three times a week
   - ☐ Four or more times a week

2. Duration of last sexual event:
   - ☐ 15 minutes or less
   - ☐ More than 15 minutes but less than 30 minutes
   - ☐ More than 30 minutes but less than 1 hour
   - ☐ More than 1 hour but less than 2
   - ☐ 2 hours or longer

"Partner" or **"Primary sexual partner"** refers to your most important or frequent sex partner, or if there is no one now, then the person with whom you had the longest sexual relationship in the past, except where noted.

3. During the last twelve months of the relationship with your

partner, did having sex make you feel (check as many as you need to describe your typical feelings):

☐ Satisfied

☐ Sad

☐ Loved

☐ Anxious or worried

☐ Scared or afraid

☐ Thrilled or excited

☐ Guilty

Answer the following questions using this scale:

1	**2**	**3**	**4**	**5**
Never or Almost Never	*Rarely*	*Sometimes*	*Often*	*Always or Almost Always*

4. __ Does sex seem to be one of the most potentially satisfying parts of life?

5. __ When considering a sexual relationship, do you think about its possible impact on the other person?

6. __ When in a relationship, do you need to feel loving toward your partner in order for you to enjoy sex together?

7. __ Would it appeal to you (if not in a relationship) to have a variety of sexual partners?

8. __ Could you enjoy having sex with someone you don't love?

9. __ If you were considering a new relationship, would you think about sexually transmitted diseases or pregnancy?

10. __ Do subtle sexual cues or messages turn you on?

11. __ Do strong, explicit sexual cues or messages turn you on?

12. __ Do you find it hard to make the transition into a sexual mood?

13. __ Do you like to be the more active person sexually, "in charge" or deciding what will happen?

14. __ Do you need to stop during sex because you feel overwhelmed or overstimulated?

15. __ Are there areas of your genitals that can be touched in a way that is painful or too intense, even when aroused?

16. __ If you are temporarily distracted or interrupted by something while having sex, does it get you out of the mood?

17. __ Do you prefer to have music on while having sex?

18. __ Do you like to talk during sex?

19. __ Do you like to have things be the same each time you have sex?

20. __ While having sex or considering it, are you easily disturbed by slight sounds, smells, seeing certain things, etc. (in the environment or the other person)?

21. __ With your primary sexual partner, do you have an orgasm (come or come to climax)?

22. __ Do you find it difficult to go right back to ordinary activities after sex?

23. __ Does sex for you have a sense of mystery or power about it?

24. __ Do you find it easy to take sex lightly?

25. __ Do you like having sex?

26. __ Do you enjoy variety in sexual activities?

27. __ Does alcohol adversely affect your sexual performance?

28. __ Have you noticed that certain medications adversely affect your sexual performance?

29. __ During the past twelve months, has your physical health interfered with your sexual activities?

30. __ During the past twelve months, have emotional problems interfered with your sexual activities?

31. __ During the past twelve months, has stress or pressure in your life interfered with your sexual activities?

32. __ Do you have a sexual fantasy while having sex with a partner?

33. __ Do you have a sexual fantasy while masturbating?

34. __ If you do have sexual fantasies, do they involve a very romantic situation?

35. __ If you do have sexual fantasies, do they involve your having power over another person?

36. __ If you do have sexual fantasies, do they involve another person having power over you?

OTHER QUESTIONS:

37. Are you currently in a relationship?
    ☐ Yes   ☐ No

38. Number of sexual partners so far in your lifetime: ____

39. Number of sexual partners you have lived with for more than one month: ____

40. Age of first sexual intercourse: ____

41. Age of first living with a sexual partner: ____

42. Number of sexual partners in last 12 months (even if sexual activity with a partner was only once): ____

43. As a child, before puberty (that is, as a girl before you began to menstruate or as a boy before your voice changed and you grew pubic hair), did anyone touch you sexually?
    ☐ Yes   ☐ No

If yes, do you think that these experiences have had any effect on your life since then?
☐ Yes   ☐ No

44. Sometimes people go through periods in which they are not interested in sex or are having trouble achieving sexual gratification. Below are just a few questions about whether you have experienced this in the past twelve months. During the last 12 months has there ever been a period of several months or more when you (check all that apply):
    ☐ Lacked interest in having sex

☐ Felt anxious just before having sex about your ability to perform sexually

☐ Came to a climax (experienced an orgasm) too quickly

☐ Experienced physical pain *during* intercourse

☐ Did not find sex pleasurable (even if it was not painful)

☐ Were unable to come to a climax (experience an orgasm)

Women: ☐ had trouble lubricating

45. On the average, in the past twelve months how often did you masturbate?

☐ More than once a day

☐ Every day

☐ Several times a week

☐ Once a week

☐ Two or three times a month

☐ Once a month

☐ Every other month

☐ Three to five times a year

☐ Once or twice a year

☐ Not at all this year

REMEMBER THE PROBLEM WITH AVERAGES

As I present the data, remember that I am generally reporting slight average differences between two groups. There is always large overlap—that is, there are many exceptions to every statement I make. You may well be one of these exceptions; this does not make you odd. Even if your experiences are unusual, they still help define what HSPs do. In this research, I found plenty of HSPs who had had every possible experience, including no sexual relationships, ever. For all of you, in sexual relationships or not, rest assured that there are many in the same situations, for many reasons.

Just for your information, I received questionnaires from 308 women and 135 men. The average age was 48 for men, 46 for women. Everyone took a short form of the HSP Self-Test as well as filling out the survey because we expected and found that some of the supposedly non-HSP nonsubscribers were actually HSPs. How many were HSPs depended on where I divided them—I tried both dividing at the midpoint of sensitivity-nonsensitivity and comparing the very sensitive to the not very sensitive. Results were about the same.

WHERE HSPs DO NOT DIFFER FROM OTHERS

HSPs and non-HSPs scored very similarly on each of the following items from the sexuality questionnaire:

- Number of sexual partners lived with (question 39).
- Duration of most recent sexual event (2).
- Sex being one of the most potentially satisfying parts of life (4).
- Being aroused by subtle cues (10).
- Difficulty making the transition into sex (12).
- Liking to be the one who is active and deciding what the two of you will do (13).
- Liking to talk during sex (18).
- Frequency of having an orgasm (21).
- Frequency of masturbating (45).
- Physical or emotional problems or medications interfering with sex (28, 29, 30).
- Having fantasies of having power over another person (35).
- Having been sexually abused, and if abused, having these experiences affect your life (43).
- Reporting a sexual dysfunction (such as lack of interest, not finding sex pleasurable, impotence, premature ejaculation) (44).
- Feelings of satisfaction, worry, excitement, or guilt during sex (3).

I found all of this rather comforting. We are equally able to see sex itself as satisfying, to be active and in charge, excited and guilt- and worry-free, and free of nonsensitivity-related sexual problems. In short, we do not seem more sexually inhibited or otherwise troubled sexually.

WHERE HSPs DIFFER FROM OTHERS

On the following questions, HSPs, whether men or women, were more likely than non-HSPs to say "often" or "almost always." All of the differences *are* statistically significant, meaning it is likely that there really is an average difference among HSPs and non-HSPs on the following items:

- Finding that sex has a sense of mystery or power about it (question 23).
- Finding it difficult to return abruptly to ordinary activities after sex (22).
- Not being turned on by strong, explicit sexual cues (11).
- Having areas of your genitals that can be touched in a way that is painful or too intense, even when aroused (15). (This was especially true for HSWs compared to non-HSWs, but was true for HSMs as well when compared to non-HSMs.)
- Needing to stop during sex because of being overwhelmed or overstimulated (14).
- Being distracted or interrupted while having sex gets you out of the mood (16).
- While having sex or considering it, being easily disturbed by slight sounds, smells, seeing certain things (in the environment or the other person) (20).
- Liking to have things be the same each time you have sex (19) and not particularly enjoying variety in sexual activities (26). (These differed for HSWs compared to non-HSWs, but even more for HSMs compared to non-HSMs.)

These results are exactly what I would expect. The first two reflect that we process experiences in a deep way. We find sexuality mysterious, powerful, and separate from the mundane. Of course it is difficult to go back to ordinary life in a casual way.

The other questions reflect the fact that our physical sensitivity and awareness of subtleties can interfere with sexuality. I asked these questions because I thought that if they were true for most HSPs, it would be a great comfort for us to know we are not alone and give us more permission to be ourselves, even when that means being overwhelmed or overstimulated sometimes, easily distracted or easily turned off, and liking things to be the same each time. (Who needs change when familiar sexuality is already mysterious and powerful?) It's all part of the package deal—if a non-HSP partner likes your intensity, he or she will have to humor your needs and preferences that inevitably come with it, just as you must humor his or her lesser sense of intensity around sex and more interest in, for example, explicit sexual cues and images. Everyone, HSP or not, has preferences about sexuality.

HIGHLY SENSITIVE WOMEN AND SEXUALITY

Sometimes the pattern of differences between HSPs and non-HSPs was different for women than for men. On the following items HSWs differed from non-HSWs (while HSMs did not differ much from non-HSMs on these items):

- HSWs were *less* likely than non-HSWs to have trouble having an orgasm or lubricating (question 44).
- *Less* likely to feel sad, scared, or afraid and more likely to feel loved (3).
- Had fewer sexual partners over her lifetime (38) and during this year (42).
- Had sex less often in the last year (1).
- Considered the impact of a sexual relationship on the other person (5).
- Were concerned before entering a sexual relationship about sexually transmitted diseases or pregnancy (9).
- Needed to feel loving toward their partners in order to enjoy sex (6) and enjoyed less having sex with someone they didn't love (8).
- Had less desire for a variety of sexual partners, even if not in a committed relationship (7).
- Were less able to take sex lightly (24).
- Liked having sex less (25).
- Were less likely to have sexual fantasies while having sex with a partner, romantic sexual fantasies, or fantasies of another person having power over them (32, 34, 35).
- Had their first intercourse later (40).

What an interesting image of sensitive women. Added to what is true of all HSPs—the intensity, being easily distracted, overwhelmed, and bothered by "little things"—HSWs seem to have orgasms more easily and find them as satisfying as non-HSWs. At the same time, they are having less sex and are slightly less likely to enjoy it. One reason for this might be that sexuality, being a source of general stimulation, is potentially a source of overarousal if life is already too full of stimulation. These results could also be due to the fact that HSPs often reported that their genitals can be touched in ways that are too painful or intense, even when sexually aroused. HSWs in particular may find it hard to complain when something hurts without feeling embarrassed, odd, cold, rejecting, or guilty that they are interfering with their partner's pleasure. But pain is pain, and HSPs do have a lower pain threshold.

Above all, this survey points out that HSWs as a group are considerate, conscientious, and discerning about who they get into bed with—they want to express their sexuality within a loving relationship. This care may explain their greater ease in having orgasms, greater feelings of being loved, and fewer feelings of fear or sadness. Smart women.

HIGHLY SENSITIVE MEN AND SEXUALITY

HSMs tended to rate themselves higher than non-HSMs on the following questions (while in general HSWs did not differ from non-HSWs on these):

- Being more likely currently to be in a relationship (question 37).
- Preferring not to have music on while having sex (17).
- Alcohol adversely affecting sexual performance (27).
- Having a sexual fantasy while having sex with a partner (32) or while masturbating (33). (What rich and busy imaginations!)

Except for the general differences between HSPs and non-HSPs, apparently HSMs are not otherwise highly different from non-HSMs. As for HSMs having their sexuality more affected by alcohol, that is what I would have predicted, given that all HSPs are more affected by alcohol, and alcohol interferes more with men's sexual performance than with women's. Thus it ought to have a differential effect on an HSM's sexual performance.

HIGH SENSITIVITY, HIGH SENSATION SEEKING, AND SEXUALITY

The questionnaire also included a brief version of the Sensation Seeker Self-Test you took in chapter 1. As I said there, this trait is independent of sensitivity—one can be strong in one, both, or neither.

Sometimes being an HSS affects an aspect of sexuality that sensitivity does not. In these cases the effect of sensation seeking is the same for HSPs and non-HSPs. Other times, sensation seeking affects an aspect of sexuality that is also affected by sensitivity. In these cases, sensation seeking adds to or subtracts from the effect on your sexuality of being an HSP. This situation is especially clear for the next result, which was true for both HSS women and men, where sensation seeking subtracts from or lessens the effect of sensitivity.

Recall one of our overall results for HSPs—on the average we prefer to do things sexually the same way each time (question 19). HSSs, however, both women and men, are *less* likely to prefer to do things sexually the same way each time. (Not too surprising.) Thus, HSP/non-HSSs most like things to be the same each time and non HSP/HSSs least like things the same each time. HSP/HSSs and non-HSP/non-HSSs are in the middle. Again, this is an example of sensation seeking lessening the effect of sensitivity, with the two temperaments in effect canceling each other out.

The other results for sensation seeking had different patterns for women and men.

Results for Women

- HSS women, compared to non-HSS women, would like more sexual partners (question 7) and have had more in their lifetime (38). HSWs and non-HSWs do not differ much in this, so the effect of being an HSS is the same for everyone. If you are a sensitive sensation seeker (HSW/HSS—or for that matter, a non-HSW/HSS), you would probably like more partners and have had more in your lifetime than a non-HSS, HSW or not.

- Women HSSs also find sex *less* thrilling and exciting (an interesting result) (3). Again, HSWs and non-HSWs do not differ much in this. So if you are an HSW/HSS, this tendency might detract from the excitement of sex for you compared to a non-HSS, HSW or not. (As with the finding above, this same difference holds for non-HSP/HSSs versus non-HSP/non-HSSs. But since this book focuses on HSPs, to keep things simple, I won't keep pointing this out in situations like this.)

- Women HSSs are more likely to think they could enjoy sex with someone they do not love (8). Since HSWs feel the opposite, this is an example of subtraction, of the two temperaments canceling each other out. So if you are an HSW/HSS, you might be in the middle on this (and thus an HSW/non-HSS would be especially low on this).

- Women HSSs find sex has more power and mystery (23). So do HSWs. Thus if you are an HSW/HSS, the traits add and you would find sex the most mysterious and powerful of any combination of temperament traits.

- Women HSSs like having sex more than non-HSSs (25). I said before that HSWs tend to like having sex a bit less than non-HSWs. So if you are an HSW/HSS, you would probably be in the middle—sensation seeking here subtracts from sensitivity, and the two cancel each other out.

- If you are an HSW/HSS, the trend is that you would have masturbated a little less often in the last twelve months (45).

- Women HSSs are more likely to have sexual fantasies while masturbating than non-HSSs (33). HSWs and non-HSWs did not differ much in this, so again, you would be more likely to do this if you are an HSW/HSS than an HSW/non-HSS.

In short, if you are an HSW/HSS, your sensation seeking adds to interest in a variety of partners, the possibility of liking sex more, enjoying sex with someone you do not love, a greater sense of liking sex, of it being even more powerful and mysterious, although it is less thrilling and you masturbate less. If you are not high in sensation seeking, however, I would argue that you are not miss-

ing anything. Why? Because, the media aside, it is just not your nature to want all the above. Horses don't eat meat, wolves don't eat
oats.

What do I say to the result that HSW/HSSs enjoy sex more? This
may only be due to the general aura of enthusiasm they seem to
bring to all relatively novel sensations and experiences, sex included. Again, before you HSW/non-HSSs get green with envy, consider the possibility that HSW/HSSs may not obtain as much pleasure as you do from activities with less sensation to them, such as
quiet reflection. The grass can always look greener, but it could be
that we instinctively choose the patch of grass that is right for our
nervous systems.

Results for Men

- Men HSSs, sensitive or not, find that emotional problems (question 30) and stress or pressure (31) interfere with sex more than
  non-HSSs do. Perhaps this is because HSSs are likely to have
  more going on in their lives. HSMs do not differ much from non-
  HSMs on this (an interesting result in itself), so being an HSS adds
  this possibility—if you are an HSM/HSS, you would be more
  likely to have this problem than an HSM/non-HSS.
- Men HSSs, sensitive or not, are less likely to have the type of sexual problem associated with lack of pleasure (44). HSMs do not
  differ from non-HSMs on this, so if you are an HSM/HSS, you are
  less likely to have this problem than an HSM/non-HSS.
- HSMs who are non-HSSs are more easily gotten out of the mood
  by being distracted during sex than any of the other groups (16).
- Men with both temperaments, HSM/HSSs, have averaged less
  than one partner this year, while the other three groups averaged
  having one partner this year (42). This could mean that if you are
  both sensitive and a sensation seeker, it is harder for you to find
  or maintain a satisfying long-term relationship. Having a narrow
  range of optimal arousal, you probably want a partner who is
  both lively and interesting and also able to be deep—plus able
  to understand a contradictory sort of man who at times wants excitement and intimacy, at times wants to be left alone.

COMMENTS FROM THE RESPONDENTS

Having looked at all these average differences, let's hear some of the individual voices of the respondents.

The Development of the Sexual HSP

Several HSPs, especially the younger ones, described a process of coming to understand their sensitive feelings about sexuality after considerable trial and error. One thirty-two-year-old woman called it the "180-degree turnaround":

> Oddly, I find that I have had quite a few more sex partners than my non-HSP female friends. Most of those occurred during my mid-twenties, a time when I was becoming increasingly (semi-consciously) aware of my high sensitivity, but actively fighting it and trying to be "normal." I had been told over and over that I was too sensitive and had to toughen up or I wouldn't go far in life. . . . Finally, though, I fell in love for real.

She then describes how the emotions and sensations at that time were frighteningly overwhelming. This relationship ended after almost three years, largely because these two lovers did not understand their temperament differences. She was shattered but never forgot the "spiritually moving quality" of their sexual moments. She has "remained celibate" for three years; her understanding of and standards for what an HSP needs had been "changed forever." She finds that just thinking about meeting a partner as a "now full-fledged HSP is a daunting task—I am taking my time to consider it."

Another woman told a similar story of having many partners in her early twenties, and at forty-seven having had no sexual partners for ten years.

> As in nearly all other areas of my life, I was not true to myself, to my HSP nature, in my early years regarding sexual experiences. The growth of self-awareness, of honoring the self, profoundly changes an HSP's perspective on sex.

On the other hand, some HSPs had sensed their difference from the start without experimentation. A twenty-six-year-old wrote about not having had sex yet because she hasn't yet felt truly in love. "I do feel intensely and I want someone to respect my sensitivity. I want and expect to enjoy sex. I do not think my sensitivity will hamper me—in fact, I think it will enhance it." But she is waiting.

HSWs are not alone in this feeling. A thirty-three-year-old HSM I interviewed said firmly that "there is only thing I know for sure—I have to be in love, have to have known the woman before. I almost wish I were different. . . . Part of the fear is rejection, so I wait to be sure I really like the person and that she likes me. And I haven't had many rejections thanks to that care."

Learning to be selective isn't unique to heterosexuals. A gay man of forty writes that he had many relationships earlier in life, but given his sensitivity, he is no longer interested in relationships that do not have "the three components" of emotional, physical, and spiritual resonance. He finds that only about 20 percent of gay men are sensitive like himself, so he knows he has to be patient and search for the right sensitive partner.

Our Greater (Not Surprising) Sensitivity to Pleasure

Many HSPs commented that their sexual pleasure was intense—possibly unusually so. For example, one woman wrote this:

> I have always been physically sensitive to sexual pleasure in that the slightest touch or caress can be the source of deep satisfaction. When being kissed, my arousal level is high and my teeth tingle, the follicles of my hair "goose bump," and I make vocal sounds of pleasure resembling soft moans.
>
> I have often wondered if my sensitive nature gave me an "edge" in terms of pleasure; I suspect so.

Another described that she becomes "overaroused" and so needs to stop her partner, whom she then helps to have an orgasm on his own, which gives her a simultaneous orgasm purely through her sensitivity to his. In her words,

In the process my torso will start to rock and I will feel some release, though not a true orgasm. Or this rocking often starts just before my partner climaxes. Then we're both moving, though not in intercourse, and then we climax together. It is almost as if I can sense things in my partner and my body reacts. It is stimulated by these intuitions.

Others noted both the pleasures and pains associated with this sensitivity. A forty-eight-year-old woman wrote that she can have "clitoral, vaginal opening, vaginal, cervical, uterine, and ovarian orgasms. I feel the HSP awareness allows things to be subdivided down into this sort of useful, usable detail."

This same woman reports that since adolescence she has been aware that she was not like others—she could tell from movies, books, and how people talked. For her, sex has always been "powerful and mysterious," while others seem able to talk about it in a shallow way that "completely jars my sensibility."

Sexual activity can sometimes be painful if everything is not exactly HSP-right. Things can change in a flash due to extremely subtle stimuli that my partner (a non-HSP) seems oblivious to. I've also had problems because of overly sensitive senses. I am very sensitive to off-odors in the genital region, for instance.

When she would ask her first partner to wash, he thought she found sex itself "dirty." She realizes now that he did not have her keen sense of smell, but there was considerable pain in her memory of these misunderstandings.

Sexuality and Empathic Connection

Many HSPs noted strong connections with their sexual partners. I already mentioned the woman who could have an orgasm while merely sensing her partner's, without any other stimulation. A fifty-five-year-old HSW wrote this:

It became clear to me during and especially at the end of my thirty-year marriage that the sexual union itself was a deep inner

communion. Often I was taking on my husband's feelings. . . .
Thus I have gained a tremendous insight into the importance of
sexual union.

The importance of an empathic connection is also demonstrated
by the fact that without it some HSPs find sexual pleasure almost
impossible, as this forty-eight-year-old woman explains:

My sexual experiences with partners have been few and far between. My marriage lasted two years. Each of my relationships with
my other partners lasted six months or less. As a super HSP (I
scored 100 percent on your self-test), it takes me longer in a relationship before I am ready to risk intimacy . . . and seldom do I
meet a man who is willing to give me that much time. . . . I have
never had an orgasm with a partner. . . . Because I do orgasm, often
intensely, when I masturbate (a skill I had to develop over time), I
feel that there is the potential to be equally orgasmic with a partner. However, I have never had the opportunity to explore that.

Obstacles to Sexuality

Although, on the average, HSPs' sexuality was not any more hampered
by sexual dysfunction, illness, stress, medications, relationship dissatisfaction, or a history of sexual abuse than non-HSPs, several individual HSPs did write that menopause, their partner's lack of interest, or
prior sexual abuse had interfered in various ways with their sexuality.

One of the most poignant stories was of how physical trauma in
childhood created sexual problems in adulthood. This was the case
of Bruce, a very sensitive man who had polio when he was seven,
so seriously that twice he thought he was dying. When he fell in
love as an adult and tried to have sexual relations with his young
wife, he was utterly unable to ejaculate. Psychotherapy uncovered
the reason: In the hospital he had mostly women nurses, all of
whom had to "violate" him (pump out his stomach and suction his
lungs), and this left him afraid to trust any woman who might be trying to get something out of his body, including his semen.

Bruce's wife has stuck by him through the years, and there have
been breakthroughs and improvements, although things are far from
perfect. Yet they find they have a deeply loving, strong relationship.

Indeed, they feel their troubles have bonded them; their having to accept this extreme "package deal" has strengthened their characters. Perhaps the message from Bruce's story is that satisfying sex may be important and worth every effort to have in a relationship, but it is not *everything*.

SOME ADVICE ABOUT SEX FOR HSPS

For the most part, the same advice for HSPs about having good close relationships in general also applies to good sexual relationships. But a few points are worth emphasizing.

About Desire

To be sexual, we must feel desire. Young men seem to have little trouble with desire, whether HSPs or not. But it is my observation that desire can become an issue for many HSWs and perhaps for HSMs too as they mature and are less driven by hormones. Problems with desire are usually psychological, not physical. People, HSPs included, have to feel real pleasure during sex, almost every time, in order to feel repeated, reliable desire. To feel pleasure, they have to be relaxed and experience little or no pain. Above all, no one is aroused sexually when *over*aroused in the nonsexual sense—after a busy day, for example. Because HSPs are so attuned to others' needs, however, we are likely to make love anyway, even when we are not relaxed or desiring it, just to please our partners. Sometimes this works out and we end up enjoying ourselves. But often when we don't really want to have sex and do it anyway, it isn't very pleasurable. So it is fairly natural and inevitable that we won't desire to do it very much the next time.

There are also all kinds of reasons to "pause to check" before surrendering to desire—worry about performing adequately, having been raised in a sexually repressive atmosphere, a history of sexual abuse, concern about sexually transmitted diseases, and doubt about the other's trustworthiness, just for starters. Because HSPs do pause more to check and reflect on possible dangers, strong reasons to suspect danger can almost paralyze our sexual desire.

What can we do about all this?

1. *Be patient.* And if you have a sexual partner, he or she needs patience too. But work actively on it. Sexual desire does not usually improve without attention.

2. *Have many dialogues* with your partner about what each of you does and does not like, rather than guess or project. (If you are without a partner, explore this topic on your own—maybe dialogue in your imagination with your sexual self.) Dialogue about sex requires trust, as does sex itself. Since you have probably frequently felt in danger of judgment or rejection in this area, trust in the sexual area has to be carefully built, dialogue by dialogue—it does not just happen.

3. *Try to do only what you truly enjoy,* which may be much less varied and exotic than what you imagine pleases others. Of course you want to consider your partner's preferences too. But you both will suffer in the long run if either of you engages in activities you truly do *not* enjoy. Your desire will evaporate. It's also possible that a sexual activity your partner likes is okay or even pleasant for you one time and decidedly not the next time. You *must* feel free to veto an activity, "midstream" even, if it is not feeling okay.

4. *If you desire sex less than your partner, the two of you should decide that you will always be the one to initiate it,* at least for a long period. It forces you to notice when you are interested, and you will be interested eventually if you feel no pressure. You *do* have your own sexual body. This strategy avoids the "couple splitting" we talked about in chapter 5—you don't want your partner to be known as the one who always feels the desire, you as the one who never does. So, do not ever have sex to please or relieve your partner, at least for awhile. If you don't feel like having sex, do not engage in it. He or she can always masturbate. (However, if there is a great mismatch between how often you and your partner would like sex, you'll probably need to explore this further, perhaps with a relationship counselor specializing in sexual issues.)

5. *Reflect on your sexual desire when you are alone,* before moving into a sexual encounter with another. Once with the other, all the sensory stimulation can distract from the body's signs of desire. Alone, you can use your fine imagination to anticipate how

it will feel to have and hold the other sexually, giving your sexual response a "jump start."

6. *Enjoy your sexual dreams* and believe them when they say you are in the mood for sex outside of your sleep.

7. *Don't worry if you have trouble with your mind wandering during sex.* Send your body to play with the other's body and trust that they will have a wonderful time. You will be present when you can be.

8. *If sexual fantasies help, enjoy them.* HSPs can worry that it isn't "right" to think of anything but their partners during sex, but sometimes we, more than others, need a boost over the wall that separates ordinary life from the altered state called sexuality. Most people have sexual fantasies even when making love with their partners, and research on the subject shows that those who do have fantasies have happier relationships than those who do not—as long as they are not having fantasies about someone they intend to have an affair with!

Other Thoughts—For Those in a Relationship

Even if feeling desire is usually not a problem for you, your temperament suggests that the following points could be important:

1. *Expect your temperament and your partner's to matter sexually,* and find ways to accept how your temperaments affect each of you. There may be some disappointment in this—perhaps your non-HSP partner will never find lovemaking as mysterious and powerful as you do, while a non-HSP partner may regret that you may never be thrilled by the prospect of getting it on in an airplane lavatory. If you are both HSPs, perhaps you are disappointed that you are both so easily gotten out of the mood. As you accept one another's natural ways, the subtle demands on each other for impossible changes should decrease, so that both of you feel freer, less inadequate or defensive. It can be quite a gift.

2. *Learn.* Get to know your sexual body and your partner's. Learn what pleases each of you and make full use of that wisdom as only an HSP can.

3. *Be flexible.* This does not mean you have to agree to something that turns you (as an HSP) off. Quite the contrary—if you are flexible, you can probably find something that satisfies both of you.

Other Thoughts—For Those Not in a Relationship

If you are not in a relationship, your sexual self is still very real and deserves attention.

1. *Enjoy sex alone.* According to my data, HSPs are just as likely to masturbate as non-HSPs, so I hope you feel at ease with solo sexuality. Everyone needs to come to their own place on the subject, but there is good evidence that masturbation is associated with health and happiness. Loving your body and inviting it often to feel its sexual energy is a fine thing to do. Those without sexual partners should not miss that self-initiated flow of energy.

2. *Nurture your passion.* If you are hoping to find a sexual partner, it is especially important to keep your sexual desire in full flower, rather than prune it back until someone comes along. Sexual desire invites desire, sexual aloofness turns it away. If you repress all your sexuality, you may not be at all aware of communicating noninterest, but you are still doing it.

3. *Remember, desire does not mean lack of discrimination,* as we sometimes see it depicted. The HSW feeling her sexual yearning is still not receptive to just anyone. The HSM feeling his body's hunger is not going to have sex indiscriminately. You can still be turned off by the person or situation, but this does not eliminate the fact of your desire. The behavioral pause-to-check and activation systems operate *independently.* You can want to plunge ahead but still pause when that is right, too.

4. *Reflect in fresh ways about having no sexual activity, if that is your choice or the result of your circumstances.* Many HSWs and HSMs have done the same. It is good to remember that in several cultures, India for example, restraint from all sexual activity is seen as an almost essential aspect of developing higher mental and spiritual powers. While this path is taken more by men, women who abstain are especially admired and even feared because of the inner strength they are thought to acquire

in this way. Priestly advisors in particular, throughout history, have often abstained from sexuality. In our culture, it is frowned upon and seen as outmoded, but obviously that doesn't make the idea entirely wrong—there may be great wisdom and benefits in thinking of your abstinence as an austerity with higher purposes.

ESPECIALLY FOR HSPS—A DEPTH LOOK AT SEXUALITY

I found much of the information I read about sexuality useful but shallow. I was determined not to leave you with the same feeling in this chapter. What follows are simply a few quotes about sexuality from persons I think of as HSPs. Basically, their words turned me on. Maybe what follows is HSP porn.

From D. H. Lawrence:

> Marriage is no marriage that is not a correspondence of blood. For the blood is the substance of the soul, and of the deepest consciousness. . . . The blood of man and the blood of woman are two eternally different streams, that can never be mingled. . . . They are the two rivers that encircle the whole of life, and in marriage the circle is complete, and in sex the two rivers touch and renew one another, without ever commingling or confusing. We know it. The phallus is a column of blood that fills the valley of blood of a woman. The great river of male blood touches to its depths the great river of female blood—yet neither breaks its bounds. It is the deepest of all communions, as all the religions, in practice, know.

Lawrence's "marital advice"?

> Vitally the human race is dying. It is like a great uprooted tree, with its roots in the air. We must plant ourselves again in the universe. Let us prepare now for the death of our present "little" life, and the re-emergence in a bigger life, in touch with the moving cosmos.

From Ranier Maria Rilke:

> Perhaps the great renewal of the world will consist of this, that man and woman, freed of all confused feelings and desires, shall no longer seek each other as opposites, but simply as members of a family and neighbors, and will unite as *human beings,* in order to simply, earnestly, patiently, and jointly bear the heavy responsibility of sexuality that has been entrusted to them.
>
> They who meet in the night to be entwined and sway in passionate lust are performing a serious work. They are gathering "sweets" and depth and power for the song of some future poet, who shall arise and speak of unspeakable bliss.
>
> The earth is full of this secret down to her smallest things. Oh, that we would only receive this secret more humbly, bear it more earnestly, endure it, and feel how awesomely difficult it is, rather than to take it lightly.

But do not worry whether you are conscious of all this, because "though they error and embrace blindly, the future comes all the same. . . . Those who live the secret wrong . . . lose it only for themselves and still hand it on, like a sealed letter, without knowing it."

From Bernd Jager:

Phenomenologist Jager describes sexual passion as a kind of rebellion of the flesh. In daily life, "the surface dominates the depth" as the head dominates the body.

> But in the world of passion the depth no longer remains mere support for a brilliant surface; it wells up and destroys the charming play of light, the brilliant outer covering of things and beings.
>
> Everything unfolds a dark substantiality with which we are secretly linked. And we ourselves commune with all these things no longer merely by sight, through inspection or deduction, but rather by means of a deeper kinship, through our flesh. . . .

We feel the turmoil of all flesh in our flesh. . . . In the world of passion we are communing vessels in which the upheaval collects itself, by which it sounds itself out and thereby slowly acquires definition. All the life here spreads in succeeding waves from the depth and the center. The surfaces here are the tight skins of drums or the blank tense steel of railroad tracks to which we press the ear to hear the rumble of an approaching event.

The approaching orgasm is like the end of a journey, at the end of which "the good helmsman, after having done all he can, ties himself to the wheel and entrusts himself to the waves to carry him. . . . At the height of passion the water steers the ship."

In the organs of sex themselves, this leap, this discontinuity, is also found. Jager sees the hands as designed to explore the outer world and to work, to obey our will. "Sexual organs are inwardly turned, brooding organs, both inept and unresponsive to a daytime world of tasks. The rise and fall of the penis is not a feat of strength, or even of agility. . . ." We cease to be workers, gripping a tool, and become gripped by the tool which is no tool at all, except perhaps as a servant of the workless world of the night.

FINAL THOUGHTS

Sexuality—Rilke's sealed letter on the serious work of gathering "sweets" and depth and power for some future poet to speak of unspeakable bliss—that is the blessing and responsibility of the highly sensitive body. It can be a different blessing, a different responsibility than the non-HSP's. Treasure that difference.

9

The Spiritual Path of HSPs:
Secure Love Leads the Way, the
Way Leads to Secure Love

In all of my interviews, HSPs readily spoke of the spiritual aspect of their relationships. Honoring this interest, the purpose of this chapter is not to report on those statements but to further them. Most of what is written on relationships has, from an HSP's perspective, a slightly superficial quality to it—how to be happy and stay happy. Left out are Spirit and its transformations, as a relationship and in relationships. I don't think a book for HSPs can omit these subjects.

We will begin by discussing what, to some of us, is the First Relationship, in all senses, which is not with our mothers or fathers but with God, Spirit, the Self. For some of us, at least, all human relationships affect and are affected by that ultimate relationship. For other HSPs, spirituality is a problematic or even avoided issue, but if you wish to explore it a little more, you may find that a return to the fear of intimacy (the topic of chapter 3) is helpful. This time, however, we will be considering the fear of intimacy with God, Spirit, or the Self. We will also consider how the inner lover guides us toward Self-intimacy and more about this form of intimacy. Finally, we will return to human love, in particular the spiritual work an HSP can do over years and years with a willing partner.

We HSPs, as the culture's priestly advisors (described in chapter 1), are the ones meant to develop the fuller understanding of the deep, sometimes dark, sometimes highly spiritual aspects of relationships. These aspects have tormented the planet, when the pain and yearning created by distorted love have been acted out through wars and cruelty. The best minds have been frustrated with the question of how to deal with the love/hate within human nature, particularly when infused with a passionate desire to serve a Greater Other, be that a lover, leader, nation, or God. These issues are HSPs' work. We ponder the real meaning of our relationships as investors ponder the real worth of their stocks (not that we don't sometimes think about stocks too). The world has enough people pondering their stocks, and if you put their information onto paper and into warehouses, they would probably cover the state of Vermont. The information on the depth (unconscious, spiritual) aspects of close relationships wouldn't fill a closet. But which topic is more likely to keep the human species around for another millennium? So, whatever the relationships you are now in—marriage, another style of partnership, friendship, familial, therapeutic—this chapter's intent is to stimulate your developing wisdom about love. Let's get to work.

SPIRITUALITY AS SEEING THE UNSEEN

We each have our own ideas about spirituality, and I wish very much to respect yours. So perhaps we need to start with making mine explicit, remembering they are only mine and are nothing you have to agree with. This way my views are not lurking between the lines, and perhaps mine being explicit will clarify yours too, so that they can be shared with others when the subject comes up. (This is also why in *The Highly Sensitive Person* and the *Workbook* I urged you to write the precepts of your religion, whatever that might be.)

My feeling is that spirit or God is everywhere, although it is, paradoxically, easier to see in the unseen. To see the unseen, start with the values behind the arts and laws of a culture—the personality behind a face. What's behind these, if we look deeply, is what John Desteian calls prevailing spirit, the often wise and well-adapted personal and collective soul (although there will be a shadow there too). If we look further into the unseen—the breath coming and going, the sap in the plant, the strange wild beauty in nature—we come to essential spirit, the mysterious instinctual juice that feeds everything, that causes us to love everything as much as we do.

Finally, for those who probe further still, there's the deepest level of the unseen, the source of essential spirit—Spirit, God, Brahman, the One, Allah, the absolute, pure consciousness. Who knows this source? In a sense, no one. But those sensitized to it, looking for it, are drawn closer. Since we HSPs are specialists in seeing what others cannot see, in intuiting what is behind the scene, you could say we have a spiritual talent—we can sniff out spirit at all these levels. Those are my thoughts on spirituality.

ANOTHER ASSET WE BRING TO RELATIONSHIPS—SPIRITUAL TALENT

My Own Evidence

Having been with thousands of identified HSPs, in groups and alone with individuals, I have made the following observations:

1. *The quality of silence.* When only HSPs are in a group, such as an audience or seminar, whether listening, waiting for me to speak, or meditating, they tend to create the type of deep silence usually noticed only in sacred places or in groups who have met for a spiritual purpose or practice. They seem to be settled into the unseen.

2. *Ethical tendencies.* HSPs tend to be considerate of others in a way that is at least superficially part of the religious attitude, as most religions describe it. We are hardly saints, and there is always a shadow side to this—for example, we may be kind partly out of a fear of others' reactions, and secretly long to be a huge bother. But anyone speaking before an all-HSP rather than mixed-temperament audience will tend to feel more heard, supported, and considered in little ways (less whispering, walking out, complaining). The unseen environment of feelings is well tended by HSPs.

3. *Eagerness for spiritual experiences.* We seem to seek spiritual experiences and therefore probably have them more often. For example, HSPs are usually comfortable moving inward in meditation, reflection, or prayer whenever I offer them the opportunity, while non-HSPs are usually uncomfortable with this offer, asking anxiously or irritably what they are expected to do. HSPs often have had spiritual experiences since early childhood, even without religious training, and agree more often with the statement

"my inner life is rich and complex." They are familiar with the inner, the unseen.

4. *Spirituality permeates life.* HSPs tend to express spirituality in all aspects of life. If asked, and even if not asked, they talk about it more than non-HSPs. We often go to religious services or spiritual or philosophical discussions. In fact, we are often the instigators. We may see our vocation, health, and just about everything else as aspects of our spirituality. So of course we see our loves and relationships this way, too—as a spiritual path to greater wisdom, humility, or unity with all of life, or as indicators of how near we are to our spiritual goal. The unseen is seen in everything.

Evidence from Genetics

What makes an HSP or anyone spiritual? In some circles it is an intellectual fashion to see religious or spiritual interest as due to weakness or ignorance—that people are spiritual when they cannot face the hard realities of life or accept the "scientific facts." This disparagement is most common among certain non-HSP warrior kings, who in my opinion often lack the HSP/priestly advisor's spiritual talent.

The warrior kings have their own talent, of course, for "facing tough facts" and plunging ahead without constantly rethinking the myriad implications, as HSPs can do. This is all well and good. But because warrior kings' tough talents are preferred in this culture, spiritual talent can be seen as no talent at all, which is not good.

A study by behavioral geneticists Kenneth Kendler, Charles Gardener, and Carol Prescott found that something like what I am calling spiritual talent is partially inherited, just as musical ability is partly inherited. They designed their research to tease out the relations among religious affiliation, vulnerability to alcoholism, psychiatric disorder, and the inheritance of any of these. They interviewed 2,000 women, including 500 identical twins and 350 fraternal twins, questioning them about three religious characteristics: personal devotion (importance of spirituality to daily life, private praying, seeking spiritual comfort), personal religious conservatism (whether they agreed, for example, that the Bible is literally true), and institutional conservatism (whether they belonged to a conservative church).

If a characteristic is largely genetically determined, the degree of similarity of two siblings on the characteristic will be highest if the siblings are identical twins (because they have identical genes). If environment is the main contributor, two siblings without identical genes are just as likely to be similar as those with identical genes. So the degree of similarity on that characteristic will be about equal for identical and fraternal twins—since the genes of fraternal twins are no more similar than any pair of siblings. (By the way, similar research on HSPs is one reason sensitivity is assumed to be inherited.)

The results were that identical twins were more similar in their degree of personal devotion than fraternal twins. That is, the tendency to have or seek spiritual experiences was inherited. But there was no difference in the similarity of identical and fraternal twins in their personal or institutional religious conservatism, suggesting that these are influenced more by the family or community than by genes.

It is also worth noting that personal devotion was less common, not more, among those who were alcoholics or depressed due to stress, and was unrelated to any psychiatric disorders. So much for the theory that religious feelings arise from weakness. Personal devotion was also greater with more years of education. So much for the theory that religious feelings arise from ignorance.

Of course this was not a study of HSPs. Finding that something is affected by genes does not say which gene is causing it. I will, however, happily wager that it is not a "religious gene," but something more basic to the nervous system—its tendency to pause and reflect, to be aware of subtle experiences. That is, its inherited sensitivity.

SPIRITUALITY IS A RELATIONSHIP

This book is about human love, human relationships. Yet there is no doubt that our ability to love each other is affected by our spirituality. I am also going to suggest the reverse, that our capacity for intimacy with the Divine is affected by our human relationships. After all, every religion and spiritual practice, from shamanism to Zen Buddhism, Shintoism to Christianity, emphasizes a relationship between the individual and spirit. How could our personal experiences with human relationships not influence our sense of our relationship with the Divine, with the Universe, with the Self?

Time out. Obviously I am going to have to come up with one term for the ultimate unseen, rather than continually saying "God, Spirit, the Divine, etc." My choice is going to be the Self, mainly because I want to discuss the Jungian concept of the ego-Self axis, such as it's described by Edward Edinger in *Ego and Archetype*. But I better explain this term, the Self. It is not some narcissistic denial of God. It is a traditional translation of an Eastern idea that our individual consciousness is part of the larger consciousness, the Self, which includes everything because everything is a manifestation of God's consciousness. It reflects the intuition that God is unknowable, but the individual self's experience of its Self is not so unknowable. Indeed, you could say that ultimately the Self is all that the individual self is ever experiencing.

Whether one is "one with God" or separate from and devoted to God makes a big difference in some theologies. Personally, I do not find the two experiences contradictory. They are more like the wave and particle nature of light—if you want to know the Self, it does no good to deny either way it can appear. The two experiences are much like our experience of human relationships—there are moments of merger and also moments of being separate enough to feel devotion toward the other.

The other half of the ego-Self axis, the ego, is merely your conscious mind. So all we have left to define is an axis. The definition Edinger is referring to is an axis as a straight-line connection between two objects, along which various positions of the two can occur. No matter how close or distant the two are, the connection remains, unseen but powerful.

Of course what we are trying to describe as an axis is actually too rich for any one metaphor. You could as easily say that the ego-Self connection is an umbilical cord to the Mother of All that sustains your yet-to-be-fully-born ego. Or the Self is a bath in which your ego bathes and a sea from which your ego has evolved, like life itself out of the oceans. These metaphors express the view that the Self is also, ultimately, the entire psyche, personal and collective, Desteian's prevailing and essential spirit combined, including all the archetypes and your individual ego too. Your ego has come out of that wholeness yet is still part of it, as a child becomes separate but still belongs to the family.

The Ego-Self Axis and Early Relationships

To many people, concepts like the ego-Self axis and spirituality are part of some transcendental world far removed from close relationships, if that world exists at all. But again, I think personal relationships and our relationship to the transcendent are intricately interwoven. When we forget this, we have lost awareness of our umbilical cord to Spirit. So let's renew some of this awareness.

According to Edinger, and also the Jungian Eric Neumann, who probably coined the term *ego-Self axis,* we come into life out of the Self, and in early childhood we are still in an unconscious unity with it. This total identification with the Self makes infants and toddlers rather charmingly grandiose and greedy, delightfully natural and strong, in an instinctual, unconscious way. (It is much less charming in an adult.) As we become more aware of ourselves, around two years, we lose some of that innocence but gain consciousness of our individuality. The separation from the Self has begun, Paradise is lost, and the axis appears—there is now a relationship.

The most prominent relationship at that age, however, is with our caretakers, so we project our receding memory of the Self onto our caretakers and have our ego-Self relationships with our parents. But gradually we realize that our parents are less than perfect—they are not the lost Self. (If this process is not gradual we may split off our parents' bad parts—for example, deny them or assign them to ourselves—or split the parent/Self so that our parents are all bad but some other real or imagined person is all good, as discussed in chapter 7.)

With this withdrawal of our projection of the Self onto our parents, we seek the Self elsewhere, maybe in a teacher or first love. When a series of special people also fail to be as whole and wonderful as the Self, we may stop seeking and decide there is no one worth idealizing, unconsciously giving up on the Self. Or we may belong to a religion that is able to absorb that projection for us—this, after all, is one reason for religion. But many people find their religions do not turn out to work for this purpose, and the doubt of the Self's existence only deepens.

HSPs, however, do not usually give up so easily. True, as young adults especially, we may decide to be self-sufficient, seek goals in this world, and forget about the fading dream. But this solution rarely works for long. For HSPs, goals that are not saturated with meaning—ultimate, spiritual meaning—just don't satisfy, as a general rule. Not knowing what to do, where to turn, we eventually reach a state of ego-Self alienation—as far away from the Self as we can be on our axis-tether. In this state, HSPs in particular will feel alone in a universe that seems empty, Godless, devoid of charm.

The Repeating Cycle for HSPs

For the non-HSP, if this alienation happens at all, it will usually be at midlife. For an HSP, I think it is often a recurring cycle of seeking in which we find or seem to find what we seek, and then are disillusioned again. Or we may be entirely blocked or stopped within this cycle. According to Edinger, and my own experience, all of this is greatly influenced by childhood experiences.

For example, someone may be stuck in the part of the cycle where they are wholly identified with the Self, like an infant. They might be involved in some kind of grandiose spirituality, certain they are enlightened or specially chosen by God to found a movement or complete some drastic mission. One must be careful to judge such callings, but it is likely that in childhood such people were intrusively overindulged—like those with the preoccupied attachment style described in chapter 3—or else abused or neglected, emotionally or physically, so that they cling to an unconscious fusion with the Self as a defense against the terror of being left alone in a hostile world (the fear of the narcissist or dismissive avoidant).

You can also be stuck at the opposite end of the cycle from total identity, in a state of alienation. This is typical for those betrayed or disillusioned by the parent/Self in a way that was too sudden or extreme. HSPs in particular can also stay far from the Self out of fear. Perhaps as a child you were overwhelmed and overstimulated by the adults around you, on whom you had projected the Self. Or perhaps a parent used you to gratify some desire—a desire to have a child prodigy, for example, or a companion, or the much more extreme case of using a child sexually. As an adult you may desperately desire closeness to the Self but unconsciously fear being overwhelmed or used. And if you were not allowed ego boundaries as a child, some of this fear may be justified. It is true that the ego can be swamped by the Self if the ego cannot hold its own.

Ego-Self Attachment Style

Neither I nor Edinger would ever reduce the nature of your relationship with Spirit entirely to your childhood issues. But it is not surprising that research has consistently found that people's images of God are similar to their images of themselves, so that, for example, those with high self-esteem tend to see God as loving. As for attachment style (as described in chapter 3), social psychologists Lee Kirkpatrick and Phil Shaver found that those with secure attachment styles perceived God as significantly more loving and less distant and controlling than insecure types. (Secures were no more likely to be religious or spiritual—this may have more to do with being an HSP. But if they were spiritual, their spirituality had a positive tone.) Among the insecure types, avoidants (they combined the dismissive and fearful types) tended to be agnostics, just as one would expect—avoiding the entire issue of a relationship, expecting no one and nothing. However, avoidants were by far the most likely to experience a sudden religious conversion (44 percent in this attachment group, 10 percent in the other groups combined).

The preoccupied types were more likely to go to extremes—to be either ardent atheists or to have had intense experiences such as "speaking in tongues." These results are just what you would expect of people who are anxiously, ambivalently preoccupied with relationships, maximizing their concern about attachment, including their attachment to the Self.

As I said in chapter 3, HSPs are no more likely to have an insecure attachment style—the odds are about fifty-fifty for everyone. When it comes to attachment to the Self or God, you may even be more secure, given your spiritual talents. Still, if you had a very insecure attachment to your earliest caretaker, you need to remember the implications of Gunnar's finding that sensitive insecure children tend to find novel experiences more threatening than other children. If this is your background to life, when you think about the universe, it cannot seem very safe. You may turn to God as the one secure fact, given your natural spiritual inclination, but it would be difficult to trust the reality of that security if your experience and your very physiology has been steeped in insecurity.

This ego-Self-axis understanding of what is underneath an insecure attachment style especially makes sense with HSPs. For example, it helps explain why insecurity in childhood can lead to more depression and anxiety for HSPs than non-HSPs in adulthood. We take the lack of a caring parent/Self to its logical conclusion—the universe is empty. There is every reason for despair, every reason to feel worthless. In Edinger's opinion, when a parent rejects a child, unconsciously both of them see the parent as God. That is, the parent is "inflated in an identification with the deity," and therefore the child experiences the parent/Self's rejection "as something inhuman, total, and irrevocable." Surely this is more the way it all happens for a sensitive child.

By understanding childhood wounds as disruptions of the ego-Self axis, we can also appreciate how religion tries to help, by explaining how much God loves and accepts us. But something inside an insecure in particular can be hard to convince.

The Blocked Ego-Self Axis and Love

Turning to the effects of the ego-Self axis on love in adulthood, when we experience our partners as rejecting, even if they are not (or not as much as we project), we could say that we are really projecting our experiences of the Self as rejecting. In this sense, one could say that the "working model" or attachment style is none other than our position on the ego-Self axis.

What is remarkable is that so many people, especially HSPs, even if abused as children or beaten down by traumas in adulthood, still can believe in God so much (recall the avoidants' sudden conversions) and still can fall in love so hard. One could call it evidence that we do carry a dream, an archetype—more or less unconscious—of a strong, stable connection to the Self. It is this memory of the Self from which we came, the axis that is always there, no matter how alienated we feel. And if we keep trying to believe in the Self or to fall in love (I will equate these for now), we may yet become secure that we can have good-enough connections to a good-enough other in a good-enough universe.

The problem comes down to becoming secure (see chapter 3). But now it is completely intertwined with spiritual security. That is, it may be hard to be close with another human, to feel true security, while there is no closeness and security with the Self. Yet the attachment research suggests that it may also be hard to be close to the Self if one cannot be close and secure within human relationships. Catch twenty-two. We have a dream/memory of love; we have a dream/memory of the Self. But for some of us it is just too difficult to trust that the dream can come true or the memory is real.

HEALING THE EGO-SELF AXIS

The "road signs" identifying routes to a secure attachment style (which I gave to you in chapter 3) can now be thought about in a new, ego-Self-axis way. For example, the healing aspect of two of these—having kind patience with yourself and new, more secure experiences—is really the Self's acceptance.

Acceptance by the Self

Wise therapists make their first priority the establishment of the idea that in the therapy hour all thoughts or feelings are acceptable (although acting on them may not be)—they are all parts of the Self's totality and not a reason one must fear or feel alienated from it. This acceptance of every impulse and aspect, no matter how seemingly unsavory, is essential to a rapprochement to the Self. Every saint has had to face his or her inner sinner and feel it was known, forgiven, God-sent, before the love between human and God felt secure.

No wonder that, in Edinger's words, "The therapist as a person becomes the *center* of the patient's life and thoughts. The therapy sessions become the *central* points of the week. A center of meaning and order has appeared where previously there was chaos and despair." The umbilical cord that has appeared through the acceptance of the therapist sends acceptance to the ego, feeding it, drawing it closer to the Self.

Whether in psychotherapy, religion, or anywhere else, when a relationship provides acceptance to the darkest parts of the personality—which insecures learned from birth to hide in order to survive—that relationship will immensely help you develop security and the courage to trust the Self and others. But this acceptance needs to continue for a long time.

The other suggestions from chapter 3 can be similarly understood in ego-Self axis terms: Grieving opens you to all feelings, all bodily experiences and emotions, which are each messages from the Self, like the images and symbols in our dreams. Individuating and meditating can be seen simply as ways to draw closer to the Self along that axis.

A Word about Dreaming and Healing

Dream work is one of the best ways to draw near to the Self, to *know* it is there and connecting with you. Every time you remember a dream and tend it by day, you will find insights you would never have thought of. Where do these come from? Every religion teaches that dreams are messages from the Self to the ego. Just one example of this teaching is from the Book of Job 30:15–18:

> In dreams, in visions of the night,
> when deepest sleep falls upon men,
> while they sleep in their beds, God makes them listen,
> and his correction strikes them with terror.
> To turn a man from reckless conduct,
> to check the pride of mortal man,
> at the edge of the pit he holds him back alive
> and stops him from crossing the river of death.

The sense of the Self in this passage makes me think of a crabby but ultimately caring parent who grabs our hand when crossing the street—a Self who wishes to hold us back alive from the edge of the pit, who wishes to terrorize us a bit to prevent our crossing the river of death into that place of alienation from the Self and empty despair.

If you don't dream very much, this may be the avoidant in you speaking ("the Self and I don't have anything to do with each other"). I challenge you to try again. If you pay attention to even the smallest fragments (and get enough sleep), the dreams will speak. You may then need help understanding what they are saying to you (they use a language unique to you, but there are still some "grammatical" points common to all dreams that will help with the decoding). You can get this from books, seminars, or Jungian therapy. But the dreams *will* speak.

THE INNER LOVER AS GUIDE TO A
STABLE INTIMACY WITH THE SELF

The inner lover—this intensely special, mysterious figure—was introduced in chapter 2, but a spiritual perspective adds a new understanding of why, for example, someone of the other, "strange" gender would so often be important to the inner life. Only this very strange, differently gendered being can carry the very strangest, most split-off parts of yourself that long to mate, merge, or create with you. The more you can love the inner lover, the more whole you are—the closer you are to the ego's acceptance of the Self, the Self's acceptance of the ego.

I do not wish to imply, however, that your dream or active-imagination interactions with your inner lover are "mere" symbols of your progress toward integration of the opposite poles of your complexes. The inner lover is how the Self relates to us in a way we as humans can understand, and what is asked of you is to tend the relationship as you would a relationship with an outer lover. However your inner lover first appears in your dreams—as a dream of an outer lover, a past lover, or a total stranger, or as a new figure in every dream—eventually he or she coalesces and becomes very real as you recognize and respond to him or her. The inner lover can become a great comfort and source of security, and also a guide to the Self or even a more accessible stand-in for the Self.

When we are drawing closer to the Self, sometimes this happy state is expressed by dreams of a marvelous wedding with the inner lover. Other wedding dreams, such as difficulty getting to a wedding, refusing to wed, or being a bridal attendant may also speak of the conditions standing in the way of your mutual love, or of integrating some opposite within you. Freudians aside, dreams about sex and trouble having sex may also be about the relationship to the Self, or this strange-gendered part of the Self, and not about physical sex at all.

If the ego-Self axis is in need of drastic healing, the inner lover will reveal that too, by appearing as a disturbing dream figure, expressing symbolically all the distortions interfering with intimacy between the ego and the Self. For example, if you are still affected by the rejection of a person on whom you projected the Self, at first your inner lover will appear as critical, unsupportive, or rejecting—even mocking.

The "rehabilitation" of a negative would-be inner lover through inner work parallels the work you must do in outer relationships, every day. As you work on the one side, the other changes. In both arenas, you may only need to learn to surrender more into this intimate union. Or you may have to stand up for yourself, or be more accepting, or listen, or convince him or her to change. Through your dreams, the Self will tell you of your progress.

For example, Elise (the HSW in chapter 3 who was working on her fear of abandonment) could not yet risk feeling love because, to her, the most salient point about love is that it always leads someday to loss. As her inner work progressed, she dreamed that a beloved dog had died (as though her psyche could not risk a dream of losing a human). In the dream she knew she was upset about the loss, but she was unable to feel anything at all. Her inner lover appeared as a monk (symbolically, still far from being someone she could marry) who held a memorial service for the dog. During the service, he cried uncontrollably for *her*, for *her* loss. Hearing his crying, Elise could feel her grief rising in her, against her will, and finally a loud, humiliating sob burst from her, there in the service. But it was all right—no one minded. After that, she felt intense, unspeakable sadness in the dream. But it was made somewhat more bearable by the example of the monk, who was performing his ritual even as he cried, clearly out of love for her.

How do you work on this inner relationship? Again, through attending to your dreams, you can begin your romance with the inner lover, and augment this with active imagination (described on p. 66). As your love for each other grows, you will be initiated into what I call the Self-intimate life.

THE SELF-INTIMATE LIFE

As the individuation process continues, the cycles of closeness and distance or total strandedness from the Self do end. Your dreams and active imagination provide an increasingly strong sense that the images and symbols you receive are messages from a Self very involved with you. You also begin to experience many more outward events as messages from the Self. It is as if there is not only less of a split between the acceptable and unacceptable parts of yourself, but between conscious and unconscious and even inner and outer life. This is, in my opinion, how HSPs in particular are meant to live.

One way to understand this situation (what Jung and later Jungians called living the "symbolic life") is to contrast it with life before that split heals. Alienated from the Self, the outer life can seem so banal and meaningless, especially to an HSP, that it can indeed feel like "the edge of the pit . . . the river of death." To dispel this emptiness, you quite unconsciously project the Self onto something tangible, like great projects at work, raising the perfect child, or even something like alcohol (spirits instead of Spirit). Frequent choices are a foolish guru or preacher who lets you do this, or an impossible love. This is behavior born of blind, instinctive spiritual yearning augmented by powerful personal complexes, like a need for basic love not received from infancy. This is "reckless conduct." It is all part of life without Self-intimacy.

Looking Back on Mark and Linda

Mark and Linda (described in chapter 5) were the couple who struggled with Linda's several infatuations and finally an affair. Linda was desperately, blindly seeking the Self—something that Mark (or anyone) couldn't be. She finally found what she sought in her spiritual practice, although at first it seemed to her that she had found what she sought in her spiritual teacher, on whom she had projected the Self. But her wise teacher rejected the projection and also told her to see her marriage to Mark as part of her path. That is, she was to see him as something the Self had given her and expected her to deal with, not without help, but not by having affairs either. Affairs would not require her to grow closer to the Self or to integrate the split-off parts in her, such as the part capable of holding Mark in such contempt that she could betray him. Seeing her infatuations as expressions of her need to be closer to the Self eventually spared Mark and Linda the pain of divorce.

Why Is Self-Intimacy Also Called the "Symbolic Life"?

Symbols are central to Self-intimacy. From the Jungian viewpoint, a symbol is a pointer to something mysterious that cannot be known directly or easily put into words. (A sign, on the other hand, such as a stop sign, points to something easily expressed in words.) But symbols are even more: Symbols carry the Self's message and the Self's energy. They are alive—as alive as any lover. If you are not conscious of just what these alive energies are, you can blindly obey them or take them literally, not as symbols, and project them onto people and situations in the world.

For example, Gillian, an HSW, was a happily married young mother who, after one day of riding lessons, found herself infatuated with the instructor. He was a champion rider in the international horse-show circuit and reputed to have brief, tempestuous affairs, although the women involved were rumored to express few regrets. Gillian's powerful attraction to him was the last thing this sensitive, conscientious wife and mother wanted to feel. What I was able to tell her (not in quite these words) was that her feeling for this man might be a message from the Self, saying that she was neglecting an important part of herself right now—a self-pleasing, wild and free sort of person who lives close to the instincts, both through sexuality and through the horses, whose animal minds one must know intimately in order to ride them as a champion. This is what the riding instructor, as a symbol, pointed to. She could choose to take the symbol literally and have the affair, or perhaps more to the point, she could choose to live as her rider-inner-lover does. But of course the very idea of doing either and destroying so many lives was terrifying. If she took the feelings more symbolically, however, they were anything but terrifying—they were a much-needed warning from the Self that she was living a one-sided life, too self-sacrificing and out of touch with her instincts.

It is not that everything must be taken so symbolically that we never *do* anything. It is important to act on the messages from the Self when we can do so honorably. In Gillian's case, perhaps in later years she will ride in horse shows, or whatever might be its equivalent for her. (And if her family is wise, they will encourage her, realizing that the sacrifice of such a hope, as described in chapter 7, will not be good for her or them in the long run.)

HSPs are usually especially concerned about making conscious, ethical choices. To do this, your choices must really be choices, not ruled by energies you don't understand. And HSPs are no more immune to unconscious compulsions than others—we may even be less immune. So you need to become very good at considering the symbolic message from the Self latent in a desire.

You may even come to understand most of your life's events as a communication from the Self, so that there seems to be an undeviating justice and blessing in all the circumstances of your life. I like Edinger's metaphor: Life's events, both good and bad, become beads strung on a string in a rosary of life symbolizing one long numinous encounter between the ego and the Self.

JOSH AND THE WATER BRINGER

As a final example, consider Josh, an HSP who was socially withdrawn and fearful. He tried to work on this by enrolling in a therapy group that taught social skills, taking some Prozac, even thinking about how his rejecting mother and absent father could have lowered his self-esteem so that he fears social rejection. But in his case, none of these often-helpful approaches helped.

One night he dreams that a monster has him in its grip. He fights and fights to no avail. That is, the Self is telling him that no social-skills training or Prozac or insight is going to kill this monster.

Josh has more dreams about the monster, who now takes other forms—as a witch turning him to stone, a desert where he is dying of thirst, and a spider holding him in a web. With some help from someone understanding dream work, he begins to think about what each image means. How do you deal with a witch? Many fairy tales provide archetypal answers to the archetypal evil antimother. But who is the witch in his life? And what about the spider? It is green. Why green? Envy? What does he think about spiders? Are they always bad?

One night he dreams of a mysterious woman who brings him water in the desert. Now he is very interested. Whether he knows it consciously, he senses that the Self has suggested some remedy. But why is the water brought by this woman? What about the feminine has he been thirsting for? He has tended to see himself as too feminine. But perhaps he is not. And so the dialogue between ego and Self begins. He is no longer gripped by an undifferentiated, compulsive instinct to withdraw from people. It has qualities, and he has some ideas for dealing with it. These ideas are not from a book or a therapist (although, again, at first one may need help to learn how to do the decoding). But the dream, the message, the wisdom is reaching him from inside himself.

Just this fact, that some answers are coming from within, began to affect Josh's need to withdraw in fear in every social situation. He even started to question whether he was really the shallow, uninteresting person he thought he was. He wondered if he was really so alone. Even if he never married, would his life really be hopeless and without meaning?

In terms of the Self-intimate life, Josh did not have a clue about it at the outset. He was completely gripped by his instinctual fear of being hurt. But the Self, through his dreams, showed him that he was behaving *as if* gripped by a monster or trapped like a bug in a web. He was so in their grip, so identified with these situations, that he was acting them out. He *was* the human held by a monster, the bug held by the web, and he might have soon been the man in love with the first woman who seemed to slake his thirst. But as he became more conscious of the inner figures as symbols, he made use of the messages in the symbols to rise above, and also deal with, his purely unconscious, instinctual response. He was no longer just someone at the mercy of a monster or a spider, or full of gratitude to a water bringer. The scary or entrancing images were lifted to another level, given meaning. His raw instinct was in a sense civilized.

Civilization is the business of the conscious, choosing ego, which considers all the consequences suggested by a series of symbols. Such a civilizing, symbolizing influence is the specialty of the HSP. That is why warrior kings have always turned to their HSP priestly advisors to explain their dreams to them.

When all states of mind, even those such as fear or shyness, can be seen as numinous encounters between ego and Self, we have achieved much of the goal of a spiritual life. Then we will find the numinous encounter even as we face the largest fears and losses, even death itself. But shyness like Josh's is a fine place to begin.

The Joining of Two Symbolic Lives

Almost every religion and spiritual tradition encourages the sacred rituals and practices to be performed in the company of others. Spiritual experiences are more powerful this way. At the same time, rituals and practices done side by side with the ones we love enrich and heal these relationships as nothing else can. If you are in a relationship and do not already follow rituals, meditate, pray, or go to religious services together, this may be an important step for you to take.

Spirituality cannot be expected to take care of every problem in a relationship, of course. It lights up the top floors, and the hard work of communicating and understanding human psychology—our complexes, shadow stuff, instincts, and symbolic expression—keeps the lights on in the lower floors. Side by side, neither leaning toward nor away but upright, two people doing their work together can become two towers of light.

Seen from afar, however, they may seem like part of one great City of Light. One of the many repeated dream symbols of the Self is the Holy City, and although I am a country girl at heart, I am imagining right now that love is about arriving home to that City, becoming one with its rhythms and life—a tower, or two towers—within the skyline of light.

SO, WHAT IS LOVE?

As we near the end of this book, we are now in a position to understand love in a radically new way. In chapter 4 I defined love rather dryly as "the desire to enter and maintain a close relationship with a particular other person," but now we can understand that particular other person to be whoever has the attributes that will allow us to project the Self onto him or her. So, in a sense, all love is directed toward the Self, toward entering the City and standing side by side with your lover there, two towers in one skyline. Even when we love a car or a dog, and certainly when we love a mother, a friend, a lover, we are trying to enter and love the Self.

In my opinion this does not mean that love of another obscures our vision of the real goal, the Self, a view implied by some spiritual traditions. Love plays more of a role than that. For one thing, as each lover disappoints us because he or she is not the Self, we search deeper within until we find what we seek. But some human loves also seem to be paths to the Self, as the Sufis described—from *fana* to *baqa,* from seeing the divine in our beloved to seeing our beloved as part of the divine (remember these from chapter 4?). For this transformation to happen, and then to stabilize so that it can weather all storms, you and your love need time.

FOR HSPS IN LONG-LASTING LOVES

HSPs are likely to want long-term relationships—we have reflected about it and suspect that here is the greatest potential for depth (even though, on the average, relationships become less satisfying with time, and half of all marriages end in divorce). Or we have less glorious reasons to want relationship stability—we dislike change, we dislike rejecting or being rejected, we are aware that endings are inevitably painful and that the alternatives probably will not be better anyway.

Whatever the reason we persist, long-term relationships of all sorts are needed to further Self-intimacy, just as Self-intimacy is required to deepen our long-term loves. In Jung's view, introvert though he was, both forms of personal growth definitely required being in a relationship.

> The unrelated human being lacks wholeness, for he can achieve wholeness only through the soul, and the soul cannot exist without its other side, which is always found in a "You." Wholeness is a combination of I and You, and these show themselves to be parts of a transcendent unity whose nature can only be grasped symbolically.

In part Jung is saying that with our lovers we can face our shadows and complexes, withdraw our projections, and accept our limits due to our personalities and temperaments, plus have our chance to transcend these limits, to be more whole, through the other possessing some of what we lack. But there's more here, I think—the suggestion that the relationship is part of the Self, a fresh symbol from the Self pointing back to the Self.

It may be that not every relationship has this strong sense of coming from the Self and returning us to it. But when a relationship does, I think it has a fated quality. An example I like, because of where I live, is the romance of the poet Robinson Jeffers and Una Call Kuster. Jeffers is famed for his verses, written mainly in the twenties, about the meaning he found in his home place, California's wild lands south of Monterey. Clearly a highly sensitive man, he fell deeply in love with Una when they met in Los Angeles, in a graduate course in advanced German. She was a dynamic, passionate, well-educated woman uniquely able to appreciate his depths. Unfortunately she was already married, to a charming but shallow businessman who had little in common with Una except the wealthy Los Angeles social set in which they had met.

Robinson and Una repeatedly tried to give up their relationship, but after a year's voluntary separation, Robinson returned to Los Angeles from Seattle and encountered Una on the street within a half hour of his arrival. The coincidence was a symbol, in Jungian terms, that neither could ignore. After more struggle—and public scandal, of course—they married and lived together for forty-four years, until her death. He built by hand for her a stone cottage and tower on a rocky point above the beach. Especially while building Tor tower, Jeffers wrote his finest poetry. The tower and the poems were in service to his love.

A love that feels fated and sacred like Robinson and Una's seems to have a life of its own. Something new has been born, a third thing, the great love itself, which is the Self present with the two lovers. This third one makes demands of the two—such as that Una and Robinson suffer public scandal, and that he build her a tower and write his poems.

Romantic relationships are not the only ones that can feel fated, sacred, guided by the Self. Friendships can as well. And one can have more than one such relationship at a time. In the example of Arthur, Guinevere, and Lancelot—one of the most fated, sacred, painful relationship triangles in history—it seems each pair had a relationship with the other that had this quality, as did the three of them together.

Whatever the form of a seemingly Self-fated relationship, it becomes—like an important dream—a message from the Self, a teaching from a spiritual master. It asks your devotion, obedience, and humble service in return for your sometimes basking in its bliss. But if it demands that the two of you fight, you must fight—as "worthy opponents," to use Haule's term in *Divine Madness*. If it demands that you forgive, then you forgive. If it demands a confession of your sins, then you confess. It may even demand that you give up each other's physical presence, but that too is in service to the love, which remains sacred and stronger than ever because of this sacrifice of your two individual desires to the Self.

How does one know the will of the Self? As always, through dreams, symptoms, "coincidences" or signs in daily life, and other pointers to the mysterious, numinous world underlying this seemingly ordinary one. You and I, as HSPs, are especially designed to decipher that will, to pay careful attention to it, to carry out its requests as best as we can, and by so doing to allow the totality of ourselves, ego and Self, lover and the Love, to have the fullest life and development. It is, so to speak, our Holy Grail.

Recalling the story of Arthur, Lancelot, and Guinevere, one might wonder why Guinevere and Lancelot's love was not punished more by God (or by the storyteller), given that the adulterous couple not only betrayed Arthur but brought down Camelot. But as Haule points out in *Divine Madness,* what is easily forgotten is that the goal of all of it—of Arthur, his kingship, Merlin, the Round Table, Lancelot, Guinevere, and Camelot itself—was the Holy Grail, a powerful symbol of the Self. In seeking the Self, every spiritual tradition tells us that there will be strange demands and dark times for all who are involved—for anything new to be born, something old must die.

HSPs especially tend not to want anything to change or die, so this message is important: In long-term relationships you must be ready to endure the nice-friendship aspect of your relationship being betrayed, perhaps through a terrible fight, in order for the passion of the Self, through essential spirit, to be reborn. Above all, you must be ready to assist in the fall of your Camelots (perhaps the projects you have undertaken together, the nice home you have created, or the children you have raised, literally or figuratively). This includes being ready for the final fall of your Camelot, the death of one of you.

When Lancelot and Guinevere retire to monastery and convent to live out their lives separately and in solitude, we tend to think of it as a penance. But perhaps it was more like the next stage of their love affair, the *baqa* we discussed in chapter 4. The Self brought them to such a level of oneness that they went with peace to their separate holy lives and deaths, always united. The Holy Spirit had weaned them from the need for each other's physical presence so that they could enjoy a more ultimately satisfying union with one another within the Self.

NOW, FAREWELL

Like Lancelot and Guinevere, it is time to wean ourselves from these words that link us, and to enjoy a subtler, continuing relationship. It is difficult to write these final lines. I feel a loss. You and I have become close. I have felt your presence always, although not knowing your name. I have tried to anticipate your needs, your questions, your troubles. But this is just my sensitive nature—you would do the same for me.

It is also this sensitive nature that makes me dislike farewells like this. But my inner lover, wise man, tries to help me with these transitions by counseling that every beginning requires an ending. So I comfort myself with the beginning you will make with someone, inner or outer, man or woman, in a new myth or a new chapter in your myth. We dream the dream onward. Good night.

Notes

Regarding this book's discussion of HSPs separate from relationships, the points addressed are well supported by research, all of which is cited in one of the following sources:

- E. N. Aron, *The Highly Sensitive Person* (New York: Broadway Books, 1997).
- E. N. Aron and A. Aron, "Sensory-Processing Sensitivity and Its Relation to Introversion and Emotionality," *Journal of Personality and Social Psychology* 73 (1997): 345–68.
- E. N. Aron, "High Sensitivity as One Source of Fearfulness and Shyness: Preliminary Research and Clinical Implications" in *Extreme Fear, Shyness, and Social Phobia: Origins, Biological Mechanisms, and Clinical Outcomes,* eds. L. A. Schmidt and J. Schulkin (New York: Oxford University Press, 1999), 251–72.
- E. N. Aron, "Counseling the Highly Sensitive Person," *Counseling and Human Development* 28 (1996): 1–7.

The notes below are usually of studies on relationships or findings about HSPs that are not found in the above sources. When I refer to my own research, it has usually been published in the above, except if it concerns HSPs' relationships or sexuality—these newest results are being first published in this book.

Introduction

p. 4 Matt McGue and David Lykken: M. McGue and D. T. Lykken, "Personality and Divorce: A Genetic Analysis," *Journal of Personality and Social Psychology* 71 (1996): 288–99.

Chapter One

p. 20 The research shows . . . similar personalities: D. M. Buss, "Human Mate Selection," *American Scientist* 47 (1985): 47–51.

p. 20 similar personalities . . . happier together: R. J. H. Russell and P. Wells, "Personality Similarity and Quality of Marriage," *Personality and Individual Differences* 12 (1991): 407–12.

p. 20 personality . . . whether matched or not: R. B. Kosek, "The Quest for a Perfect Spouse: Spousal Ratings and Marital Satisfaction," *Psychological Reports* 79 (1996): 731–35.

p. 22 John Gottman: J. M. Gottman and N. Silver, *The Seven Principles for Making Marriage Work* (New York: Crown Publishers, 1999).

p. 27 Carl Jung defined introversion: C. G. Jung, *Psychological Types,* vol. 6, *The Collected Works of C. G. Jung,* ed. W. McGuire (Princeton, N.J.: Princeton University Press, 1971).

p. 29 Carl Jung talked about sensitivity: C. G. Jung, *Freud and Psychoanalysis,* vol. 4, *The Collected Works* (1961).

p. 29 Albert Mehrabian: A. Mehrabian and E. O'Reilly, "Analysis of Personality Measures in Terms of Basic Dimensions of Temperament," *Journal of Personality and Social Psychology* 38 (1980): 492–503.

p. 29 Alexander Thomas and Stella Chess: A. Thomas and S. Chess, "Temperament and Cognition: Relations between Temperament and Mental Test Scores," in *Temperament in Childhood,* eds. G. A. Kohnstamm, J. E. Bates, and M. K. Rothbart (Washington, D.C.: American Psychological Association, 1994), 377–87.

p. 29 Janet Poland: J. Poland, *The Sensitive Child* (New York: St. Martin's, 1996).

p. 32 "bold" fish: D. S. Wilson, K. Coleman, A. B. Clark, and L. Biederman, "Shy-Bold Continuum in Pumpkinseed Sunfish *(Lepomis Gibbosus):* An Ecological Study of a Psychological Trait," *Journal of Comparative Psychology* 107 (1993): 250.

p. 32 Research comparing elementary school children: X. Chen, K. Rubin, and Y. Sun, "Social Reputation and Peer Relationships in Chinese and Canadian Children: A Cross-Cultural Study," *Child Development* 63 (1992): 1336–43.

p. 34 "varied, novel, complex . . .": M. Zuckerman, *Behavioral Expressions and Biosocial Bases of Sensation Seeking* (New York: Cambridge University Press, 1994), 27.

p. 35 "casual and hedonistic . . .": M. Zuckerman, "Impulsive Unsocialized Sensation Seeking: The Biological Foundations of a Basic Dimension of Personality," in *Temperament: Individual Differences at the Interface of Biology and Behavior,* eds. J. E. Bates and T. D. Wachs (Washington, D.C.: American Psychological Association, 1994), 224.

Chapter Two

p. 44 "strange gender" . . . They may be angels. . . : P. Young-Eisendrath, *You're Not What I Expected: Love After the Romance Has Ended* (New York: Fromm International Publishing Corporation, 1997), 24.

p. 47 exerting their influence: L. L. Carli, "Gender, Interpersonal Power, and Social Influence," *Journal of Social Issues* 55 (1999): 81–99.

p. 47 underestimate their abilities: R. C. Barnett and G. K. Baruch, *The*

Competent Woman: Perspectives on Development (New York: Irvington Publishers, 1978).

p. 47   paid less: S. Faludi, *Backlash: The Undeclared War Against American Women* (New York: Crown, 1991).

p. 51   "but everyone else . . .": W. Pollack, *Real Boys: Rescuing Our Sons from the Myths of Boyhood* (New York: Henry Holt and Company, 1998), 6.

p. 51   "Boys are enlisted . . .": S. Koffman, "Sensitive Men—Their Special Task," *Comfort Zone: The HSP Newsletter* 1 (1) (1996): 14.

p. 51   Brian Gilmartin: B. G. Gilmartin, *Shyness and Love: Causes, Consequences, and Treatment* (Lanham, Md.: University Press of America, 1987).

p. 52   negative effects on young men: for example, R. Bly, *Iron John: A Book About Men* (Reading, Mass.: Addison-Wesley, 1990).

p. 54   "can have an extremely . . .": Gilmartin, *Shyness and Love,* 400.

p. 61   research shows . . . "feminine" way: L. K. Lamke, D. L. Sollie, R. G. Durbin, and J. A. Fitzpatrick, "Masculinity, Femininity and Relationship Satisfaction: The Mediating Role of Interpersonal Competence," *Journal of Social and Personal Relationships* 11 (1994): 535–54.

p. 61   Recent videotaped research . . . did not differ: L. A. Pasch, T. N. Bradbury, and J. Davila, "Gender, Negative Affectivity, and Observed Social Support Behavior in Marital Interactions," *Personal Relationships* 4 (1997): 361–78.

p. 61   Research indicates . . . least happy marriages: W. Ickes, "Traditional Gender Roles: Do They Make, and Then Break Our Relationships?" *Journal of Social Issues* 49 (1993): 71–85.

p. 61   less responsive to marital therapy: N. S. Jacobson, W. C. Follette, and M. Pagel, "Predicting Who Will Benefit from Behavioral Marital Therapy," *Journal of Consulting and Clinical Psychology* 54 (1986): 518–22.

p. 61   strong evidence that such marriages: R. B. Stuart, *Helping Couples Change: A Social Learning Approach to Marital Therapy* (New York: The Guilford Press, 1980), 264.

p. 61   The fact is . . . polarized, and likely to end: L. J. Roberts and L. J. Krokoff, "A Time-Series Analysis of Withdrawal, Hostility, and Displeasure in Satisfied and Dissatisfied Marriages," *Journal of Marriage and the Family* 52 (1990): 95–105.

p. 61   Christopher Heavey: C. L. Heavey, C. Layne, and A. Christensen, "Gender and Conflict Structure in Marital Interaction: A Replication and Extension," *Journal of Consulting and Clinical Psychology* 61 (1993): 16–27.

p. 66   Robert Johnson: R. Johnson, *Inner Work* (San Francisco: Harper San Francisco, 1989).

p. 67   Recent research . . . our first reactions: P. G. Devine, "Stereotypes and Prejudice: Their Automatic and controlled components," *Journal of Personality and Social Psychology* 56 (1989): 680–90.

Chapter Three

p. 73   Researchers find that people in close: M. D. Sherman and M. H. Thelen, "Fear of Intimacy Scale: Validation and Extension with Adolescents," *Journal of Social and Personal Relationships* 13 (1996): 507–21.

p. 75   Elaine Hatfield: E. Hatfield, "The Dangers of Intimacy," in *Communications, Intimacy, and Close Relationships,* ed. V. J. Derlega (New York: Academic Press, 1984), 377–87.

p. 90   "working model": J. Bowlby, *A Secure Base: Clinical Applications of Attachment Theory* (London: Routledge, 1988).

p. 91   "false self": D. W. Winnicott, *Maturational Processes and the Facilitating Environment* (London: Hogarth Press and the Institute of Psychoanalysis, 1965).

p. 92   the following four statements [adapted from]: K. Bartholomew and L. M. Horowitz, "Attachment styles among young adults: A test of a four-category model," *Journal of Personality* 61 (1991): 226–44.

p. 94   about 50 percent [and percentages for next three styles]: M. Diehl, A. B. Elnick, L. S. Bourbeau, and G. Labouvie-Vief, "Adult Attachment Styles: Their Relations to Family Context and Personality," *Journal of Personality and Social Psychology* 74 (1998): 1656–69.

p. 95   Your parents were probably unresponsive: D. J. Siegel, *The Developing Mind: Toward a Neurobiology of Interpersonal Experience* (New York: Guilford Press, 1999).

p. 95   But laboratory studies . . . signs of dissociation: Ibid.

p. 96   a study of eighteen-month-olds: M. Gunnar, "Psychoendocrine Studies of Temperament and Stress in Early Childhood: Expanding Current Models," in *Temperament: Individual Differences,* eds. Bates and Wachs (Washington, D.C.: American Psychological Association, 1994), 175–98.

p. 97   greater general well-being . . . more self-confident: K. A. Brennan and P. R. Shaver, "Dimensions of Adult Attachment, Affect Regulation, and Romantic Functioning," *Personality and Social Psychology Bulletin* 21 (1995): 267–83.

p. 97   more balanced and realistic: M. Mikulincer, "Attachment Style and the Mental Representation of the Self," *Journal of Personality and Social Psychology* 69 (1995): 1203–15.

p. 97   stick to the task: Y. Lussier, S. Sabourin, and C. Turgeon, "Coping Strategies as Moderators of the Relationships Between Attachment and Marital Adjustment," *Journal of Social and Personal Relationships* 14 (1997): 777–91.

p. 97   alcohol . . . or . . . eating disorder: Brennan and Shaver, "Dimensions of Adult Attachment."

p. 97   prefer to have secure partners: H. Latty-Mann and K. E. Davis, "Attachment Theory and Partner Choice: Preference and Actuality," *Journal of Social and Personal Relationships* 13 (1996): 5–23.

p. 97   happier in relationships: R. R. Kobak and C. Hazan, "Attachment in Marriage: Effects of Security and Accuracy of Working Models," *Journal of Personality and Social Psychology* 60 (1991): 861–69.

p. 97   less distant, defensive, or distressed: E. C. Klohnen and S. Bera,

"Behavioral and Experiential Patterns of Avoidantly and Securely Attached Women Across Adulthood: A 31-Year Longitudinal Perspective," *Journal of Personality and Social Psychology* 74 (1998): 211–23.

p. 97   less frustrated . . . or fearful of abandonment: Brennan and Shaver, "Dimensions of Adult Attachment."

p. 97   angry less often . . . more positive outcomes: M. Mikulincer, "Adult Attachment Style and Individual Differences in Functional versus Dysfunctional Experiences of Anger," *Journal of Personality and Social Psychology* 74 (1998): 513–24.

p. 97   trustworthy friends and to accept their faults: Brennan and Shaver, "Dimensions of Adult Attachment."

p. 98   turn to their partners for support . . . give support: J. A. Simpson, W. S. Rholes, and J. S. Nelligan, "Support Seeking and Support Giving within Couples in an Anxiety-Provoking Situation: The Role of Attachment Styles," *Journal of Personality and Social Psychology* 62 (1992): 434–46.

p. 98   positive emotions . . . relationship satisfaction: J. A. Feeney, "Adult Attachment, Emotional Control, and Marital Satisfaction," *Personal Relationships* 6 (1999): 169–85.

p. 98   when separated from their partners: B. C. Feeney and L. A. Kirkpatrick, "Effects of Adult Attachment and Presence of Romantic Partners on Physiological Responses to Stress," *Journal of Personality and Social Psychology* 70 (1996): 255–70.

p. 98   sex without feeling love: Brennan and Shaver, "Dimensions of Adult Attachment."

p. 98   How do you recognize: M. Main, "Cross-Cultural Studies of Attachment Organization: Recent Studies, Changing Methodologies, and the Concept of Conditional Strategies," *Human Development* 33 (1990): 48–61.

p. 98   "earned secures": Siegel, *The Developing Mind*, 91.

p. 100   but it can be overridden: Siegel, *The Developing Mind*.

p. 103   Peter Kramer: P. D. Kramer, *Should You Leave? A Psychiatrist Explores Intimacy and Autonomy—and the Nature of Advice* (New York: Scribner, 1997).

Chapter Four

p. 104   "Love is a set of . . .": A. Aron and E. N. Aron, "Love and Sexuality," in *Sexuality in Close Relationships,* eds. K. McKinney and S. Sprecher (Hillsdale, N.J.: Lawrence Erlbaum, 1991), 25.

p. 105   doctoral dissertation on love: A. Aron, *Relationship Variables in Human Heterosexual Attraction* (Doctoral Dissertation, University of Toronto, 1970).

p. 105   an academic book on falling in love: A. Aron and E. N. Aron, *Love as the Expansion of Self: Understanding Attraction and Satisfaction* (New York: Hemisphere, 1986).

p. 105   articles for scholarly journals: For a review, see A. Aron and E. N. Aron, "The Self-Expansion Model of Motivation and Cognition in

Close Relationships," in *The Handbook of Personal Relationships*, 2nd ed., eds. S. Duck and W. Ickes (Chichester, U.K.: Wiley, 1997), 251–70.

p. 107   our research . . . asked people to tell the story: A. Aron, D. G. Dutton, E. N. Aron, and A. Iverson, "Experiences of Falling in Love," *Journal of Social and Personal Relationships* 6 (1989): 243–57.

p. 108   "individuals to focus . . .": H. E. Fisher, "Lust, Attraction, and Attachment in Mammalian Reproduction," *Human Nature* 9 (1998): 23.

p. 108   biologists have suggested pheromones: M. Kodis, D. Moran, and D. Houy, *Love Scents: How Your Natural Pheromones Influence Your Relationships, Your Moods, and Who You Love* (New York: Dutton, 1998).

p. 110   emotions toward that object: A. Tesser, "Self-Generated Attitude Change" in *Advances in Experimental Social Psychology*, vol. 11, ed. L. Berkowitz (New York: Academic Press, 1978), 289–338.

p. 111   the famous "bridge study": D. G. Dutton and A. Aron, "Some Evidence for Heightened Sexual Attraction under Conditions of High Anxiety," *Journal of Personality and Social Psychology* 30 (1974): 510–17.

p. 111   research that followed: C. A. Foster, B. S. Witcher, W. K. Campbell, and J. D. Green, "Arousal and Attraction: Evidence for Automatic and Controlled Processes," *Journal of Personality and Social Psychology* 74 (1998): 86–101.

p. 112   "love appears to be . . .": E. S. Person, *Dreams of Love and Fateful Encounters: The Power of Romantic Passion* (New York: Penguin Books, 1989), 264.

p. 112   "both some guarantee . . .": Ibid.

p. 112   also tried situations: A. Aron, *Relationship Variables*.

p. 113   John Desteian: J. A. Desteian, *Coming Together—Coming Apart: The Union of Opposites in Love Relationships* (Boston: SIGO Press, 1989).

p. 115   John Haule: J. R. Haule, *Divine Madness: Archetypes of Romantic Love* (Boston: Shambhala, 1990).

p. 115   especially for the fearful . . . styles: A. Aron, E. N. Aron, and J. Allen, "Motivations for Unreciprocated Love," *Personality and Social Psychology Bulletin* 24 (1998): 787–96.

p. 116   "in order to force . . .": C. G. Jung, *Visions Seminars* (Zurich: Spring Publications, 1976), 110.

p. 116   Jung would always say: V. Harms, *The Inner Lover* (Boston: Shambhala, 1992).

p. 123   well-established psychological fact: L. D. Ross, T. M. Amabile, and J. L. Steinmetz, "Social Roles, Social Control and Biases in Social-Perception Processes," *Journal of Personality and Social Psychology* 35 (1977): 485–94.

p. 124   about 11 percent: A. M. Pines, *Falling in Love: How We Choose the Lovers We Choose* (New York: Routledge, 1999).

Chapter Five

p. 128   Research shows . . . two similar partners: A. Caspi and E. S. Herbener, "Continuity and Change: Assortative Marriage and the Consistency of

Personality in Adulthood," *Journal of Personality and Social Psychology* 58, (1990): 250–58.

p. 143 "requires a conscious effort . . .": Kramer, *Should You Leave?*, 198.

p. 144 When you choose [paraphrased from]: D. Wile, *After the Honeymoon: How Conflict Can Improve Your Relationship* (New York: Wiley, 1988).

p. 144 "the imaginative work . . .": Person, *Dreams of Love and Fateful Encounters*, 264.

Chapter Six

p. 156 more insecurity, negative emotion: B. R. Karney and T. N. Bradbury, "Neuroticism, Marital Interaction, and the Trajectory of Marital Satisfaction," *Journal of Personality and Social Psychology* 72 (1997): 1075–92.

p. 164 According to Jung: Jung, *Psychological Types*, vol. 6, *The Collected Works*.

Chapter Seven

p. 172 weekly self-descriptions: A. Aron, M. Paris, and E. N. Aron, "Prospective Studies of Falling in Love and Self-Concept Change," *Journal of Personality and Social Psychology* 69 (1995): 1102–12.

p. 172 decline in relationship satisfaction: Karney and Bradbury, "Neuroticism, Marital Interaction, and the Trajectory of Marital Satisfaction."

p. 172 initial surveys: A. Aron, C. C. Norman, and E. N. Aron, "Couples Shared Participation in Novel and Arousing Activities and Experienced Relationship Quality," *Journal of Personality and Social Psychology* (2000).

p. 172 Charlotte Reissman: C. Reissman, A. Aron, and M. R. Bergen, "Shared Activities and Marital Satisfaction: Causal Direction and Self-Expansion versus Boredom," *Journal of Social and Personal Relationships* 10 (1993): 243–54.

p. 173 In another experiment: Aron, Norman, and Aron, "Couples Shared Participation in Novel and Arousing Activities and Experienced Relationship Quality."

p. 175 first observed about women: J. Gottman and N. Silver, *The Seven Principles for Making Marriage Work* (New York: Crown, 1999).

p. 175 In dialogue: Young-Eisendrath, *You're Not What I Expected.*

p. 178 marital researchers: Gottman and Silver, *The Seven Principles for Making Marriage Work.*

p. 180 here are some ways: Six of these are from Ibid., adapted for HSPs.

p. 181 fully 80 percent: Ibid.

p. 182 signs of disengagement: Ibid.

p. 183 signs of trouble: Ibid.

p. 184 unfulfilled hope: Ibid.

p. 184 meaning in their work: B. Jaeger, "The Highly Sensitive Self-Employed," *Comfort Zone: The HSP Newsletter* 4 (2) (1999): 13.

p. 187 "A person who is aware . . .": Desteian, *Coming Together—Coming Apart*, 37.

p. 189   John Gottman: Gottman and Silver, *The Seven Principles for Making Marriage Work.*

p. 193   "A general and merely academic . . . But they show up. . .": C. G. Jung, *The Practice of Psychotherapy,* vol. 16, *The Collected Works* (1985), 294–95.

p. 194   Research shows . . . store all their: C. J. Showers, "Compartmentalization of Positive and Negative Self-Knowledge: Keeping the Bad Apples Out of the Bunch," *Journal of Personality and Social Psychology* 62 (1992): 1036–49.

p. 195   further research . . . about their partners: C. J. Showers and S. B. Kevlyn, "Organization of Knowledge about a Relationship Partner: Implications for Liking and Loving," *Journal of Personality and Social Psychology* 76 (1999): 958–71.

p. 196   only 1 percent: Gottman and Silver, *The Seven Principles for Making Marriage Work.*

p. 196   In a survey: "Psychotherapy," *Consumer Reports* November (1995): 734–39.

Chapter Eight

p. 219   research on . . . fantasies: J. J. Griffin, *Sexual Fantasy, Extramarital Affairs, and Marriage Commitment* (Doctoral Dissertation, California Graduate School of Family Psychology, 1990).

p. 221   "Marriage is no marriage . . .": D. H. Lawrence, "Marriage and the Living Cosmos," in *Challenge of the Heart: Love, Sex, and Intimacy in Changing Times,* ed. J. Wellwood (Boston, Shambhala, 1985), 166.

p. 221   "Vitally, the human race . . .": Ibid., 169.

p. 222   "Perhaps the great renewal . . .": R. M. Rilke, "Advice for a Young Lover," in *The Art of Staying Together: Embracing Love, Intimacy, and Spirit in Relationships,* ed. M. R. Waldman (New York: Jeremy P. Tarcher/Putnum, 1998), 171.

p. 222   "They who meet in the night . . .": Ibid.

p. 222   "The earth is full . . .": Ibid., 170.

p. 222   "though they error . . .": R. M. Rilke, "Learning to Love," in *Challenge of the Heart,* 264.

p. 222   "the surface dominates . . . But in the world . . .": B. Jager, "Passion and Transformation," in *Challenge of the Heart,* 218.

p. 222   "Everything unfolds a dark . . .": Ibid., 218–19.

p. 223   "the good helmsman . . .": Ibid., 220.

p. 223   "Sexual organs are . . .": Ibid., 221.

Chapter Nine

p. 227   Kenneth Kendler: K. S. Kendler, C. O. Gardener, and C. A. Prescott, "Religion, Psychopathology, and Substance Use and Abuse: A Multimeasure Genetic-Epidemiologic Study," *American Journal of Psychiatry* (1997): 322–29.

p. 229   Edward Edinger: E. F. Edinger, *Ego and Archetype: Individuation and the Religious Function of the Psyche* (New York: Penguin Books, 1972).

p. 232   research . . . people's images of God: P. Benson and B. Spilka, "God Image as a Function of Self-Esteem and Locus of Control," *Journal for the Scientific Study of Religion* 12 (1973): 297–310.

p. 232   Lee Kirkpatrick: L. A. Kirkpatrick and P. R. Shaver, "An Attachment-Theoretical Approach to Romantic Love and Religious Belief," *Personality and Social Psychology Bulletin* 18 (1992): 266–75.

p. 233   "inflated in an identification . . . as something inhuman . . .": Edinger, *Ego and Archetype,* 39–40.

p. 234   "The therapist as a person . . .": Ibid., 40.

p. 240   Edinger's metaphor: Edinger, *Ego and Archetype,* 117.

p. 243   "The unrelated human being . . .": Jung, *The Practice of Psychotherapy,* 244–45.

p. 243   Robinson Jeffers: J. Karman, *Robinson Jeffers: Poet of California* (Brownsville, Ore.: Story Line Press, 1996

Index

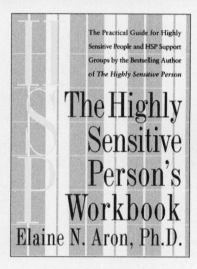